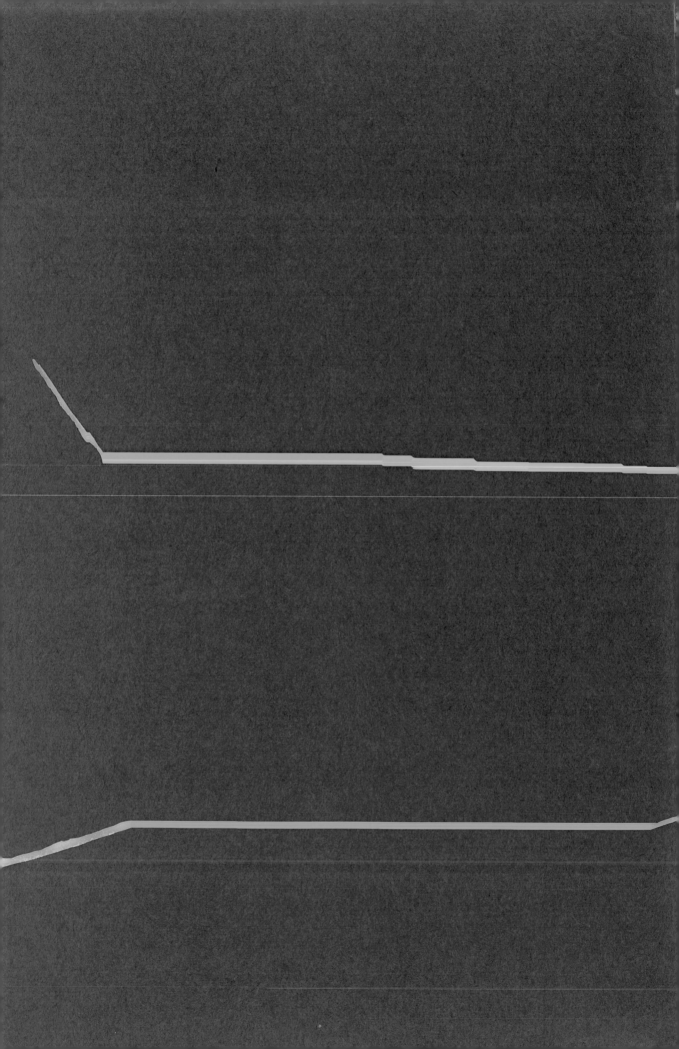

BUILDING

ORGANIZATIONAL

FITNESS

BUILDING

ORGANIZATIONAL

FITNESS

Management Methodology for Transformation and Strategic Advantage

Ryuji Fukuda

Translated by
Noriko Hosoyamada

PRODUCTIVITY PRESS | PORTLAND, OREGON

Originally published as *Manejimento Kaihatsu no Susume* (Tokyo: Japanese Standards Association), © 1994 by Ryuji Fukuda.

English edition © 1997 by Productivity Press, a division of Productivity, Inc. Translated by Noriko Hosoyamada with editing by Neil DeCarlo.

Additional copies of this book are available from the publisher. Discounts are available for multiple copies through the Sales Department (800-394-6868). Address all other inquiries to:

Productivity Press
P.O. Box 13390
Portland, OR 97213-0309
United States of America
Telephone: 503-235-0600
Telefax: 503-235-0909
E-mail: service@ppress.com

Book and cover design by Bill Stanton
Cover photograph by Barry Kaplan
Graphics and composition by Boston Graphics, Inc.
Additional composition by William H. Brunson Typography Services
Printed and bound by Edwards Brothers in the United States of America

Library of Congress Cataloging-in-Publication Data

Fukuda, Ryūji, 1928–
    [Manejimento kaihatsu no susume. English]
    Building organizational fitness : management methodology for transformational and strategic advantage / Ryuji Fukuda.—English ed.
      p. cm.
    Includes bibliographical references and index.
    ISBN 1-56327-144-3 (hc)
    1. Production management.   2. Production planning.   I. Title.
TS155.F77513 1997
658.5—DC21   96-51744
                                                                 CIP

02 01 00 99 98 97   10 9 8 7 6 5 4 3 2 1

CONTENTS

CHAPTER 2 | ORGANIZING ACTIONS FOR IMPROVEMENT/ TRANSFORMATION: THE POLICY/OBJECTIVE MATRIX 27

CHAPTER 6 | USING WINDOW ANALYSIS FOR ACCURATE FACT FINDING AND EFFECTIVE COUNTERMEASURES 163

CHAPTER 7 | STOCKLESS PRODUCTION AND SEDAC 187

CHAPTER 8 | IMPROVING AND MAINTAINING ORGANIZATIONAL FITNESS   217

PUBLISHER'S MESSAGE

Management is often called a science, which means that if we consistently apply proven managerial techniques we should all get substantially the same results. It happens when we mix chemicals; it can happen with machines on the factory floor. But when it comes to managing people, we see wide variances in our results. So then is management really a science? According to Ryuji Fukuda it surely is, if we use proven reliable methods.

This has been Mr. Fukuda's evolving theme for the past 30 years: to find and then apply in a practical way the world's best management concepts. He has been very consistent and very successful in that endeavor. And as you will see from this marvelous book, the ability to manage scientifically and successfully is something universal and available to us all.

Back in the spring of 1981, on my first study mission to Japan, I met Ryuji Fukuda, who was then a managing director of Sumitomo Electric. I was very impressed with his openness to teach American senior managers about some of the most effective management concepts being used in Japan. Total quality management (TQM), just-in-time (JIT), total productive maintenance (TPM), and other approaches were quite hidden from us at the time. This meeting with Mr. Fukuda began my incredible journey of discovery in Japan. His openness and excitement were contagious. He was the first to share some of the new and very powerful techniques being used by the Japanese to improve their quality and productivity.

Later in 1981, he came to America to speak at a Productivity conference at the Waldorf Astoria in New York City. Once again he gave us something unique: a challenge to learn what the Japanese were doing differently in their thrust for world class competitiveness. It all began with Ryuji Fukuda. I am very grateful to him, as two years later his *Managerial Engineering* became the book that launched my publishing company. And I am very proud to publish his third book in English, which explains in detail the steps necessary for senior managers to meet and beat their international competitors. In 1981 there were many secrets kept from us; today the secrets are all in the open. Left for us is the hard work necessary to apply them.

Building Organizational Fitness intends to demonstrate how a company can carry out companywide transformation and proceed toward the fast-track path. In Chapter 1 Mr. Fukuda presents seven conditions for us to examine and apply:

1. *Top management commitment—everyone is committed to improvement—must be communicated and practiced*

What exactly is this commitment and how must we communicate it? How often and when do we practice it? And how do we get the feedback that the commitment is there and happening at all levels?

2. *Superior development capabilities*

Are all assets—people as well as equipment—operating at their highest level of proficiency? To what extent do we invest in the continuous development of our human resources? Do we challenge people to learn and grow every single day?

3. *Superior managing capabilities*

What are the factors that advance our management capabilities?

4. *Effective in-house education and on-the-job coaching*

What is an effective in-house education program? What is the difference between on-the-job training and on-the-job coaching?

5. *Total active participation of staff departments*

How do you take senior management's goals and deploy them throughout the organization? How do you get buy-in at every level and in every part of the organization?

6. Enabling structures to promote improvements in daily work

What tools and techniques will promote and stimulate people to improve every day? How do we get feedback that tells us whether the improvement process is working?

7. Enabling structures that encourage creative improvements by integrating knowledge and experience

How can we take all learning from passive listening to experiencing?

Later chapters of the book expand on this approach and introduce four key methods for implementing it. Chapter 2 introduces the Policy/Objective Matrix, a powerful tool for deploying and implementing improvements aligned with top management's strategic planning. Chapter 3 describes the SEDAC method, an expansion of Mr. Fukuda's unique CEDAC approach for creative, participative problem solving. Chapter 4 focuses on the improvement process and SEDAC's role in testing new ideas and learning from failures. Chapter 5 describes uses of SEDAC in staff functions such as engineering. This chapter introduces SEDACs on arrow, FMEA, and PDPC diagrams for specific types of problems or improvements, and shows how SEDAC might be used for equipment-related problem solving in TPM.

Chapter 6 introduces a third method, Window Analysis. This important tool helps managers determine whether a problem relates to lack of a known standard or to nonadherence to a known standard—which points the way to the kind of solution to implement. In Chapter 7 Mr. Fukuda talks about Stockless Production as a fourth key approach for competitiveness. Chapter 8 deals with ways to maintain the results of improvement over time.

On my second trip to Japan in the fall of 1981, Jack Warne, president of Omark Industries, and I found a book written on Toyota's just-in-time production system. Jack and I immediately bought 500 copies each. He gave one copy to every manager in his company and asked them to read one chapter at a time in small study groups within their plant. "Can we apply these ideas at Omark?" he asked.

Within one year Omark was able to reduce inventory levels by half, reduce factory floor space by half, and become the best example of just-in-time in America.

I recommend you follow Jack Warne's approach with the book you are now holding. Take the scientific approach to learning from this book. Read only Chapter 1. If it excites you, buy additional copies for your entire senior staff. Ask them to read only the first chapter. Meet with the group a week later and ask, "What do you think about the ideas in the book? Can we apply them here?" Then each week meet again for 30 minutes to address one fundamental question: "How can we apply the ideas presented in the book in our company?"

I guarantee you success.

The most powerful way to transform your company is to get your senior staff into executive study groups to learn the very latest concepts, to talk about them, and to apply and experience them. What works, you keep and improve on. What doesn't work is an opportunity to learn from your mistakes.

Ryuji Fukuda is a conceptual genius with the ability to synthesize the world's best managerial techniques and put them together in a new framework for you to use successfully. He has a proven track record:

- A professor of engineering at Kobe University

- In charge of all production at Sumitomo Electric Co. (the GE of Japan)

- A managing director of Meidensha Electric Co.

- A top independent management consultant and advisor to the Japan Management Association whose ideas have been implemented at Sony, Timken, Fiat, and many other companies in Japan, the United States, and Europe

- Author of *Managerial Engineering, CEDAC,* and other books, articles, and papers

- A winner of the prestigious Deming Prize

- Selected as the top lecturer at the Japan Management Association

In this book Ryuji Fukuda shares a lifetime of insights with us. Leaders in every industry can profit from understanding his tested strategies and techniques.

I'd like to thank the people who helped make this publication possible. First, of course, is Mr. Fukuda, whom I am honored to have learned a great deal from over these many years. Great appreciation must also be given to Noriko Hosoyamada, who has worked with Mr. Fukuda extensively in Japan and in the West and has produced a careful translation of this book; and also to Neil DeCarlo for his editing of the translation.

Within Productivity, thanks go to Diane Asay, editor in chief; Karen Jones, senior development editor; Connie Dyer, director of TPM research and product development; Mary Junewick and Susan Swanson, production editors; and Bill Stanton, art director and designer. Thanks also to Julie Zinkus, copyediting; Marianne L'Abbate and Marvin Moore, proofreading; Boston Graphics, Inc., illustrations and composition; and William H. Brunson Typography Services, final page typography and layout.

Norman Bodek
Publisher

PREFACE

Undoubtedly, the most urgent task for companies today is to take a hard look at the future. Business leaders are preoccupied with how to win in the game of growth and profits and how to fully invest their energy and resources in achieving their goals. More importantly, executives and managers are becoming aware that they need to conduct their business in a way that is respected both inside and outside their countries. In these times more than ever, the challenge is to foster a unique brand of intellectual creativity in the organization and use it to achieve excellent and consistent results.

To remain competitive, companies must nurture a strong capability for self-development and a strong corporate culture, both of which form part of the foundation for improvement. Whatever the future may bring, we will always be engaged in improving the quality of our work, products, and services. Specifically, this entails developing and accumulating knowledge about how to do our jobs better, creating better flows of information, and strengthening our will and ability to do our jobs right. Clearly, the requirement to do all these is expected to grow in importance rather than dwindle. In this kind of working environment, it's necessary for people to develop a sense of responsibility and a proclivity for sincere work, mutual trust, and the notion that working hard to be better is a virtue. In this book, I discuss technology in two broad categories:

1. *Intrinsic technology,* which refers to the essential techniques and methods for conducting work and achieving tasks, and

2. *Management technology,* which refers to the techniques and methods for improving the quality or quantity of tasks. It's important to note that the original meaning of management technology implies and requires high morale of the people involved in its development and application.

In support of the foundational elements of improvement discussed above—self-development capability and corporate culture—this book introduces several key management technologies and describes their successful application in many Japanese, U.S., and Italian companies. Through these technologies, companies the world over have achieved remarkable results and have become more competitive. For your reference, the two primary management technologies described here are:

The P/O (Policy/Objective) Matrix. Through examples of P/O Matrix application at many companies, this book introduces how to develop policies and objectives for overall improvement plans, how to identify and organize improvement teams, and how to remove anticipated obstacles to improvement.

SEDAC (Structure for Enhancing Daily Activities through Creativity). SEDAC has contributed to quick and effective achievement of improvement objectives. The SEDAC case studies covered in this book include its application in staff areas, where participation in companywide improvement greatly influences the overall success of the organization. Specifically, the features of SEDAC are:

- Professionalism and purposiveness

- Real-time collection of on-site and actual information

- Effective use of idea generation methods for improvement

- Confirmation and standardization of results through trial and error

- Development of professional sensibilities for prediction

- Learning by translating information into basic knowledge (discussed here through a TPM [total productive maintenance] application example)

- Diagnosis and correction of improvement activity deficiencies

- Simultaneous implementation of the items listed above

Other management technologies covered in this book include *Window Analysis*, a method for classifying and analyzing problems from a viewpoint of management actions required, and *Stockless Production*. This approach helps companies reduce work-in-process and lead time in an effective and easy-to-understand manner.

Of course, just understanding management techniques intellectually doesn't mean you know how to use them. Practice is critical. To ensure continued practice by everyone concerned, an organization must have an enabling structure that allows people to practice while doing their jobs. Also, through continuous implementation, it's important to add new and improved features to your management technologies.

I believe that managerial skill is developed through experience. For this reason, my intention is not to force fixed concepts and techniques on the reader. Further, I don't believe the techniques covered in this book are the only ones that will be used in years to come. As someone with a certain amount of experience, my intention is to expose readers to the details of the above-mentioned techniques. They, in turn, can decide how they might apply them in their organizations. My suggestion is for readers to stop reading from time to time and think about the details of their own unique situations. Also, I encourage readers to improve the utility of the management technologies and systems in this book through continued creativity, refinement, and practice.

Naturally, I am indebted to many people. First of all, special thanks go to my client companies, who willingly agreed to cooperate and share their materials and successes. Although limited space prevents the listing of everyone in these companies, I thank all of them for their inspiration. It's truly been a pleasure to work with each and every one.

As for the Italian companies introduced in this book, Dott. Ing. Carlalberto Da Pozzo of Galgano Associati was responsible for collecting and collating the information they provided. Regarding information gathered from U.S. companies, I thank Ms. Toni Davies, formerly of Productivity, Inc., for her dedicated assistance. I would also like to note that these companies were guided and consulted mainly by Galgano Associati in Europe and by Productivity, Inc., in the United States.

I also would like to thank Dr. Makoto Kawane, chairman of Tayca; Dr. Yoshio Kondo, professor emeritus of Kyoto University; and Mr. Sanshi Sakabe, president of Dynic, for their long-term friendship and inspiring suggestions.

Really, this book is a sequel to *Managerial Engineering,* which was translated and published in 1983 by Productivity, Inc. For their hard work in preparing this book for publication in English, I am indebted to Norman Bodek and Robert Shoemaker of Productivity, Inc., and to Steven Ott, Diane Asay, and Karen Jones of Productivity Press. Last but not least, special thanks go to Ms. Noriko Hosoyamada, translator, and Mr. Neil DeCarlo, editor, for their teamwork in ensuring an accurate and smooth translation from the Japanese original.

Managing for Shaping the Future

IMPROVEMENT, INNOVATION, AND TRANSFORMATION

Improvement, innovation, transformation, renewal, and change—the list goes on. In this book, we don't plan to be confused by terminology. Instead, we will define key words at the onset, keeping them as simple as possible.

Let's start with *transformation.* Transformation occurs when people inside an organization realize they have reached a higher level through continuous improvement and technological innovation. While improvements are the individual actions required to achieve transformation, transformation is the state that results from such improvements. From this standpoint, I agree with Professor Dan Dimancescu, who points out that continuous improvement has been a key factor in the transformation of Chrysler Corporation (Dimancescu 1994).

Now let's move on to *improvement* and *innovation.* The prevailing image for improvement is small change, while innovation refers to breakthrough. Although in general these definitions hold true, it's not always easy to draw a clear line between improvement and innovation. They are interrelated. Sometimes, after basic technology is developed through continuous improvement, innovations flourish. On the other hand, the application of innovative technologies may create the need for improvement activities.

In this book, improvement is used in a broad, generic sense, which often includes innovation. So please don't take improvement to mean only small changes in the workplace.

MANAGEMENT MUST ALWAYS TRANSFORM

The success of management is determined by creativity and teamwork at all levels of the organization. Such creativity and teamwork, of course, need to focus on keeping pace with the speed of innovation and change in the external environment. In response to change, many companies all over the world have been striving for companywide transformation. With their own methods and styles, some have achieved significant success while others are still working to get there. To ensure achievement of long-lasting results, it's necessary to clarify the purpose of companywide improvement and transformation. Indeed, countless numbers of improvement and implementation methods for companywide transformation have been introduced in the market. Unfortunately, with so much at their fingertips, people often jump into the *how to* before they clearly understand the *why*.

Table 1-1.
Purposes and Assessment of Companywide Improvement and Transformation

Purposes	Assessment Targets	Assessment Indicators
1. Significant contribution to achieving the business/profit plans (Securing profit)	Results	• Performance vis-à-vis business plans (e.g., performance indices of achieving sales turnover, profit margin, and business plans) • Management indicator trends (e.g., sales growth rate, sales profit ratio, profit rate, labor productivity, sales at breakeven point)
2. Accumulation and standardization of know-how learned from the improvement process, which enables human resources and technologies to develop (Strengthening improvement and development capability)	Processes	• Accumulation of intrinsic technologies* (number of technological standards, research papers, and patents) • Accumulation of management technologies** (amount of standardized know-how and quality index of know-how)

*   Intrinsic technology refers to the essential techniques and methods for conducting work and achieving tasks.
** Management technology refers to the techniques and methods for improving the quality or quantity of tasks.

What would you say if a junior member of your company asked, "Why do we have to implement companywide improvement?" My explanation is summed up in Table 1-1, which shows the purposes of companywide improvement, as well as the measures needed to assess company progress toward those purposes

Securing Profits

Obviously, one of the main reasons for companywide improvement is to achieve the company's business/profit plans. In Figure 1-1, the outer circle represents a company's business plans, which are translated into daily business activities for making profits. The inner circles represent companywide improvement initiatives, which focus on daily business activities that greatly contribute to achieving business plans. Other aspects of Figure 1-1 will be explained later. Our intent here is to point out that improvement initiatives are part of the annual business/profit plans.

This may be obvious, but I'll say it anyway. Profits are not the only reason a company exists. A company exists to serve society and earn its respect. Today, more than ever, many companies are seriously asking themselves what they should do to be respected. To earn respect, a company's success should include its ability to provide a stable and

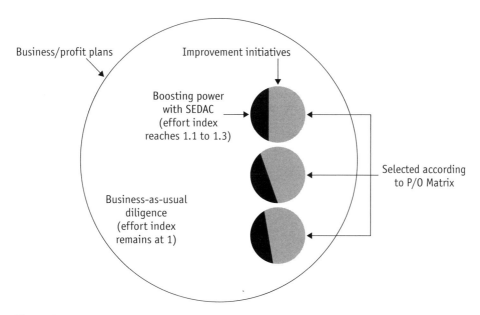

Figure 1-1.
Achievement of Business Plans

comfortable life for employees and to contribute to society with quality products and services. For these reasons as well, a company should be able to turn a profit.

Fostering and Using Improvement and Development Powers

Another very important reason to implement companywide improvement is to foster, utilize, and build the company's improvement and development powers. Since the early 1980s, I have worked with many companies as a consultant and have closely observed their companywide activities. While some companies achieved their business plans almost perfectly year after year, others did not. At the end of the year, despite their rigorous efforts, many companies still fell short of their goals. Nevertheless, over time, some of them managed to transform themselves into much stronger organizations and even went on to achieve or surpass their targets.

The question here is what makes companies different? Of course, what and how improvement projects are chosen impacts whether or not a company achieves its business plans. These, however, are not the only reasons, nor are they the fundamental ones.

When companies discuss resources, they often refer to people, technologies, money, information, and time—all in the same breath. Yet each of these is different and each possesses different characteristics. For example, time is the same for your company as it is for your competition. Money, on the other hand, can be intentionally manipulated and moved around depending on a company's situation at any given time.

What about people and technologies? (Technologies, by the way, are not limited to manufacturing industries; nonmanufacturing industries have technologies too.) Both people and technologies should be developed over time, a process that is possible only by building up one's operational, organizational, and managerial powers year after year. Some companies purchase technology rather than developing it, but this is the exception rather than the rule.

To improve and transform, companies must continuously strengthen their people and their technologies. Simply borrowing or purchasing either resource will eventually lead to failure. Even if a company works hard one year, it cannot expect to improve these resources immediately. Developing people and technologies requires well-planned, continuous, and long-term effort. The difference between companies that achieve their business plans and those that don't lies in their ability to accumulate powers over time—power to organize, work continuously, and develop. Without making a conscious effort to accumulate such powers, each year's hard work just repeats itself and ends in disappointment. On the flip side, accumulating powers positions a company to succeed in related projects as well as new challenges. As a matter of fact, the more powers a company accumulates, the smoother its business goes.

How Are Powers Accumulated?

In Japan, we often suggest basing performance evaluations not only on results, but also on the process used to achieve results. It's important, though, to go beyond emotional evaluations. Saying that someone worked hard or had a good attitude is not enough. The evaluation criteria must be clear and should include the following two questions:

1. What has the person *learned* by working hard? In other words, what new findings were made as a result of the improvement process?

2. Has the know-how been *refined and formatted* for future use? In other words, can the knowledge gained be transformed into viable information that others can use to guide them in similar cases?

When we work wholeheartedly, whether our results end in failure or success, our intrinsic and managerial knowledge expands. In this age of tough competition, hard work should include learning lessons from our efforts. This means we ought to extract the essence of individual experience and transform it into guiding rules that can be applied widely across the organization. If you really take a scientific approach to your work, you will accumulate know-how, transform the company, and give yourself a competitive edge.

How Do We Know We Are Making Progress?

Item 2 in Table 1-1 shows examples of indicators that measure how well process objectives are achieved. For intrinsic technologies, it shows the number of technical standards, the number of research papers, and the number of patents. Management technologies, on the other hand, are another aspect that may not be as readily understood. Let's look at some examples.

The Takasago Works of Mitsubishi Heavy Industries manufactures machinery for the electric power industry, including large-scale rotary machines, such as steam turbines for fossil fuel and nuclear power plants, gas turbines, hydro and wind power equipment, and refrigeration systems. The plant's purchasing department took up an improvement initiative for material procurement practices. By effectively managing budget and material purchasing costs, and by strengthening value analysis (VA) practices, they were able to substantially reduce cost.

In the process of achieving this result, the purchasing department developed and standardized nine new work procedures and techniques as indicated in item 2 in Table 1-2. At the same time, department employees grew through their experience. By applying their newfound know-how, they are sure to do an even better job in the future.

For example, one of the nine new work procedures helped Takasago Works deal more effectively with vendors on its VA proposals. The com-

Table 1-2.
Building Improvement Powers
(Purchasing Department, Takasago Works, Mitsubishi Heavy Industries)

Status of Improvement Activities			
1. Number of SEDAC cards		(April 1988 to January 1989)	
Problem cards	Improvement cards	Standard cards	"First-class" cards
621	587	224	22
2. "First-class" procurement work procedures and techniques			
Cost Reduction		Work Process Improvement	
1. Mandated VA proposals from vendors with a project cost quotation of ¥5 million or more 2. Developed a profile of subcontractors in need of guidance and improvement 3. Developed a checklist for processing work orders for local subcontractors who perform retrofit and maintenance services 4. Encouraged more competition among vendors (both domestic and foreign); enforced new vendor award criteria, when bid prices are the same		1. Reinforced the basic work rules and promoted the streamlining of work procedures through departmental audit 2. Installed dedicated "hot file" racks for specified delivery slips in the material handling office 3. Developed procedures and techniques for processing consumption taxes imposed on direct imports 4. Upgraded computer communications to enable direct input of purchase order files from the production control system to the procurement management system 5. Reinforced predelivery coordination practices to streamline indirect work, such as unloading and storage	

pany learned the key points of this procedure from a year's worth of requiring vendors with a project cost of ¥5 million ($50,000)* or more to submit VA proposals. Then they standardized their know-how, which is now available for all department employees and should soon help them become more effective VA promoters.

The SEDAC cards in item 1 of Table 1-2 will be discussed further in Chapter 3, but need some explanation here. (SEDAC stands for Structure for Enhancing Daily Activities through Creativity.) The number of problem cards (621) represents the purchasing department's list of problems, which need to be solved to achieve improvement objectives, overcome past obstacles, remedy undesirable situations, and remove the causes of problems.

The number of improvement cards (587) represents the number of ideas generated by department team members to resolve the above issues. The number of standard cards (224) represents the number of ideas tested and considered effective.

From the standard cards, "first-class" cards were chosen based on their originality, ingenuity, creativity, or on the results they generated. The contents of both the standard and the first-class cards were compiled in nine work procedures and techniques, shown in item 2 of Table 1-2.

Converting a person's knowledge into information to share with colleagues is essential for company growth. This example shows us that, for a company to grow, it is essential to convert an individual's know-how into transferable information.

WHAT SHOULD MANAGEMENT TECHNOLOGIES BE USED FOR?

People have long extracted the essence of excellent individual work experience and have formalized (standardized) it into know-how—or a better way of doing their jobs. This is often called *management technology* and is turned into standards, manuals, or textbooks.

An easy-to-understand example of this extraction process is the case of Frank Gilbreth, one of the pioneers of industrial engineering (IE). To put what he learned from his teacher into action, Gilbreth traded his business suit for working clothes and became the apprentice of a bricklaying

---

*Translator's note: A U.S. dollar equivalent for Japanese yen figures is given in parentheses throughout this book. For simplicity, the conversion rate of $1.00 to ¥100 is used.

craftsman. As such, he not only attentively observed a veteran craftsman, but also gained firsthand experience in bricklaying. Gilbreth developed his findings into the well-known *principles of motion economy.*

Essentially, Gilbreth's principles taught people how to do manual operations efficiently. For example:

- Use both hands simultaneously, rather than using one hand

- Minimize the number of movements, such as loading and unloading of work pieces and tools

- Combine tools, if more than two tools are used

- Facilitate movement

Gilbreth extracted the universal essence of the good craftsman's excellent work and formulated it into principles others could learn.

Gilbreth's principles apply not only to bricklaying, but to all other jobs that involve movement. Anyone who learns these principles and adapts such principles to a specific task can do the job more efficiently than if he or she tried to do it "their own way" from scratch. Is it surprising that Gilbreth's principles are still embodied in today's machine tools? Machine tools handle multiple jobs simultaneously, just like a human uses both hands. Once the machining center chucks a workpiece, it does not release the piece until all possible machining jobs are done. In this way, no loading/unloading and no transfers are necessary.

The process of extracting and accumulating know-how was traditionally considered the job of a few chosen experts, such as Gilbreth. But why should we rely on experts? Why shouldn't we, as a group of people, become our own experts? By doing so, we can extract the essence of our own excellent work experience and results. We can then formalize (standardize) this essence to strengthen our know-how and manuals—our management technologies. By adopting this approach, we become more efficient and effective.

The Effectiveness and Limitations of Management Technologies

Generally speaking, an organization consists of regular experienced people, a large number of "developing" people, and a handful of expert

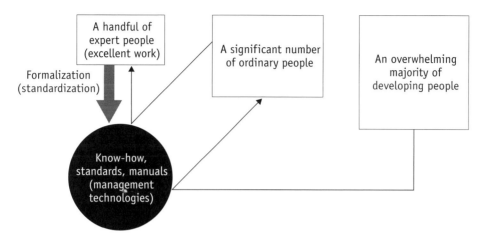

Figure 1-2.
Effectiveness of Management Technologies

people. By using management technologies, the developing employees can learn to do their jobs as well as regular experienced people within a relatively short time. Moreover, through the use of management technologies, regular experienced people can work as well as expert people. Figure 1-2 shows this transfer of know-how. This is the role of management technologies—no more and no less.

Even so, management technologies fall short of duplicating the level of work done by that small handful of truly excellent people—the masters of their trades. The work of these masters almost always involves gut feeling—something unwritten or unexplainable that enables them to perform exceptionally. Of course, there are the few exceptions. Some jobs are so prescriptive that they allow little or no room for gut feeling. Many accounting jobs, for example, are performed precisely, by the book, exactly as prescribed by work manuals.

The point is this: We cannot discuss the accumulation of know-how in one broad brush, since some industries and jobs are more difficult to standardize than others. However, we should strive to find ways of standardizing even seemingly difficult work functions. Although their effectiveness may vary, management technologies help people in the ways discussed above.

From the viewpoint of the true masters, manuals are nothing but a collection of *known* techniques. Yet these very manuals are undoubtedly good for developing people and for regular experienced people, who constitute the majority of people in most companies.

I once saw a TV program featuring the topic "Are management technologies useful?" Those who participated seemed to come from different groups, which are covered in Figure 1-2. Perhaps reflecting on their personal experience, they argued about whether management technologies are useful or not. In my opinion, this was a waste of time. Management techniques always possess benefits and limitations and should be applied accordingly.

Types of Management Technologies and Their Users

The standards or manuals (management technologies) mentioned in Figure 1-2 come in two types: procedures and techniques. *Procedures* outline the basic steps for performing jobs. They are like the fundamental movements in a sport. Except for a few instances in which new procedures are developed, efforts to standardize procedures mostly add to, complement, or simplify existing ones. *Techniques,* on the other hand, are the ways in which jobs are performed well. As indicated in the example of Takasago Works, Mitsubishi Heavy Industries, new-job know-how is developed through standardizing the techniques by which jobs are performed.

In both cases, to use management technologies effectively, it's important to know the purpose and role of each technology and to know the users. It's also important to continuously accumulate new know-how on an ongoing basis.

Let me digress a bit. Japan is said to possess construction technology used in building large bridges and tunnels, such as the Honshu-Shikou bridge and the English Channel tunnel. This strength is attributed to the accrual of necessary engineering information and manuals as well as development of people with the talent to design and construct such big projects.

Don't get me wrong—it's a fact that truly excellent jobs can only be done by a handful of experts. But this doesn't devalue management technology. Like any useful system, we just have to understand its strengths as well as limitations.

THE SPEED OF TRANSFORMATION IS A FUNCTION OF ORGANIZATIONAL FITNESS

Figure 1-3 depicts my experiences with the pace of transformation at various companies. The left column lists the stages of companywide transformation, with a short description that represents the situation observed at each different level of progress. Above stage 0 (pre-improvement) progress is made at five levels. These range from the stage where some people have begun improvement activities but have not coordinated efforts as a company (stage 1), to the stage where more than 80 percent of the people in the company, beginning with top management, share a feeling of success and optimism about measuring up to benchmarks (stage 5). Stage 5, then, is the level at which companywide transformation is realized.

Different slopes depict different speeds of progress. If an organization is currently situated at point A, it will take a considerable amount of time to reach the success line at the top. If it sits at point B, the organization can expect to reach the success line much more quickly.

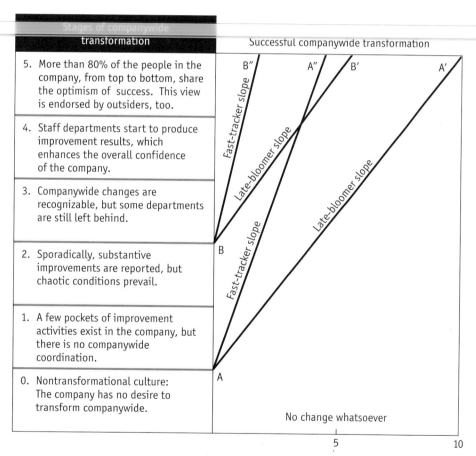

Figure 1-3.
How Long Does It Take to Achieve Companywide Transformation?

The horizontal axis depicts time. Even if companies start from the same point—point A, for example—they should not expect to reach the success line at the same time. Determining an expected time to reach the success line is a function of the following factors:

- Top management's commitment to companywide transformation

- Management leadership

- The existing level of intrinsic technology

- The capability for managing companywide activities

- The methods of promoting companywide activities, and

- The surrounding business environment

These factors will be discussed in more detail in the next section.

Depending on how well the organization practices these factors, its path to success will vary. Fast-trackers, for example, will reach the success line more quickly (point A to A″). Late bloomers, on the other hand, will reach success much further in the future (point A to A′). Of course, within the space of any given year a fast-tracker company can move toward the late-bloomer slope and vice versa.

Naturally, the current improvement fitness level of a company—the assets built up over time—greatly influences the speed at which the company transforms. As things get better and the company starts to see its efforts accelerate, a positive cycle begins to turn. Knowing this fact, it's my hope that top management will lead its companywide transformation efforts in a way that puts them as close to the fast-track path as possible.

As discussed above, even though the speed of progress varies, once an organization begins its improvement efforts, things get better. The only exception is when the company doesn't have the will or desire to transform on a companywide basis. If this is the case, no change whatsoever will occur.

One final point: The conditions for effective and efficient companywide transformation are universal—there are no important differences between companies of different nationalities or industries.

SEVEN CONDITIONS FOR THE FAST TRACK

Table 1-3 lists seven conditions for taking the fast-track path to company-wide transformation depicted in Figure 1-3. When a company lacks these conditions, it swings to the late-bloomer path in proportion to its shortage level. This book intends to demonstrate how a company can carry out companywide transformation and proceed toward the fast-track path, regardless of its country or industry.

It's easy for an outsider to give advice like "you must" or "you should" to those involved in the company's business. Just giving advice, however, will not help change reality. Instead, from my limited experience, I would like to offer practical structures to help the reader's continuous efforts to achieve companywide transformation—structures that have been tried, tested, and universally applied. But before we discuss specific implementation plans in the chapters that follow, the seven conditions for fast-track transformation are explained below.

Condition 1: Top Management Commitment

Having met with many top and middle managers, I've never met one who said, "I'm not committed to improvement." Everyone is committed to improvement. Yet commitment is only meaningful when it's communicated and practiced. Through many consulting assignments, I've learned that the driving force behind persistent management commitment is a sense of accountability, or morale, which in this instance refers to *a sense of sincerity about one's job*. When morale is low, nothing happens.

Commitment from top management is so important that even if a company lacks other fast-track conditions, it can still be successful if the

Table 1-3.
Seven Conditions for Fast-Track Companywide Transformation

1. Top and middle management commitment to companywide transformation
2. Superior in-house development capabilities
    - Intrinsic technologies, mainly by R&D department
    - Management technologies, through daily work
3. Superior managing capabilities
4. Effective in-house education and on-the-job coaching
5. Total active participation of staff departments in companywide improvement
6. Enabling structures to promote improvement in daily work
7. Enabling structures that encourage creative improvement by integrating knowledge and experience

majority of top and middle managers persevere in their desire to change the status quo and improve the company. They are the only ones who can open the path of companywide transformation. Although some readers may find their companies lacking many favorable (fast-track) conditions, it's my sincere hope that they will never give up and, as a result, will succeed.

Condition 2: Superior Development Capabilities

To achieve companywide transformation, it's vital for the company to have high-level technologies, both intrinsic and managerial. Even more important, a company must possess an in-house capability for developing these technologies. Suppose, for example, a company comes across a new management technique, but only 80 percent of it applies to the business. If this company does not possess the capability to develop management technology, it will probably become disturbed over the portion that doesn't apply. As a result, rather than tailoring the 20 percent to make the technique usable, the company is likely to discard the technique entirely.

Intrinsic technologies are developed internally by the research and development department. But how should a company develop managerial technologies in-house? This issue will be addressed in various parts of this book, including "Study Group Activities for Companywide Integration" in Chapter 4 (page 111).

Condition 3: Superior Managing Capabilities

Unassumingly, I once asked the people at Sumitomo Kashima Works, "What do you think of your works?" Their reply went like this:

- We are gentlemen.

- We have a rich history. We are free and open-hearted. We are both young and old.

- We have a strong sense of responsibility and pride.

- Every day is not totally enjoyable. But if you do your part whole-heartedly, someone in the company always helps you.

- The job here is demanding, but we are persistent.

- We work with an open heart, which is important for constant learning.

A high level of management capability means, I believe, that an organization has achieved a state similar to what the people at Kashima Works describe above. In addition to the characteristics found at Kashima Works, outsiders take note of the following when they encounter well-managed companies:

- A lively atmosphere

- Good interemployee relations

- A strong sense of manager responsibility

- Courteous telephone responses

- A well-set but relaxed pace

- No mistreatment of weaker or slower people

The list goes on and on. All of these characteristics, by the way, are interrelated. When a company practices one, it often practices others. Don't be fooled—these are important characteristics for any company, and none of them can be developed overnight.

With a full heart: create excitement, dreams, and technology. This was Sony Inazawa's 1993 companywide transformation slogan, which was developed over the span of five meetings by both managers and first-line employees. While it may seem somewhat flowery and rhetorical, this slogan gained the employees' enthusiastic support because Sony Inazawa embodied a lively atmosphere. Perhaps it was because the company actually created excitement, dreams, and technology.

Condition 4: Effective In-House Education and On-the-Job Coaching

Any discussion of organizational education and training includes both on-the-job and off-the-job training. The question, however, is whether on-the-job training really follows off-the-job training. At the end of an off-the-job training course, the instructor often tells the class, "Please apply what you've learned on the job." Unfortunately, the class frequently takes this to mean, "We will do nothing."

The right side of Figure 1-4 shows the ladder of continuous improvement, while the left shows its individual rungs. The rungs symbolize

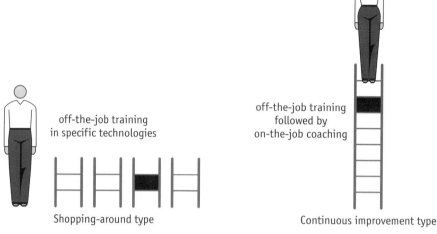

off-the-job training
in specific technologies

Shopping-around type

off-the-job training
followed by
on-the-job coaching

Continuous improvement type

Figure 1-4.
Getting the Most from Education and Training

training received off the job, such as quality control and industrial engineering training (management technologies) or equipment maintenance and microelectronics application training (intrinsic technologies). While intrinsic technologies tend to be applied immediately after such training, this is not always the case with management technologies.

How then can managers help employees transfer off-the-job training into applied daily work? The answer is through thoughtful *on-the-job coaching,* which is even better than on-the-job training. In the role of coach, managers and supervisors show employees how to apply specific work techniques soon after the techniques have been learned. In this way, the ladder of continuous improvement is extended upward.

Some people may mistakenly think that the ladder of continuous improvement is extended by learning without coaching. People who believe this "shop around" for good training. They send their employees to one course, another one, and then another, and so on. The employees may pick something up here and there, but without coaching nothing really happens. It's not because the training wasn't any good (although that is sometimes true also).

After the training, managers must educate and guide employees in applying it to daily work. In this situation, customs such as long-term employment and seniority systems are helpful, although on the surface they may seem traditional and unnecessary. The reality is that without these customs, the ingrained belief that senior employees guide and teach junior ones would not exist. And without these customs, senior employees are likely to feel threatened by junior employees, or they might become concerned that junior employees will someday abandon the company. Enthusiasm for coaching, therefore, can be damaged by the absence of long-term employment and seniority customs.

While Japanese companies have relied on these favorable business customs for quite a while, they must continue to deal with the tough issues of lifetime and seniority-based employment in a changing economic environment. It's easy for many companies to take these customs for granted, just as one might overlook the importance of air and water in everyday life—a point that will be discussed further in Chapter 8.

Earlier, I mentioned that I prefer on-the-job coaching over on-the-job training. What I mean is that it's not enough just to *train* employees to apply what they have learned. In addition, the manager must *encourage* employees to blend their own thinking and experience with what they have learned.

For example, employee A presents a project report. Employee A's manager reads it and tells him, "If you had analyzed the situation using the statistical techniques you learned in the last training course, your conclusion would be better." "So," the manager says, "I will give you a week. Compare the two groups of data using the statistical test method you learned. Come back and report your professional findings."

If the managers or senior members coached their employees this way, the employees would learn the importance of working with data objectively. They would also learn the merit of applying statistical techniques that enable them to do a better, more efficient job than they could do strictly on their own. At the very least, this provides an important opportunity for employees to think. Also, by applying what they have learned, employees will see value and begin to enjoy learning.

Condition 5: Total Active Participation of Staff Departments

In general, the reality of companywide improvement has manifested only in line organizations. Staff functions haven't traditionally participated and, when they have, it's been on the surface. Part of the reason for this is that staff people think they're already serious about doing their jobs well. Consequently, even after the company launches new companywide improvement efforts, they feel they have nothing more to contribute.

In light of this, I would like to redefine what improvement means for managers and staffers by asking the following question: "What (quality and quantity) in your work process or products has become better today than it was yesterday?" Just working as earnestly today as you did yesterday is not enough. You must make a conscious effort, every day, to answer this question.

In making improvements and contributing to transformation, managers and staffers are expected not only to correct existing deficiencies, but also to take steps toward making significant changes. The idea is to challenge current practices, question the necessity of these practices, and start anew. I experienced this type of situation many years back, when the then-popular test-lot manufacturing method was challenged. Focusing on a small test lot in advance of final manufacturing, this method determined optimal manufacturing conditions. By switching to a standard QC method, however, the dispersion of product quality was reduced by two-thirds and manufacturing throughput time was cut in half.

As shown in Figure 1-5, in general the difference between good performers and poor performers among first-line employees varies by no more than 20 percent. Staffers, however, vary by as much as 500 percent! Even more shocking, the difference often reaches 1,000 percent at the mid- and top-management levels. Given this, it is not hard to see why a poorly performing manager can make an organization ten times worse than it was before. Since the participation and effort of managers and staffers have such a dramatic impact on performance, we expect their participation in companywide improvement to contribute substantially to results.

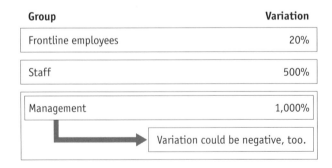

Group	Variation
Frontline employees	20%
Staff	500%
Management	1,000%

Variation could be negative, too.

Figure 1-5.
Variation in Work Performance

Condition 6: Enabling Structures to Promote Improvement in Daily Work

As discussed earlier in Table 1-3, themes for companywide improvement should be selected from daily business activities. No matter how innovative the theme may seem, it still has to be translated into everyday work tasks to be achieved. For this reason, daily work should not be viewed as small, insignificant jobs and should not be considered separately from improvement and innovation efforts. Companies make profit from every employee's daily work contribution.

If you don't adopt this view, you may get caught in the same trap we once did. All week we were busy doing our regular daily jobs (which were important), which left us wondering when we would have time for improvement projects. As it turned out, the only time left was during the weekends.

Unless we structure in the time to carry out improvement activities on a daily basis as part of our regular jobs, people will say, "We're too busy to improve." What they're really saying is, "We can improve when things are slow" or "Only less busy departments can improve." The truth is, busy departments need to improve and innovate more than any so they can carry out their jobs more efficiently. For example, back when the consumption tax was introduced in Japan, I visited a company's accounting department, which was very busy preparing the organization for the new tax system. They were so busy they couldn't handle their planned improvement projects. In such a case, the priority improvement theme should have been to introduce and implement the consumption tax system smoothly.

To carry out daily work improvement activities, it's essential to designate the most important work—work that is pressing and needs to be done now—as improvement themes. Furthermore, such a structure should enable employees to contribute to improvement while carrying out their daily jobs. Specific structures for doing this will be introduced in later chapters (the P/O Matrix in Chapter 2 and SEDAC in Chapter 3).

Condition 7: Enabling Structures That Encourage Creative Improvements by Integrating Knowledge and Experience

To promote improvement, an enabling structure should integrate everyone's knowledge and experience and encourage new, creative ideas. *Everyone's knowledge* refers not only to the knowledge of people inside the company, but to all available knowledge in the world. The idea is to take advantage of all available and new knowledge to realize our improvement theme. Such knowledge comes in many forms: books, reports, technical papers, and videos to name a few.

In this age of rapid progress, knowledge and information change constantly. In the midst of all this, employees turn over too. Such a turbulent environment requires organizations to have an enabling system or structure by which they can accumulate and hand down knowledge and information.

An enabling structure is indispensable for accumulating existing knowledge and information and for coming up with new ideas. Such a structure facilitates improvement activities by encouraging the participation of frontline employees, managers, supervisors, and staffers, who provide support according to their professional knowledge. Also, an enabling structure draws unique advantages and ideas out of diverse constituencies and integrates them for effective action.

SOME CHARACTERISTIC EXAMPLES

In the previous section, I introduced seven conditions that enable an organization to achieve significant improvement results. This section introduces a few typical examples of organizations that embodied these conditions and achieved significant results.

Universal Applicability

Figure 1-6, a process quality defect index from September 1987 to January 1988, shows improvement trends in several of Sony Corporation's overseas plants. One of the world's leading electronics manufacturers, this company has developed and introduced many products that were first to market in Japan and the world. As the graph shows, each plant is measured against an average quality defect index of 100 as of January 1987.

In May of 1986, the Sony U.K. plant held its first SEDAC session in Wales at the Brigend plant. Since then, similar sessions have been held at other plants. In just 12 to 18 months, all the Sony plants achieved remarkable reductions in process quality defects—reductions of 80 percent or more! And as of March 1988, these overseas plants matched the quality defect levels of their Japanese counterparts. Needless to say, Sony's suc-

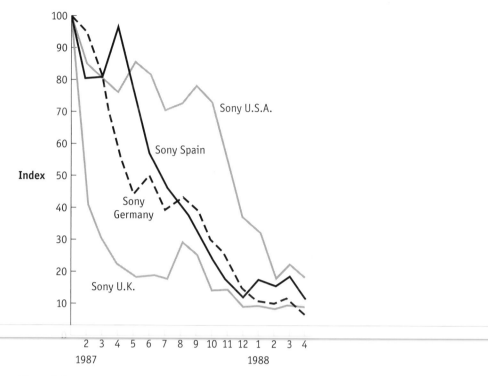

Figure 1-6.
In-Process Quality Defect Rate (Sony Group, Consumer Electronics)

cess with these overseas plants has given the company important information for formulating future business strategies.

For any technique to be useful, it must have wide applicability—anyone should be able to apply it anywhere. The plants mentioned in Figure 1-6 all operate in different social and economic environments and in different cultures. For example, the Sony Germany plant in Stuttgart has employees from 21 different nations. This cultural diversity, however, should not be a barrier to successfully carrying out improvement initiatives.

Urgency and New Challenge

Figure 1-7 shows an improvement case involving Sony Senmaya, a Sony group company whose main business is manufacturing information equipment for car CD players and telephones. This plant succeeded in reducing a process defect rate of 13 percent—a commonly accepted rate at the time—to less than 1 percent within a year. Just one result of this

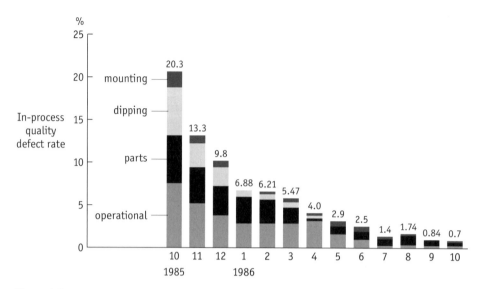

Figure 1-7.
In-Process Quality Defect Rate on a Mounting Line (Sony Senmaya)

success was landing an OEM production contract with Nissan Motors. At the beginning of this project, everyone thought the goal of less than 1 percent process defects was impossible. With the total cooperation of Sony Corporation's AS division headquarters, however, the plant was able to conclude this project successfully and lay the foundation for an OEM production contract initiated years later in 1989 with Ford Motor Company. The bottom line? In just one year, from October 1985 to October 1986, the manufacturing plant achieved dramatic improvement results.

Why did Sony achieve such good results? Mainly, it had a sense of urgency. Excellent leadership played an important role too, since this was a new challenge that had no precedent. Additionally, SEDAC helped by facilitating cooperation between the Sony Senmaya manufacturing plant and division headquarters. After going through the SEDAC process, one team member said he felt as if he could have a meeting every day with different colleagues who, in actuality, were far apart. This person highlights that having prompt access to accurate information is a key to success.

In-House Education: The Basis for Improvement Activities

The Bucyrus, Ohio, plant of Timken, an American manufacturer known for its tapered roller bearings, conducted various improvement activities using the Policy/Objective Matrix and SEDAC. (See Chapters 2 and 3 for more information on the P/O Matrix and SEDAC.) Because of its outstanding improvement, *Industry Week* magazine recognized this plant in 1992 as one of America's best plants. To merit such a distinction, the Bucyrus plant had to achieve excellent results through continuous improvement, demonstrate high manager/employee morale, and effectively implement characteristic improvement activities. Partly due to SEDAC, the Bucyrus plant achieved its targets for 30 of 50 improvement projects and cut plantwide quality problems in half. They achieved these results by reducing bearing machining process quality defects by 30 percent, cup finishing quality defects and rework by 50 percent, and three other product defect rates by 19, 35, and 78 percent respectively.

The Bucyrus plant achieved these results largely because it committed itself to SEDAC, which provided special training to 112 plant employees, including 23 managers and staffers, 35 supervisors, and 54 operators.

Today it's rare, even in the first-line workplace, for a supervisor or staffer to solve a problem alone. The Bucyrus plant succeeded because it garnered the cooperation of many people, functions, and departments. By training everyone throughout the ranks with the same curriculum, and by encouraging people to use common techniques, the entire plant was able to contribute and work together toward common goals. Certainly, Timken's Bucyrus plant teaches us that in-house education is an important part of an effective improvement infrastructure.

Improvement That Reflects Each Company's Individuality

In November 1992, SEDAC users met for a workshop in Rome, where 30 companies throughout Europe participated and where 8 companies made presentations. Many said that the P/O Matrix and SEDAC contributed to improved performance in their companies.

Table 1-4 shows the results achieved by the Rome Airport Company (Societa Aeroporti di Roma) in Italy, which has 6,500 employees working around the clock to service airlines from 76 nations. As you might imagine, an aircraft receives many services from many airport vehicles after landing and before takeoff. For this reason, the company decided to use SEDAC to help reduce service vehicle fuel costs.

The company began by running simulations to determine optimal operating schedules for various service vehicles. When these schedules were actually implemented, however, the vehicles often encountered unanticipated situations and problems. When these arose, service vehicles deviated temporarily from the rules while continuing to serve customers—

Table 1-4.
Improvement of Airport Operations Using SEDAC
(The Rome Airport Company, Societa Aeroporti di Roma))

Number of employees: 6,500	1992
• Reduced fuel consumption of service vehicles used in the airport 　　Fuel consumption of aircraft service vehicles 　　(Annual savings of $200,000)	−16%
• Reduced maintenance personnel injuries 　　Lost-time injuries of maintenance personnel	−30%
• Reduced total paper consumption in the airport administration 　　Volume of paper consumption	−23%

the airlines and their passengers. Later, after operations were again under control, SEDAC was used to generate ideas for preventing the same deficiencies from recurring. By following this approach, the company's 441 automotive department people—35 managers/leaders and 406 employees—refined their operating schedules. In addition, they used the successfully tested SEDAC improvement cards to develop 20 know-how booklets for airport vehicle operations.

In the service industries, it's easy to achieve nominal cost reductions while neglecting the goal of *customer satisfaction*. Such cost reductions, however, are suicidal. Without falling into this trap, the Rome Airport Company achieved fuel cost reduction savings of approximately $200,000.

During this same period, the maintenance department of the Rome Airport Company began a corrective maintenance project to improve measures on the failed parts and systems of maintenance equipment for airport vehicles. They didn't want to simply repair equipment to its original condition; they wanted to reduce the rate of accidental maintenance equipment failure and, as a result, reduce maintenance personnel injuries. Furthermore, the administrative department reviewed and upgraded the airport's forms and baggage tags, as well as the purpose behind them. As a whole, the company has achieved the results shown in Table 1-4.

Of course these activities did not begin smoothly or happen automatically. They required exceptional effort from both managers and team leaders, who gradually moved the organization toward improvement. In fact, the general manager who headed the whole effort said that, at first, not everyone understood what needed to be accomplished. He had many meetings with employees in which he communicated the purpose and objectives of the project, appealing to the employees by saying, "Let's improve the quality of our work and provide better service to customers." To accomplish this, he felt it was essential for everyone to understand how important their jobs were. While making progress with SEDAC, incidentally, the airport improved cross-functional coordination along with its work atmosphere.

As a side note, whenever I work with these companies I avoid using the term *Japanese-style management*. It's true that, while implementing companywide improvement/transformation to achieve business objectives, companies often develop traits seen in Japanese companies. However, in such companies, these traits are by-products; they are not the result of directly pursuing such traits as Japanese-style companies do. My point is this: I believe that each company's improvement and transformation initiative should have its own distinct individuality and management system.

HOW LONG DOES IT TAKE TO BECOME A FIRST-CLASS COMPANY?

One of the questions most frequently asked by top management, especially in the West, is "How long does it take to reach the success line and become *first class in transformation?*" I forced myself earlier in Figure 1-3 to give you some numbers. Based on my experience, the answer is at least three years, although it can take up to ten.

Many factors, of course, influence which progress slope (see Figure 1-3) the company takes. For example, the amount of effort a company expends on transformation, especially at the beginning, affects how long it takes to reach first-class status.

In the United States, business process reengineering is said to have a success rate between 30 and 50 percent. Reengineering, if it is to succeed, needs top management leadership. From my own experience, I am convinced this is true. Let us say, for example, that a company begins a reengineering project and succeeds within three years. For this to happen, the company surely must have developed a certain capability for companywide improvement. Without such a basic capability, even with excellent ideas, success is unlikely.

On the other hand, it is possible for a company to succeed, regardless of its improvement culture, if it has superior top management leadership.

This is true not only for reengineering, but for any initiative that requires companywide involvement. So what does it mean to have excellent top management—a must for companywide transformation? And what are the systematic and specific means by which this leadership is translated into action? These topics will be discussed in the next chapter on the P/O Matrix.

Organizing Actions for Improvement/Transformation: the Policy Objective Matrix

Perhaps many readers feel they know a lot about policy management, or management by objectives (MBO). Since "knowing" and "doing" are two different things, this chapter lays out my experience with clients in developing and implementing a practical methodology for what I call policy/objective management.

MANAGING IMPROVEMENT ACTIVITIES

Management transformation cannot be achieved through external forces. People must continuously think and act for themselves. The P/O Matrix and SEDAC (discussed in Chapter 3) are implementation vehicles for internally driven transformation. When used properly, these vehicles enable companies to make deliberate, efficient, and effective steps toward their transformation goals. In this chapter, we cover the P/O Matrix.

The Policy/Objective (P/O) Matrix is a tool for visualizing and translating top management's commitment to improvement and transformation into concrete actions. It compiles information on annual policies/objectives at different levels of the organization and links this content from the top of the organization to the front lines. It also ensures cross-functional cooperation. In short, the P/O Matrix is a technique by which to manage companywide activities to achieve policies and objectives.

Specifically, the P/O Matrix aims to:

1. Provide a company with an enabling structure for achieving priority business plans and for making yearly progress toward management transformation.

2. Prevent a company from falling into an undesirable state of affairs, such as the separation of management transformation efforts from efforts to achieve annual business plans. When this happens, a company treats management transformation as a mere slogan or temporary program and considers it separate from regular, ongoing work.

3. Facilitate the planning and establishment of policies and objectives that specify what, why, who, how, and how much to accomplish during a given term.

4. Capture, document, and coordinate a company's highest priority tasks.

5. Develop business plans by integrating the knowledge and experience of all employees and by networking all parts of the company, beginning with top management.

6. Allocate resources for improvement (people, technology, money, information, and time) in a way that is optimal for the whole company.

7. Provide an enabling structure for interdepartmental cooperation, since many priorities require the efforts of more than one department.

8. Make plans visible to anyone in the organization at any time.

9. Help a company respond quickly to changes in the surrounding environment.

10. Provide an enabling structure for anticipating and removing obstacles while proceeding with plans.

11. Prevent a company, when it becomes busy, from making excuses for not improving.

12. Help a company use its full companywide capabilities to carry out plans.

13. Periodically examine and study a company's performance in implementing priority improvement plans (at the end of any term) and incorporate findings into the P/O Matrix practices for the next term.

MAKING TOP MANAGEMENT COMMITMENT TANGIBLE

Combining Policy Management and Management by Objectives

The primary purpose of the P/O Matrix is to deliberately promote and manage improvement activities in a way that achieves the goal of company-wide transformation. Before plunging into the details of how the P/O Matrix is applied, however, a little background is in order.

The origin of *management by objectives* is attributed to a German sociologist, who said, "When people are given specific objectives, they are motivated to work harder and do a better job." According to one definition, management by objectives (MBO) is a management system that aims to achieve the objectives of a company by having each individual in the company set personal objectives that specify what, by when, and how much they will achieve (Ishikawa 1981). Yet many have argued that while defining the end result is important, the management process involved in producing that result is equally or even more important. This process is called *hoshin kanri,* or policy management, first introduced by Bridgestone Tire in Japan.

In recent years, MBO and policy management have shed light on each other, and whichever name is used, they both tend to include objectives and processes. This book, therefore, doesn't attempt to separate the two; instead it uses the term *policy/objective management,* because in practice both objectives and processes are necessary.

Having said this, based on my experience, I don't think it's necessary to develop objectives to the level of each individual, as mentioned in the previous definition of MBO. Rather, it is sufficient to stop developing objectives at the work unit or group level—a point I will elaborate later. For now, suffice it to say that people usually do not have the luxury to work on individual improvement projects or objectives in addition to those of their work unit or group. Even when they do, it's rare that such projects can be accomplished with individual effort alone. They usually require the contributions of other people. One exception: if an effort is geared toward clarifying each person's role in achieving unit projects or objectives, it may be beneficial to deploy objectives down to the individual level.

As Table 1-1 (page 2) showed, there are two purposes for companywide improvement and transformation.

- Securing profit

- Strengthening improvement and development capability

There was a time in the past when companies supported and encouraged any and all improvement projects, without systematically managing them. Perhaps this strategy was necessary back then, when the primary concern was to have people in the company, especially first-line employees, familiarize themselves with improvement activities. In today's climate, however, we can no longer afford such a strategy; instead, we have to manage our improvement activities systematically.

While there are virtually infinite opportunities, large and small, for improvement in any company, we have to allocate highly finite improvement power (total power generated by people, technology, money, information, time, and other resources) to priority improvement projects. Therefore, to constantly achieve priority business plans, it's essential to manage improvement activities in a well-planned and continuous manner.

In this context, a frequently asked question is "Where do we start our companywide improvement activities?" My answer is to begin with policy/objective management. By doing so, a company manages its improvement activities from the very start.

Achieving Objectives as Planned

Figure 2-1 depicts a management system for organizational improvement. It begins at point A, where top management establishes what it intends to accomplish, and ends at point D, where a review is conducted to determine if objectives have materialized as intended. Point D is where actual performance is compared against plan.

After top management's policies are established at point A, they are deployed to the business unit or department level, shown as line B. This is where business unit objectives for achieving top management's policies are developed by articulating why, what, how much, how, by when, and who.

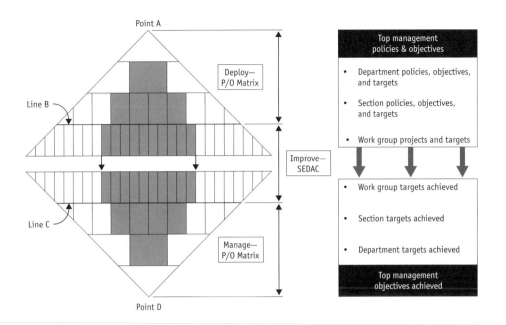

Figure 2-1.

Organizational Management for Improvement

Next, these objectives are broken down into actionable projects, indicated by line C, which are implemented by mobilizing the full improvement power of the organization. The results of each individual improvement project are then summed up, and, if all goes well, the intention of top management is achieved at point D.

Specifically, top management's intent should encompass both purposes of companywide improvement:

1. Profit and performance-related plans:

   • The amount of dollar savings that can be expected to result from improvement activities during the specified period (in support of the business/profit plan)

   • What needs to be accomplished during the specified period, even though monetary payback is not expected during the specified time (to better prepare the company for the future)

2. Improvement- and development-related plans:

   • The amount and type of intrinsic and management technology that should be accumulated and standardized while improvement activities are carried out during the specified time period (to strengthen the company's improvement and development capability)

The first step toward achieving companywide improvement/transformation is to create an enabling structure, such as a P/O Matrix, that is capable of mobilizing and focusing the company's resources on its goals. The following sections of this chapter, therefore, discuss the details of the P/O Matrix.

HOW TO BUILD A P/O MATRIX

The P/O Matrix is a concrete expression of a company's commitment to business improvement, beginning with the commitment of top management. As such, it aims to:

1. Visualize the relationship of the following items on a single piece of paper:

   • A business unit's priority policies for companywide improvement during the current period and for the next two to three years, if necessary

   • Improvement objectives for the current period, including the measures and means to achieve them

   • Targets for each improvement project

   • The overall results expected from all improvement projects

2. Align the contents listed above throughout the organization, from top management to the business units, departments, sections, and still smaller organizational units as necessary to clarify the relationship chain.

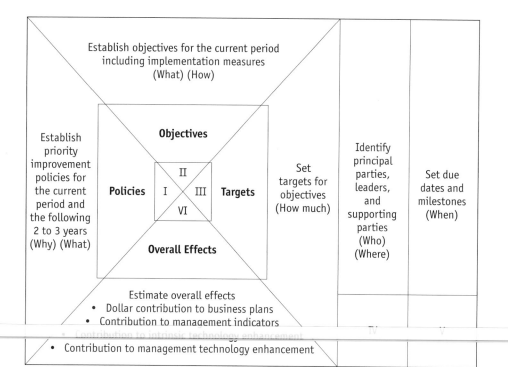

Figure 2-2.
P/O Matrix Contents

To compile the necessary information in a simple way, I decided to use the basic format of one of the seven new QC tools*—the X-type matrix**—and to call it the *P/O (Policy/Objective) Matrix*. Figure 2-2 describes what should be written in each section of the matrix. When a P/O Matrix is prepared, only the key points of each section should be recorded. If more detailed information is necessary, appropriate personnel should include it on a separate sheet of paper.

Section I: Policy

Technology Assessment

After considering what should be done for this term and for the following two to three years, each business unit writes its priority policies in Section I of the P/O Matrix. Naturally, each unit bases its policies on the purposes of companywide improvement stated in Table 1-1. Thus, for Section I of the matrix, each unit selects business activities that will significantly contribute to achieving the company's business plans and to strengthening and accumulating improvement and development capabilities needed for future growth.

Whether the business unit is identifying the priority policies for the current period or looking forward to the next two or three years, it's important to understand such important factors as market trends and customer requirements. These factors are linked with the unit's own competitive technology to develop a scenario for success.

Without a clear direction, improvement efforts become haphazard. Therefore, the top and middle managers of a company are expected to think constantly about the company's direction (or policies) using tools like the market/technology matrix shown in Figure 2-3.

It should be noted that the column for *existing intrinsic technologies* in Figure 2-3 is not a place to simply list the products produced by the business unit using such technologies. Rather, the key question is "What are the seeds of technology that differentiate the unit from others in terms of production methods, quality, and product performance?" Using this process, or conducting a technology assessment of the business unit or company, the unit identifies what existing technologies provide a competitive edge.

Whatever the reason, many Japanese companies often lack this technology perspective and tend simply to keep pace with others. (Hopefully, the reason for this is not because they're afraid their technologies are not unique.) This is paradoxical because if a company does not have superior technologies, it is likely to be drawn into a muddy price war. Such a situation, of course, is undesirable because the company would be settling for overcompetition and low return-on-investment rates, negative realities of Japanese business in general.

Just as the business unit performed an existing intrinsic technology assessment, it should also clarify its management technologies through a management system assessment. For example, SEDAC, discussed in

Market \ Technology	Existing Intrinsic and Management Technologies	Related Intrinsic and Management Technologies	New Intrinsic and Management Technologies
Existing Market	1	4	7
Related Market	2	5	8
New Market	3	6	9

Figure 2-3.
Improvement Direction (Market/Technology Matrix for Policies)

Chapter 3, is a management system for effectively implementing improvement projects. Also, Stockless Production, discussed in Chapter 7, is a management system for controlling the flow of materials and information for production.

The *related intrinsic and management technologies* shown in the middle column of Figure 2-3 refer to technologies that are extrapolations of the technologies discussed above. The right column is for new technologies and new management systems that are not just linear developments from the past, but are created through new combinations of existing technology or represent new technology altogether.

New Viewpoint—*VALUE*

Figure 2-3 also lists three views of the market. When considering a market, it's important to look at it from the customer's viewpoint. A good explanation of this viewpoint is given in a book titled *Strategic Integration for Greater Market Adaptability "SIGMA,"* which proposes to create business strategies that incorporate a slice of *value for the customer* (Kansai Industrial Engineering and Management Systems Society 1993).

Producer's Viewpoint	Customer's Viewpoint
• Quality → Zero Defects • Cost → Product Price • Delivery → Production Lead Time	• **V**aried Needs Satisfaction • **A**menity • **L**ow Risk • **U**ser Costs Minimum • **E**ffective Availability

Source: Kansai Industrial Engineering and Management Systems Society,
*Senryukuteki Togo Seisankanri Sisutemu "SIGMA" (Strategic Integration for Greater
Market Adaptability)*, Nikkan Kogyo Shimbun, 1993.

Figure 2-4.
Customer VALUE

Figure 2-4 illustrates this perspective by comparing the conventional producer-oriented viewpoint of quality, cost, and delivery (or production lead time) with the viewpoint of the customer. This figure uses the acronym *VALUE* to describe the customer's perspective. VALUE consists of the following elements:

1. *Varied needs satisfaction:* Fundamental customer value is provided when a product satisfies the true reasons why each customer buys it. The producer's viewpoint becomes *a shift toward the production of numerous models.* From the customer's side, however, only one model meets the particular needs of each customer just right.

2. *Amenity:* In addition to the practical functions of a product, features that appeal to the customer's senses add value. An example would be the self-esteem a product with a personalized design delivers, or the feeling a customer gets when getting hold of the very latest technology.

3. *Low risk:* These product features provide great value and free the customer from worry about failure or trouble. Such features also include after-sale services in case the product fails and requires immediate and complete repair.

Quality is a generic term that covers these first three aspects. In the past, however, when a manufacturing department discussed quality, they usually meant not producing defects or not passing defects to the customer.

4. *User costs minimum:* Producers often think of a product in terms of its initial cost to the customer, or price. However, the purchase

price is often only a partial cost for the customer, the tip of the iceberg. Companies should aim for a low life cycle cost to the customer.

5. *Effective availability:* Value means customers can use the product when they need it, with no wait. Often, people talk about *shortening delivery time,* a producer-oriented concept. The customer, on the other hand, is concerned not with shortening delivery time, but with having the product available *on time.*

When we say *market* in Figure 2-3, we are looking at developing new value for the customer from his or her viewpoint. In increasing profits, therefore, we should enhance customer value in addition to employing conventional measures of cost reduction. In the language of TQM, such an approach is creating *positive quality* or *attractive quality.*

To accurately understand market trends and customer requirements, it's important to establish a structure for collecting and compiling customer information. Part of this entails gathering customer information from first-line managers and employees who are in direct contact with markets. The other part entails translating such customer information into a form that can be used to facilitate top-management decision making. The bottom line? Without sound customer information, it's difficult to correctly assess market conditions.

Internal Market

Now let us expand the way we think about the market. So far, we've only discussed the market for final products. What about the market for staff functions? Who uses their professional expertise?

Suppose, for instance, the accounting department currently provides important accounting data to other departments by the fifth of each month. The user departments constitute the existing market (level of service) for the accounting department. If, however, the accounting department improves its processes in a way that allows it to provide data each day, the additional departments that might benefit from this value-added service constitute the related market (an expanded level of service).

Furthermore, what if an accounting department expands its services to include not just *after-the-fact* data, but also *before-the-fact* data by authorizing new accounting rules or calculating profit-loss while planning equipment investments? In this case, the accounting department creates a new market. To do so, of course, it needs to augment its conventional accounting techniques with new technologies, such as management accounting.

Whatever the case, an organization starts with the first box in the grid in Figure 2-3, *serving the existing market with existing technologies*. The remaining eight boxes represent choices the organization can make, based on where it wants to be in two to three years. For example, if the head of the accounting department determines that the company will need authorization to conduct profit-loss assessments in three years, the department develops a plan for entering *serving this new market and accessing the required technology* in box 9 in Figure 2-3. Then the department head makes this a policy.

In general, each business unit or department is responsible for developing its own priorities related to technology and to needs of external and internal customers, and for documenting them in Section I of the P/O Matrix. Figures 2-5 and 2-6 on pages 40-43 show how this was done at the Sony Mizunami plant for the Manufacturing Department and for one section within that department.

Catchball

A necessary condition for establishing policies is to engage in dialogue, or "catchball" communication. Part of this entails managers' fully explaining and convincing other members of the business unit why particular issues have been selected as priority policies of the unit. In such a forum, employees, as well as managers, should be free to express their opinions. It is this back-and-forth communication that we call catchball.

Shoichi Tamura explains the catchball process using an easy-to-understand illustration shown in Figure 2-7. The symbols ◎ , ◉ , and ○ in the figure represent different levels of the organization from higher to lower.

For example, the head of this business unit adopts four priority policies: A, B, C, and D. At the next level, the department director examines the four priorities and takes up A and B, as they are closely related to the work in his/her department. Also, the department director adds priority E, which is important to his/her department only. In this scenario, the higher-level policies C and D are determined to be unrelated to this department.

A similar process takes place at lower levels, where policies are deployed and developed further down into the organization. At each level of the organization, indispensable open discussions are held with higher

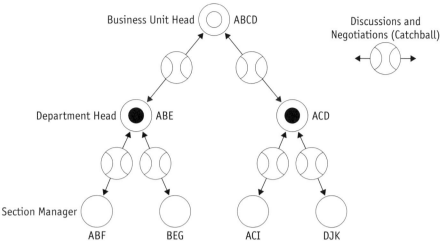

Source: Shoichi Tamura, *Ohanashi Hoshin Kanri (A Tale of Hoshin Kanri)*, Japanese Standards Association, 1987, 60.

Figure 2-7.
Example of Priority Objective Deployment (Catchball)

and lower levels. Just to clarify, at the division level, catchball discussions are held with the corporate (higher) level as well as the district (lower) level.

People often ask me if higher-ranking people, for example the president, should first come up with policies and cascade them down to the next layer. My answer is that, just like playing catch, anyone can start the process of policy catchball. Depending on the situation, the most appropriate party should take initiative. As depicted in Figure 2-7, for example, the president may throw the ABCD ball first. Or the president may receive both the ABE and ACD balls first and decide to drop E, because it doesn't have companywide implications. In this scenario, the president then issues ABCD as the company's policies. In general, it's good to avoid the scenario in which lower ranks do nothing to their P/O Matrix unless their president or business unit head issues policies. However, since the business situation is different for every company, there is no clear-cut rule for who should initiate the catchball process.

Ideally, the P/O Matrix catchball process should begin naturally as part of ongoing conversation. In this vein, the purpose of the P/O Matrix is simply to confirm these ongoing talks and document them to complete the companywide linkage of priorities between higher- and lower-ranking organizations. The idea here is that the higher and lower echelons of an

Manufacturing Department

C1	C2	C3	C4	C5	C6	C7	No.	Objective
○							15.	Achieve zero accidents and injuries
○	○	○					14.	Reduce scrap rate (effective utilization of resources)
○	○						13.	Develop human resources
	○		○				12.	Implement the ISO 9002 quality system
	○	○			○		11.	Promote labor savings
	○	○					10.	Smoothly launch new technologies and new models
	○	○		○			9.	Conduct VA and CD on raw materials
	○	○					8.	Rebuild production plans
	○		○				7.	Achieve zero market claim (due to Manufacturing)
	○	○	○				6.	Reduce warranty quality defects (due to Manufacturing)
	○	○	○			○	5.	Reduce pressure resistance defects
	○	○		○			4.	Promote each section's BIG EGG program
	○	○			○		3.	Improve equipment availability
	○	○			○		2.	Shorten processing time
	○	○				○	1.	Reduce process quality defect rate

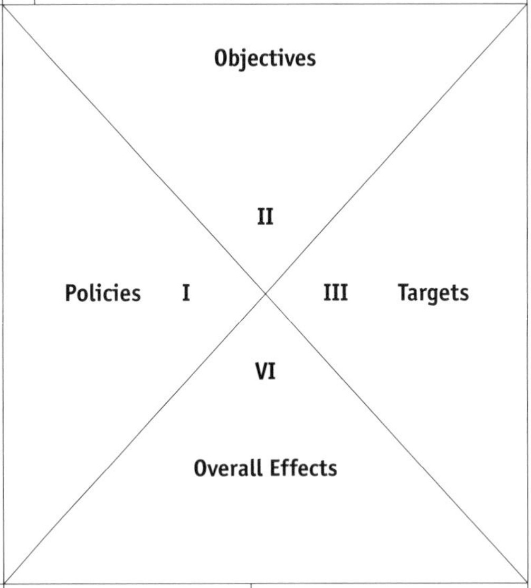

Column headers (left to right):
- C1: Create pleasant and vital workplace
- C2: Enhance technological development and improvement capability
- C3: Increase profit margin
- C4: Improve quality and reliability
- C5: Promote the BIG EGG program
- C6: Enhance production capability
- C7: Reduce quality defect losses

Central diagram labels:
Objectives — Policies I — II — III — Targets — VI — Overall Effects

C1	C2	C3	C4	C5	C6	C7	Target	Value
		○	○		○		Sales/term	A yen
	○	○	○	○	○	○	Gross profit/term	B yen
		○	○	○	○	○	Number of PCN/term	50
	○	○	○	○	○	○	Number of ECN/term	30
	○	○	○	○	○	○	Improvement effects/term	C yen

Figure 2-5.
P/O Matrix for First Half of 1993 (Sony Mizunami, Manufacturing)

Approved by	Reviewed by

◎ Principal party   ○ Supporting party

Target	Implementing parties → Manufacturing Section 1	Manufacturing Section 2	Manufacturing Section 3	Manufacturing Section 4	Equipment Maintenance Section	Improvement Promotion Section	Engineering Department	Quality Assurance Department	Improvement Management Department	General Affairs Department
(row)		○	○	○	○	○	○			◎
(row)		○	○	○	○		○	◎		○
(row)	○ ○		○	○	○	○	○	○		◎
(row)	○		○	○	○	○	○		◎	
(row)	○		○	○	○	○		◎		
(row)	○	◎	◎	◎	◎	○	○	◎	○	
(row)	○		○	○	○	○		◎	○	○
(row)	○		○	○	○	○				◎
(row)	○		○	○	○	○		○	◎	
(row)	○		○	○	○	○		◎	○	
(row)	○		○	○	○	○		◎	○	
(row)	○	◎	◎	◎	◎	○		○		○
(row)	○	◎	◎	○	◎	◎		○		
(row)	○	○	○	○	◎			○		
(row)	○	◎	◎	◎	◎			○	○	

IV

Remarks
PCN: New standards of operation, equipment, and inspection
ECN: New standards of design, technology, parts, and materials

Manufacturing Section 4

Objectives

Create pleasant and vital workplace	Enhance technological development and improvement capability	Improve profit margin	Launch new models	Promote BIG EGG	Improve equipment availability	Reduce process quality defect rate	No.	Objective	1/4 of the previous term (monetary value)	1/2 equipment down time, *b%* availability
○							15.	Create accident-free work environment		
○	○						14.	Develop employees, improve skills		
	○						13.	Implement the ISO 9002 quality system		
	○	○					12.	Shorten tact time		
	○	○					11.	Improve daily input/output curve on SEDAC		
	○						10.	Achieve zero market claim (due to Manufacturing Section 4)		
	○	○					9.	Reduce electric discharge and stray light quality defects		
	○		○				8.	Introduce the new model by using SEDAC/Arrow Diagram		
	○	○		○			7.	Save labor by operations improvement		
	○	○		○			6.	Reduce 25-inch CRT costs		
	○	○			○		5.	Shorten setup time		
	○	○			○		4.	Reduce equipment failures by preventive and productive maintenance		○
	○	○				○	3.	Reduce miss-landing defects	○	
	○	○				○	2.	Reduce baking defects	○	
○	○	○				○	1.	Reduce AG screen quality defects	○	

Policies I   II   III **Targets**   VI   **Overall Effects**

Create pleasant and vital workplace	Enhance technological development and improvement capability	Improve profit margin	Launch new models	Promote BIG EGG	Improve equipment availability	Reduce process quality defect rate	Overall Effects		1/4 of the previous term (monetary value)	1/2 equipment down time, *b%* availability
		○	○		○		Sales/term	A yen		○
	○	○	○	○	○	○	Gross profit/term	D yen	○	○
		○	○	○	○	○	Number of PCN/term	20	○	○
	○	○	○	○		○	Number of ECN/term	10	○	○
	○	○	○	○	○	○	Improvement effects/term	E yen	○	○

Figure 2-6.
P/O Matrix for First Half of 1993 (Sony Mizunami, Manufacturing Section 4)

	Approved by	Reviewed by

◎ Principal party   ○ Supporting party

Implementing parties

Target / Action	General Affairs Department	Improvement Management Department	Quality Assurance Department	Engineering Department	Improvement Promotion Section	Equipment Maintenance Section	Group 2	Group 1	Implementation Schedule (4 5 6 7 8 9)
Zero industrial and traffic accidents	◎					◎	◎	○	← →
5S JR implementation	◎						○	○	← →
100% participation of education and training		◎	○				○	○	← →
Perfect execution of internal audit findings			○	◎			○	○	← →
1/4 up from the previous term		◎		○			○	○	← →
Throughput time target		◎	○	○			○	○	← →
1/5 of the previous term (monetary value)			○	◎			○	○	← →
1/3 of the previous term (monetary value)	◎		◎		○	◎	◎	◎	← →
Process cleanliness target (dust count)			◎			○	○	○	← →
Die date adherence, quality target achievement		○		○		◎	◎	◎	← →
Employee/term target				○		◎	◎	◎	← →
2-inch cost target, c % defect rate				○	○	◎	◎	◎	← →
Setup time target				○	○		○	◎	← →
				○	○		○	◎	← →

Implementation Schedule — V
Implementing parties — IV

Remarks

PCN: New standards of operation, equipment, and inspection

ECN: New standards of design, technology, parts, and materials organization communicate all the time, not just when completing their P/O Matrices.

I once watched the movie *Field of Dreams,* in which the hero's father died when he was a young boy, but appeared to him later. In a heartwarming scene, the still-young father played catch with his grown-up son. Catchball played in a company should be the same kind of mutual interchange. It shouldn't be a formal ceremony where one person always throws the ball first.

Section II: Objectives

Selection

After having developed priority improvement policies for the current period and for two to three years into the future, a business unit selects specific improvement projects and determines the measures and means by which it will accomplish these projects. Together, these projects and their respective measures and means become the objectives of the business unit.

Since all companies possess limited resources for improvement—people, technology, money, information, time—it's important that we understand clearly why we are giving priority to certain objectives. In light of the overall purpose for implementing improvement activities, the following criteria should be used for selecting objectives:

- Will the objective contribute greatly to achieving the company's business plans for the current period?

- Will the objective contribute greatly to achieving the business unit's business plans for the current period and for the following two to three years?

- Will the objective contribute to developing and accumulating necessary improvement and development capabilities for the current period and for the following two to three years?

Both this process of selecting objectives and the next process of setting targets for Section III in Figure 2-2 require a chain of catchball throughout the ranks of the company.

Differentiating Selected Objectives

When implementing objectives documented in the P/O Matrix, some points should be remembered. In Figure 1-1 on page 3, the outer circle represents the business plans for the entire company, while the smaller inner circles represent the priority objectives entered into the P/O Matrix based on selection criteria from answering the three questions in item 1, above.

In Figure 1-1, a baseline "effort index" of 1.0 indicates that jobs are carried out with business-as-usual diligence; this is indicated by the white area inside the large circle and the gray area in the smaller circles. Some tasks require more diligence than that required to complete routine jobs. We give these tasks a higher effort index, for example 1.1 to 1.3; this increased effort is indicated by the partial black shading in the smaller circles. These circles, then, represent P/O Matrix priority tasks that require a greater amount of ingenuity to accomplish efficiently and effectively. Of course, an organization should carry out all its work with a slant toward more effective and efficient performance. This, however, is an ideal. The reality is much more difficult to achieve. I'm sure readers know from experience that no matter how many posters and slogans you use, they don't do much by themselves.

My point is that if the intention is to carry out P/O Matrix objectives with as much effort as other items in the business plan, there is no sense going through the objective selection process. Therefore, the improvement objectives selected in Section II of the matrix should be tackled with conscious effort. They require originality and ingenuity over and above that applied to regular, daily work.

As mentioned before, just saying *should* and *must* really doesn't help. For this reason, we introduce a few case examples in Chapter 3 to illustrate how to enhance the effort index within the limitations of people, money, information, and time. (The effort index shown in Figure 1-1 is a conceptual value, not a hard value. It simply points out the need to enhance our efforts in implementing improvement objectives compared with daily jobs.) Also, Chapter 3 addresses how to involve many people, who are busy with daily jobs, in achieving improvement objectives.

Section III: Targets

Target Setting

After deciding what to improve (Section II), it's time to establish targets for selected objectives. This is achieved by developing an indicator, or multiple indicators, that will sufficiently show whether or not the objective's initial aims are materialized when indicator targets are met. Although it depends on the improvement project, usually multiple indicators are better than one, as they can more clearly show the structure of a problem and the reasons for improvement.

Let me illustrate with an example. In Sony France's Alsace plant, the human resources department took up an improvement project with the theme "Reduce Absenteeism." While the plant thought a lower absentee rate was its main concern, the true concern was to make the plant more attractive for all employees. Therefore, I suggested they change their theme to "Make Sony France an Attractive Place for Everyone to Work."

To measure and monitor progress, I recommended conducting an employee survey every six months or so. Such a survey assesses and quantifies employee satisfaction by assigning a value to each question. For example, respondents answer each question on a scale of 0 to 4 (very dissatisfied, dissatisfied, neutral, satisfied, and very satisfied). The total scores for all respondents then yield an overall score for the project. If the score improves with each survey, the company can conclude that the situation is improving. In this context, it's important to note that such a survey will never come in with a perfect score, since there is no end to human desire.

Having said this, absenteeism may still be an indicator. The idea is to avoid using absenteeism as the *only* indicator, because people may become so preoccupied with improving this indicator that, in spite of their good intentions, they end up paradoxically creating an unattractive work environment. Since the location of the Alsace plant was formerly a vineyard, there are vine trellises on plant premises. In support of the objective to make Sony France an attractive place for everyone to work, one employee suggested installing benches under the trellises, so people could enjoy lunch during the fine, pleasant days of spring and fall. This suggestion may not have been offered if the project theme was simply to reduce absenteeism.

Whenever possible, it's preferable to have numerical targets for project indicators. Sometimes, however, this is not possible, as is the case for measuring certain staff functions. What is most important is to first clarify what needs to be accomplished before worrying too much about how to measure it. When the aims are clear, the measures will follow.

Responsible Decision Making

For most managers, making decisions based on objective data is fairly routine and straightforward. Managers who cannot make decisions based on subjective data, however, aren't really qualified as managers. I'm sure some readers may have been involved in projects that go nowhere because of such managers.

The perception that objective, quantifiable data is scientific and credible, while subjective data is not, is inaccurate. Whether objective or subjective, data can be valid or invalid. It all depends on the quality of data. Data that appears objective on the surface, for example, may in reality be inaccurate or biased. In such a case, data is meaningless. On the other hand, subjective data can be quite meaningful, especially when those involved can say with sincerity and confidence that it represents reality in the best possible way.

All in all, we should avoid making arbitrary decisions. We should base our decisions on objective data whenever possible. And to fulfill our obligation as managers and employees, we should be confident that our conclusions are correct when they are based on sound judgment derived from subjective data.

Section IV: Principal and Supporting Members and Leaders

Project First, Then Members

To implement the objectives selected in Section II of the P/O Matrix and to achieve the targets in Section III, it's necessary to identify the principal department, as well as the supporting departments, responsible for each objective. After this is accomplished, they are documented in Section IV of the P/O Matrix, Figure 2-2. As the case examples in Figures 2-5 and 2-6 demonstrate, in general the names of the group, section, and department are recorded. If necessary, other business units of the company and/or other associated companies may be included as well.

After improvement objectives and targets have been established, improvement activities are implemented at the daily-job level. Determining who is involved in each improvement project is usually an obvious function of the nature and size of the project, as well as organizational structure. One of the P/O Matrix rules is that all departments that ought to work together naturally become involved in the project. In this vein, the more important the project is, the less likely a single department or section will complete the project alone.

When interdepartmental cooperation is necessary, a company may have a habit of organizing a special task force. This habit should be stopped. Instead, a company should develop the habit of assembling members from different departments to work together naturally according to the purpose of the project. The point is that whatever structure an organization has, it inevitably possesses both positive and negative features. Since the current organizational structure is more than likely in place because the positive outweighs the negative, an organization should rely on its current structure to implement improvement projects—not isolate people on a task force.

An ideal organization is one that can act promptly and garner its total capabilities in pursuit of key objectives. It aims for fusion rather than division, pluralistic cooperation rather than specialization, and networking rather than rank stratification—all extremely important principles of the P/O Matrix. Of course, finalizing and confirming project team membership requires time and effort, which are expended during the company-wide review and negotiation process. This process will be covered in more detail later.

Best Leader and Best Members

Determining the principal department for Section IV of the P/O Matrix also entails selecting a leader, or person in charge of the project. In the same way the principal department is selected naturally based on the improvement project, so too the designated leader is a natural consequence of the situation at hand. This task is not so difficult. After considering the project theme and scope, and the job responsibilities of different individuals, the leader is usually identified with ease. Of course, if the logical individual is already fulfilling a leadership role for multiple projects, the next best person is selected. Finally, this principle applies to selecting team members as well. The best team leader and team members are selected based on project theme, scope, and requirements.

Section V: Scheduling

In general, an organization prepares a P/O Matrix every six months or year, an activity that determines the duration of supporting projects. An organization may also develop an implementation schedule for each project. If desired, as shown in Figure 2-6, Section V of the P/O Matrix may be laid out in a Gantt chart format. When more detailed information is required, a detailed Gantt chart or arrow diagram may be attached to the P/O Matrix.

Section VI: Overall Effects

Section VI documents improvement project contributions to the achievement of companywide targets at the end of the term. In other words, it asks how much the improvement themes identified in Section II are expected to contribute to the overall business plan by achieving the targets set in Section III. This section also documents the improvement and development capabilities that will be fostered and accumulated as a result of the implementation of projects. Since space is limited, a brief description of items and target values is sufficient here.

Figures 2-8 and 2-9 are examples of P/O Matrices for the engineering and planning/development departments of Dynic, a specialty fabric manufacturer in Japan. As for capabilities to be developed and accumulated, the engineering department wrote, "improve capabilities for new product development to assure a profit rate of 28 percent or more," "establish three or more new technologies," and "establish at least one new system." In the case of setting a target like "establish three or more new technologies," it is essential that the people involved have a clear understanding of what they mean. In this case, what kind of concrete technologies will they develop and how will they measure whether or not these technologies have been developed? The same discipline should also apply to the identified capability "establish at least one system."

Of course, all the information discussed above does not have to be documented on a P/O Matrix. It can be written horizontally, for example, in a way that lists policies, objectives, implementation targets, and overall targets. When one item has more than one related item, however, it's easier to show this mutual relationship with a P/O Matrix. As shown in Figures 2-8 and 2-9, the ○ mark designates where related items intersect.

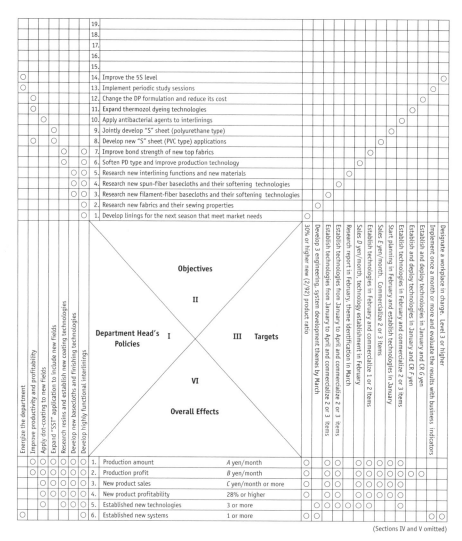

(Sections IV and V omitted)

Figure 2-8.
Plan Deployment Matrix for Term 129, Second Half
(Fabric Engineering Department, Dynic)

When to Prepare a P/O Matrix

Next, let's discuss a sample schedule for developing the P/O Matrix. Depending on the situation, the sequence of events may vary. Suppose, for example, a company's fiscal year starts on the first of April, as is the case for many Japanese companies. During the first and second week of January, the president introduces his or her policies. In response, business unit heads or department heads develop their policies for the coming fiscal year. These policies are then communicated in detail throughout the

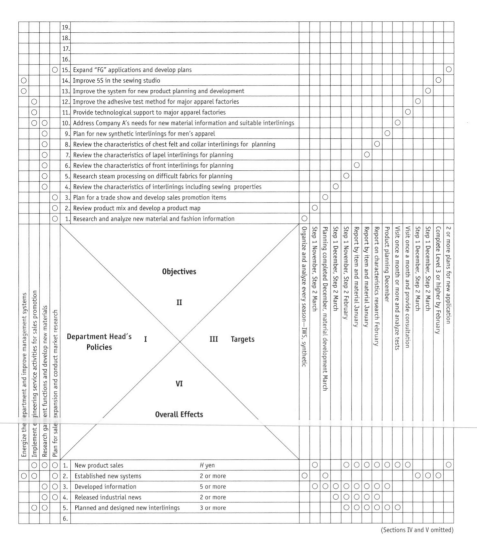

Figure 2-9.
Plan Deployment Matrix for Term 130, Second Half
(Fabric Planning and Development Department, Dynic)

(Sections IV and V omitted)

company, along with the reasons why they have been adopted and the economic and industrial conditions surrounding the company.

Because these policies will become the company's strategies, full discussions are expected during the policy development, or catchball, process. Since it's common for first-line managers and staffers to have a good grasp of what's going on in their work areas and an excellent feel for workable strategies, top management is encouraged to listen to their opinions with an open mind. Also, first-liners should take the initiative to convey their ideas, which grow out of valuable experience, to top management in an honest effort to contribute to their decision-making power.

Let me digress a bit. We should be careful to draw a clear line between management policies and philosophies. Since policies are synonymous with strategies, they are always subject to discussion and change. Philosophies and principles, on the other hand, are not. For example: "We will contribute to the development of society through our business," "We will contribute to the happiness of mankind and the improvement of culture," and "We value trust and will not pursue unearned money," are expressions of management philosophies or attitudes over time. The difference between P/O Matrix policies and these philosophies is that policies are subject to change, while philosophies are basically fixed.

Let's go back to the P/O Matrix schedule. During the third and fourth weeks of January, the department head and his or her direct reports, as well as other members of the department as needed, discuss what projects to adopt as priority objectives. This is where catchball, or the exchange of ideas, takes place.

During the first and second weeks of February, target values for the selected objectives are developed. Since we must work within resource limitations, a necessary condition for setting objective and target values is that they are achievable by exerting considerable effort and by using existing improvement and development capabilities. In this vein, we must carefully avoid creating an unachievable wish list or "castle of sand."

One question many companies ask when just beginning to use the P/O Matrix is, "On what basis should we determine that improvement targets are achievable with considerable effort?" My answer is, "That's why we have veteran managers like you, who can use their professional judgment to make accurate estimations. If there were set rules for such estimates, we would have the computer do it."

Also, part of establishing target values entails involving accounting personnel, who calculate the projected monetary contribution of each project to the profit plan. These amounts should be documented in Section VI of the matrix, "Overall effects." It's important to remember, as discussed earlier, that the expected development of management know-how and capability development should be documented in this section as well.

In calculating the monetary value of improvement effects, companies must be careful to develop a habit of including only the amount calculated as profit according to the existing accounting system. Some time ago at a conference, one company's presentation claimed a large dollar contribution from its companywide small group activities. In fact, the number was so large that it exceeded the total profits of the whole company! This claim could have been the result of the company's leniency in allowing each individual group to calculate monetary contribution separately, and then mechanically adding these amounts. Although I'm certain the presenter had no ill intention, this was an embarrassing moment for the company.

Moving along into the third and fourth weeks of February, the organization decides which department should be the principal department for each project and which departments should contribute as supporting members. If necessary, the organization also develops implementation schedules at this time.

Two final notes. One, the above schedule is an example of P/O Matrix development at a department level. For section-level matrix development, the same process should be followed, only two weeks later. Two, P/O Matrix objectives and targets are often written in an abbreviated manner. It is, therefore, often useful at the implementation stage to break objectives and targets down further with a systematic diagram such as the one shown in Figure 2-10.

Integrating with Culture

In the early 1960s, many Japanese companies tried to use imported management by objectives. At that time, the emphasis was placed on developing individual policies, objectives, and targets. Since all employees were members of the same organization, however, it was difficult for individuals to come up with items that were different from those of the groups or sections. As people found unique ways to express their individual objectives, it really just became an exercise in semantics for many Japanese companies.

After individual employees came up with improvement items and targets, they were supposed to sign off on them and present them to their bosses. Depending on the company culture, this method may or may not have motivated employees. The key point is that it's important to develop policies with a mind for the national and organizational culture and to adapt one's management practices accordingly. Incidentally, from my observations, the cultural differences between different companies in the same country are usually greater than the differences between countries.

The rule to remember for management system development is to retain the fundamentals while integrating specific methods and practices

Policy: Promote PM and improve its methods

Objectives / Targets	Section Name	Broken-down Objectives	Broken-down Targets
Eliminate hidden failures $C_p \geq 1.33$	Engineering	Improve process capability (machining equipment)	Calculate C_p value and keep the level 1.33 or higher. 8 applications/Q2
Improve availability 85% OEE (overall equipment effectiveness) of targeted equipment	Engineering	Improve and implement maintenance checksheet	1/3 reduction of downtime due to maintenance deficiency
	Machinery	Improve minor stoppages (As, M, FH)	10% increase in performance efficiency
	Electrical	Improve availability by TPM	85% or higher OEE
	Manufacturing 1	Improve OEE (RAM 1-1)	77% → 85% or higher
	Manufacturing 1	Improve OEE (RAM 1-3)	82% → 85% or higher
	Manufacturing 1	Improve OEE (MA-1, -AF)	80% → 85% or higher
Improve part fabrication processes Labor-hours down 2,250/month	Machinery	Shorten cycle time at the By A and FH lines.	20% reduction
	Machinery	Shorten setup time at the P transfer line.	30% reduction
	Machinery	Shorten setup time of the By general-purpose milling machine	50% reduction
	Chemical	Simplify the P5 process	50% labor-hours reduction
	Chemical	Improve the cleansing process	Elimination of cleansing process
Improve assembly processes Labor-hours down 2,333/month	Electrical	Review the soldering process	One soldering personnel reduction
	Electrical	Improve the mounting method for multiple loading	Three AM personnel reduction
	Manufacturing 1	Reduce cycle time (RAM 1-1, 1-3)	10% or higher
	Manufacturing 1	Reduce cycle time (MA-1, -AF)	10% or higher
	Manufacturing 2	Improve work efficiency (use of jigs, line balancing)	85% → 92% or higher total productivity
	Manufacturing 3	Improve 6C process	30% or higher efficiency increase
	NIPS	Develop and propose an evaluation method for assembly friendliness	Application of current ordering, complete the list for jig introduction

Figure 2-10.
Systematic Diagram for Breaking Down Objectives (Sendai Nikon)

into the culture where they are applied. History teaches us that no efforts are successful when local people are forced to change their culture.

Responsibility for Saying No

Suppose the fiscal year begins in April and the final draft of the P/O Matrix is developed by the middle of March. The remaining time should be used to confirm and make adjustments to the contents of P/O Matrices throughout the company. This is especially true for those organizations identified as supporting parties, so they experience no surprises when improvement activities start in the beginning of April.

Sometimes, an organization that has been nominated as a supporting party finds it impossible to support the project. In such a case, management needs to review the project to determine if the company can implement it without that organization's support or if, perhaps, target values need to be revised. These adjustments should be completed by the end of March.

During this coordination period, if a manager feels it is impossible to cooperate with another organization on a particular project, it's that manager's responsibility to say no. If this reality is known in March, the other organization has time to make adjustments accordingly. However, if the manager waits until October to say no, the other organization suffers. The lost seven months cannot be reclaimed. As Dr. Eizaburo Nishibori, one of the founders of Japan's quality movement, said, "Responsibility should be fulfilled before the fact, not after."

The P/O Matrix is prepared according to the schedule discussed above. No matter how excellent the P/O Matrix may be, it's useless if not developed on time. It's also useless if its contents are not used to guide the organization toward its objectives. The next section, therefore, will address how to use the P/O Matrix.

HOW TO USE THE P/O MATRIX

Visible Management

The P/O Matrix is an extremely effective tool for accurately and quickly communicating top management's policies and improvement intentions to the entire company. It also enables a company to thoroughly understand how much the improvements its project teams make will contribute to the overall business/profit plans. Furthermore, the P/O Matrix visually shows what areas are targeted for accumulating know-how and intrinsic management technology.

In practice, managers share such information with employees and use the matrix to manage companywide improvement activities on a daily basis. At Sony Inazawa, for example, each contributing group's or section's P/O Matrix is posted adjacent to the bulletin board that monitors the progress of improvement activities. By doing this, employees can clearly understand how their improvement projects link with companywide improvement efforts.

True Volunteerism

In the past, it was generally believed that people would take responsibility for policies and objectives only if they are developed in a bottom-up manner, not if they were deployed in a top-down manner. Is this really so? As a long-time practitioner working with companies, I've witnessed many scenarios and situations, and in my experience it's common for even self-determined policies and objectives to be forgotten.

On the other hand, I've seen cases where top-down policies and objectives were well implemented and results were achieved as planned. In light of such diverse experience, my conclusion is that the issue is more complex than just whether policies and objectives are self-determined or deployed top-down. From my experience, I've learned that people are motivated only when they thoroughly understand *why* policies and objectives (self-determined or top-down) are needed at a given time.

It's natural for an organization to gather important information at the top and middle management levels. After studying and analyzing such information, top and middle managers make their judgments and announce their policies, objectives, and targets, along with the reasons they were chosen.

Sometimes, in an attempt to push decision-making autonomy down the organizational chain, business units, departments, and individuals are asked to voluntarily come up with their own objectives and activities. Although this can be a valuable process if managed properly, often it results in a vicious circle in which voluntary actions are only voluntary on the surface; in reality, they're forced behavior. In such cases, information tends to be poor in quality, objectives and targets hold only marginal value, decisions are a mere formality, and responsibility for implementation is quite vague. The net result, as touched on earlier, is that true volunteerism never becomes a reality and nobody really feels responsible for improvement projects, even when they are not implemented. For this reason, even when the P/O Matrix is developed in a top-down manner, the approach should emphasize open communication and full explanation and understanding, not forced deployment. Full explanation and understanding foster ownership, motivate people and draw out their *true voluntary natures,* or good will towards completing top-quality work.

When Are People Most Motivated?

It should be understood that the P/O Matrix is a necessary tool for maintaining high morale. When people are given worthwhile tasks, a scenario for success, and the reasons (not just lip service) for project implementation—all by-products of the P/O Matrix—they become motivated.

I learned this lesson in a rather unhappy way from my experience as a general manager of a deficit-ridden factory. Toward the end of my third year, the factory improved and became profitable as a result of everyone's efforts and the positive impact of an improved economy. Shortly after this fortunate reversal occurred, a foreman told me a shocking story. He said, "When you first came to this factory, you said it was notorious for deficits and asked us to work hard to make it profitable. Unfortunately," he continued, "your speech reached no one's heart. We believed the factory was in the red because of shoddy management, including the general manager, not because of employees. However, a year later, you told us that such and such measures would eliminate the factory's losses. You shared the data and convinced us with your scenario for success and with reasons we could believe." The foreman then said, "It was only then that we believed we could do it and became motivated."

Strengthening Leadership for Improvement

The following are often cited as basic management capabilities for executives and managers:

- Outlook: To develop a scenario for success, including the feasibility of and measures for achieving it

- Organization: To unite employees and other departments, as needed, toward common goals

- Persuasion: To lay out a direction, determine priorities, and explain why they are necessary

It's my hope that executives and managers will use the P/O Matrix to strengthen their management capabilities. In doing so, it's important that they review and analyze the results achieved at the end of the implementation period against initial plans laid out in the P/O Matrix.

According to Ms. Noriko Hosoyamada, formerly a quality manager at Florida Power & Light, Dr. W. E. Deming changed the familiar PDCA cycle (plan, do, check, and act) to PDSA (plan, do, study, and act), to encourage more in-depth examination and analysis (Hosoyamada 1992). I also encourage the earnest study and analysis of results achieved to learn which of the management capabilities—outlook, organization, or persuasion—was inadequate or in error. In this way, excellent executives and managers can seize precious opportunities to learn. After all, such opportunities for real-life learning are truly few and far between.

By studying the results of the P/O Matrix, managers and executives continue to develop themselves, and each time they learn something, they make a slight improvement over those who do not. Over time, these differences add up and become clearly noticeable. This learning process is also important for developing new management technologies. As a consultant, I've recognized that the behavior of excellent companies is the same as that of excellent individuals—the more excellent they are, the more open-minded and willing they are to learn. Perhaps the plain truth is that they're excellent because they're always learning.

One last observation: I've noticed that my client companies get better each year at completing and using the P/O Matrix. My conclusion is that, as a result, their executives and managers are also getting better at their jobs.

Quick Response to Changes in the Surrounding Environment

When I came up with the P/O Matrix methodology, some people objected, saying, "We've been flexible in responding to turbulent changes in the surrounding environment. The P/O Matrix seems to slow us down."

This is an understandable concern. In fact, I'm aware of many cases where the use of MBO disrupted a company's ability to respond quickly to a changing business environment. In response to such an argument, however, I recommend updating the contents of the P/O Matrix as the surrounding environment and organizational priorities change. In making such changes, responsible managers should take the initiative to obtain their bosses' concurrence in allowing them to revise the P/O Matrix without hesitation.

Earlier, I used the example of the accounting department at one of my client companies. When the time came for that department's improvement project follow-up review, I visited the company. During my visit, one of the accounting department's section managers gave the following excuse for not working on any of the planned improvement projects: "Goodness gracious! An unexpected big job came to us. We had to prepare the company for the new consumption tax. Therefore, we haven't been able to work on any of the planned P/O Matrix improvement themes." Instead of making such an excuse, when he was given this big job, the manager should have revised his P/O Matrix to include the theme *smoothly introduce and operate a consumption tax system*. Items he could have designated for measurement include:

- Complete the preparatory work for the tax system introduction by the target date.

- Publish a guide for handling the consumption tax.

- Achieve error-free application of implementation rules.

Inevitably, companies face situations that require them to stop or delay improvement projects in progress. When this happens, it's necessary to add new projects to the P/O Matrix and communicate what should be done with other projects by clearly indicating *stopped* or *delayed* on the matrix. Sometimes new projects are added to the matrix while existing themes are continued. However, this can be risky, as it may result in completing all projects halfway.

Another example of shifting demands and changes in the business environment is a manufacturing department that experiences a sudden, unexpected increase of orders for specific items. If the manager in charge feels that responding to such orders is the most important job, the improvement theme *increase production of product A by X percent* should be added to the P/O Matrix.

Items for measurement might include:

- Achieve monthly production of X units.

- Maintain a defect rate of less than Y percent.

- Maintain an equipment productivity rate of Z percent or higher (if increased production requires the use of old, inefficient equipment).

In this scenario, the manager has a golden opportunity to improve production plans, quality control practices, and equipment and maintenance techniques while carrying out daily operations. And through the implementation process, the manager can expect the following results: increased profits due to additional production, improvement of equipment and tools due to the need for increased maintenance, stable quality as a result of using well-maintained equipment, and the development of production plans that are responsive to increased demand. Meanwhile, managers should develop a habit of consciously learning from the results derived from newly added projects.

In response to unforeseen events, like a sudden increase in production demand, managers may need to take initiative and discontinue other improvement projects originally planned and documented on the P/O Matrix. Responsible managers should take speedy action to revise their matrices with their bosses' concurrence. Then their departments will not end up saying, "Regrettably, due to an unexpected demand for production, we couldn't make progress on our improvement projects." Instead, managers should use the P/O Matrix to respond quickly to changing situations, thereby providing guidance and direction to employees who are most affected by sudden external changes.

Committing to Profit

When introducing the P/O Matrix, the following objection is also frequently expressed: "We had a tradition of running our business with business/profit plans. Since we already have business/profit plans, generating policy/objective management plans is like making a roof over a roof."

It's true, the contents of the P/O Matrix are included in the business/profit plans. The objectives listed on the P/O Matrix, however, are the most important actions for achieving profit and organizational fitness. For this reason, P/O Matrix objectives and targets stand above other general tasks of daily operations. As such, they require great and steady effort in fully using improvement and development capabilities and in achieving results. A technique known as SEDAC, discussed in Chapter 3, can be used to facilitate such effort.

So, P/O Matrix objectives and targets not only help secure profits but also strengthen and accumulate improvement and development capability. In short, the P/O Matrix highlights excellent opportunities for sharpening skills while accomplishing important work.

The key to success in implementing improvement activities is to have a structure or system that promotes improvement in daily work. The more an organization struggles with daily operations, as mentioned earlier, the more it needs an enabling structure for improvement. If an organization considers improvement activities to be separate from daily work, it may fall into the undesirable pattern of doing "regular" jobs during the week and "improving" only during weekends. To avoid this, and to manage improvement activities within a companywide network, the P/O Matrix plays a very important role. By using the matrix well, improvement activities can be promoted in a planned, specific, and continuous manner.

Removing Obstacles

There is still another important use of the P/O Matrix. In Japan and other countries, many conferences are held to share and study the results of companywide improvement activities. These conferences are good opportunities to share successful improvement case studies and to learn from others. Typically, such conferences are held for three days, with two and a half days allocated for presentations and the remaining half day for a panel discussion on why companywide improvement activities fail or how to successfully implement companywide improvement activities. During these sessions, people often bring up obstacles that prevent them from promoting companywide improvement. A representative listing of such obstacles is found in Figure 2-11.

For example, one of the most common obstacles is, "We are too busy doing daily work and have no time left for improvement activities." People also say, "We lack necessary improvement resources, such as people, technology, and money." Another common problem is a lack of management interest in improvement activities. In many cases, bosses do encourage and praise people when things are going well; however, when things are not going well, people have noted that their bosses are often unable to provide effective coaching when it is needed most.

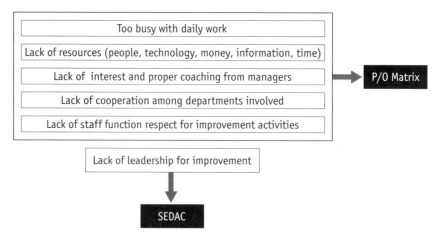

Figure 2-11.
Obstacles to Companywide Improvement

Furthermore, people say, "Departments that are supposed to work together don't cooperate." This type of comment points to the need for a structure that enables people to work together across department and section boundaries. Most big-payoff projects with serious implications for the company cannot be implemented by just one department. The greater the expected effect, the more necessary it is to have interdepartmental cooperation.

Still another issue often raised is whether or not staff functions are participating. For me, it's hard to imagine that companies still aim for dramatic improvements without involving their staff or professional groups. To overcome this situation, it's important that we promote companywide improvement with the total and active participation of staff departments.

Clearly, there are many obstacles that can impede the smooth implementation of improvement activities. As with any effort, it's better to address such obstacles from the outset, rather than wait to deal with them individually when problems arise. This is another important function of the P/O Matrix. Here, we should remember once again Dr. Nishibori's saying, "Responsibility should be fulfilled *before the fact,* not after." This is true especially for managers and executives, who should scope out and think through their projects before they impose them on the organization.

Now let's discuss how the P/O Matrix addresses specific obstacles listed in Figure 2-11. The first obstacle is that people are too busy to improve. The P/O Matrix counters this obstacle by documenting objectives that are connected with daily business activities and that are integral to what people do every day in their jobs. Here the idea is that organizations need to improve the activities that consume them each day. Usually the reason people say they are too busy to work on improvement projects is because they have selected the wrong projects. Although this may sound strange, many are not aware of this simple fact.

To address the issue of lack of resources (people, technology, money, information, and time), the P/O Matrix narrows down the number of improvement objectives to a manageable few. These objectives, and their targets, become the priorities an organization can achieve with existing resources.

Lack of interest from the boss is also addressed by the P/O Matrix through the catchball and objective/target-selection process. After engaging in the P/O Matrix process covered earlier, managers cannot be indifferent to achieving objectives and targets. If, on the other hand, improvement themes are chosen arbitrarily, progress tends to be limited and managers tend to lose interest.

As for lack of cooperation of supporting departments, the P/O Matrix identifies beforehand who should work together, in Section IV. Nevertheless, even after supporting departments are identified, sometimes actual implementation activities don't proceed as planned. For this reason, the managers who authorize the P/O Matrix are responsible for making sure their departments or sections carry out the stated obligations. The P/O Matrix documents the involvement of supporting departments with the expectation of full cooperation, not just cooperation when it's convenient or when workloads are slow.

Usually there are reasons why supporting departments do not cooperate. In such cases, the departmental manager who authorized the P/O Matrix is responsible for finding out what these reasons are and determining the necessary adjustments to make. The important point to remember is that the P/O Matrix is not just a document, a shell to fill in with words. Rather, it is a living tool used to manage the business.

Another obstacle removed by the P/O Matrix is the problem of staff participation, which will be covered in more detail in Chapter 5. In some cases, staffers look down on improvement projects, feeling they are too good to participate. In other cases, they may give the appearance of participation while not really participating in a substantive way.

The reality is that staff function involvement in companywide improvement makes a critical difference in results achieved. Staff involvement is, in fact, a necessary condition for successful companywide improvement. Nevertheless, I often encounter staff departments that are not involved in companywide improvement. Why is this? The answer can be illustrated by one of my failures.

When I was an engineer in a production engineering department, the companywide improvement promotion office ordered all the company's staff departments to organize improvement teams in the tradition of the line organizations. Eight of us who worked in the same group formed a team. The promotion office then said we should name our team, and we did so with no problem. The next step was to come up with an improvement theme. Here we stumbled. Each of us in the department was already working on different projects to improve and maintain quality, equipment, and productivity. This made it difficult to come up with a common project we could all pursue.

Finally, we selected the improvement theme: "Don't let the phone ring more than three times. (Answer the phone quickly)." As I remember, the theme of the design group, our neighbor, was to "Reduce paper waste."

If we, as young engineers, had taken such minor themes seriously and worked hard on them, we'd have been crazy. It simply wasn't the best use of our expertise. This experience taught me that it's important to first identify priority improvement themes and targets, and then identify the members whose daily work intersects with those themes. In this way, regardless of the organization or function, the best people are chosen to serve as team members for specific improvement projects—whether line or staff or both. Themes first, members second. Instead of coming up with themes for themes' sake, establish important themes, then choose team members on that basis.

Production engineers who assist plant people, therefore, may become team members if the selected theme intersects with what they do. Invariably, staff members must participate on the teams of organizations they serve. It's simply not optional. In fact, supporting staff members are often involved in five to ten improvement projects at any given time.

As for R&D departments, their work is always a strong candidate for improvement projects. Professionals in these departments should ask questions like, "What have we done better this time compared with last time?" "What new demands have we challenged ourselves with?" A good example of asking this last question is found in the companywide improvement slogan of Tayca, a leading specialized chemical company in Japan, which says, "We try the new." This slogan reflects a basic attitude toward improvement that challenges the status quo, regardless of what job or rank one holds in the organization.

The remaining obstacle, lack of leadership for improvement, will be discussed in Chapter 3 and following chapters. The effective actions of using the P/O Matrix and the reasons for effectiveness are included in Table 4-1 on page 98.

A Long Way, But...

In this chapter, we have covered many points about the P/O Matrix. It's nice if managers can apply these principles and techniques smoothly, but often actual implementation is difficult. For example, even if people practice catchball, they may not be able to reach conclusions immediately. Or project implementation may produce unsatisfactory results. All such situations reflect an organization's level of management capability, as mentioned earlier. An undesirable level of management capability may be the result of poor practices perpetuated over time. Although it may not take as long to correct such practices as it did to build them, naturally some time will be needed.

Even if implementation is imperfect, the important point is to follow the scientific method: study the results of implementation, learn from experience, and improve implementation during the next cycle. It's a certainty that people improve their skills by developing and using the P/O Matrix.

Finally, it is my hope that executives and managers take the first step and begin to rotate the upward PDSA cycle, always coming closer to the ideal. This alone will be rewarding for those just beginning companywide improvement. Remember, Rome was not built in a day.

Strengthening Improvement Power Through SEDAC

CREATIVITY AND EVERYDAY BUSINESS

Even in a difficult economic environment, it's possible for a company to develop excellent strategies along with accompanying policies and objectives. Yet no matter how outstanding, strategies are useless if a company lacks the ability to translate them into reality. That is why this chapter is devoted to SEDAC, an improvement methodology for effectively developing the ability to make strategies take shape and form in an organization.

What then is SEDAC? As spelled out in Figure 3-1, the acronym SEDAC stands for "structure for enhancing daily activities through creativity."* SEDAC has its roots in the brainstorming and KJ methods, and was developed as a management technique for generating ideas among people of different professional backgrounds. As such, it facilitates improvement and standardization as part of daily work. The important point here is that we must not assume daily activities are small and unimportant matters. Quite the contrary. No matter how large or small a project may be, it's always implemented at the level of daily work. Whether large or small, progress is made only by translating overall objectives into daily actions.

---

*SEDAC was named by Noriko Hosoyamada, the translator of this book and formerly a QC Manager at Florida Power & Light Company, the first overseas recipient of the Deming Application Prize in 1989.

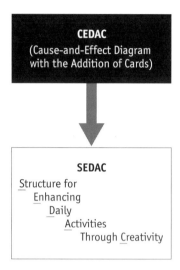

Figure 3-1.
What Is SEDAC?

The reason SEDAC includes the words *enhancing* and *through creativity* is because it's essential to be creative in a way that directly impacts improvement aims, such as improving processes or enhancing the quality/quantity of work outcomes. After all, humans are uniquely capable of thinking and generating new ideas.

By *structure,* I mean something like the flexible body of a living creature. Management techniques always involve people. And since they are widely applied in different organizations, industries, and nations, they must be highly flexible and adaptable while at the same time provide necessary structure.

FROM *CEDAC* TO *SEDAC*

SEDAC is an evolution of a method known as CEDAC, which stands for "Cause-and-Effect Diagram with Addition of Cards." The CEDAC method was first developed and used in Japan by the Standardization Study Group of Sumitomo Electric Industries. In 1978 the group introduced the CEDAC method to the public in an article in the journal *Standardization and Quality Control* that was awarded the Nikkei QC Literature Prize from the Deming Prize Committee. During the 1970s and 1980s, CEDAC was introduced and applied in many Japanese, North American, and European companies. Since that time, new features have been added to the method, and the name was changed to SEDAC to more accurately describe its function. Now SEDAC is applied widely in the manufacturing sector as well as in a variety of service sector organizations. To avoid confusion, therefore, this book uses SEDAC throughout.

HOW TO DEVELOP A SEDAC

Before developing a SEDAC, an improvement theme, a target, and its due date must be established. Also, the leader and members of the SEDAC project must be identified. Both these tasks are accomplished according to the process discussed in Chapter 2 on pages 44–48.

Depending on the nature of the problem selected for improvement, SEDAC can take different forms. Many people are familiar with the basic SEDAC format on a cause-and-effect diagram. However, SEDACs can also take the form of flowcharts, arrow diagrams, failure mode and effects analysis (FMEA), and process decision program charts (PDPC). These various forms are summarized in Table 3-2 on page 85. Before getting into the discussion of how to use different types of SEDACs and how to transition from the P/O Matrix to SEDAC, it's important that we cover some SEDAC basics. It's my hope that, by grasping the gist of how to develop a SEDAC, readers will find the rest of this chapter easier to understand. Such an understanding is essential, because SEDAC is a handy tool for improvement, not just a mere concept.

For simplicity's sake, the steps of SEDAC will be explained in the form of the cause-and-effect diagram (see Figure 3-2). This is a structured, systematic chart that shows the relationship between the causes (or factors) and the effects (or characteristics) of quality and process problems. Because of its shape, the cause-and-effect diagram is often called a fishbone diagram. People at the Fukiai Plant, Kawasaki Steel, first used the cause-and-effect diagram in 1952 when they were organizing many possible causes for quality defects under the guidance of Dr. Kaoru Ishikawa,

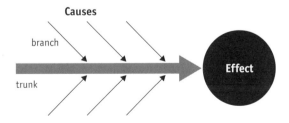

Figure 3-2.
A Cause-and-Effect Diagram

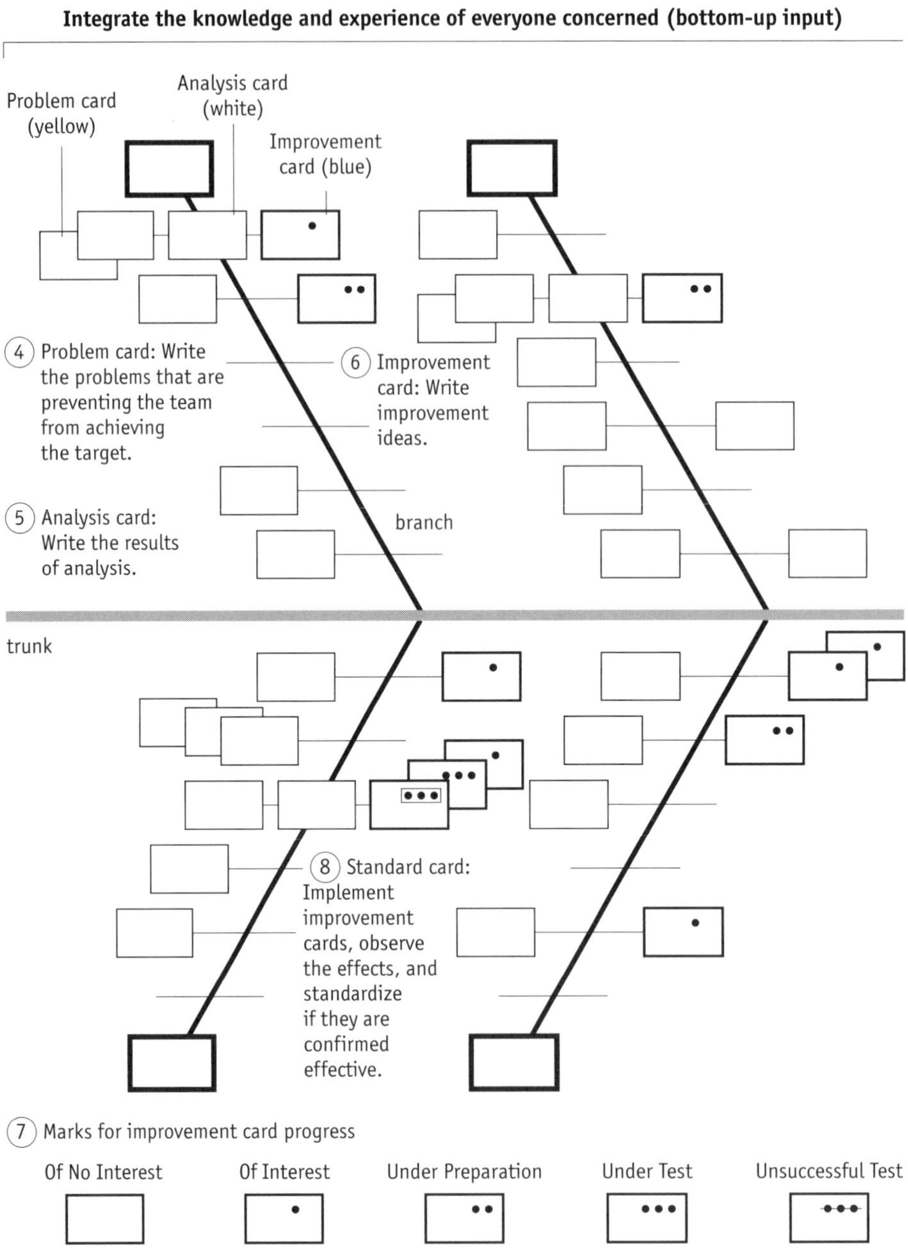

Figure 3-3.
Structure for Building a SEDAC

then a professor at Tokyo University. Since then, the cause-and-effect diagram has been applied widely in Japan and in other countries.

A key aspect of SEDAC is that it is developed in plain view, so everyone can see it at all times. A SEDAC is developed in ten steps, as shown

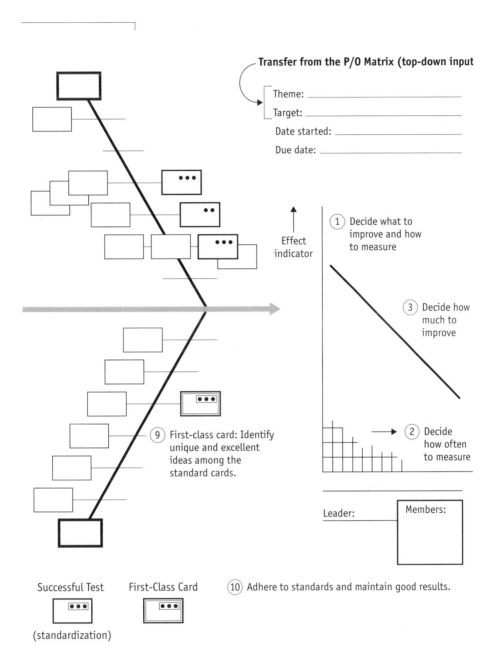

in Figure 3-3. Table 3-1 describes each step in detail. SEDAC differs from the conventional cause-and-effect diagram in that it plots quantitative data over time on the effect side of the diagram. This data—the targeted effect—is directly derived from targets identified in the already completed P/O Matrix.

Although it may not always be possible, depending on the selected effect indicator, the general rule of thumb for setting targets is to improve by at least 30 percent. The reason for this is because when the gap between the target and the current level of performance is small, it's difficult to determine whether the target was achieved by chance or by improvement actions.

The left of the diagram—often called the "trunk" and "branches"—is the cause side. This is where new ideas are generated, based on the integrated knowledge and experience of all people concerned. After steps 1, 2, and 3 are completed, step 4 entails writing *problem cards*, the purpose

Table 3-1.
Steps for Building a SEDAC

	Description	Remarks
Effect Side		
(1)	• Confirm what to improve by when. • Decide how to measure.	Refer to the objectives selected on the P/O Matrix.
(2)	• Decide how often to measure.	The shorter the measuring interval, the more active the improvement project becomes (i.e., every lot, every day, etc.).
(3)	• Confirm how much to improve.	Refer to the targets set on the P/O Matrix.
Cause Side		
(4)	• Develop problem cards: To achieve the target, team members write observed facts, obstacles, causes, and investigation items on cards. • The team leader collects problem cards, categorizes them, and places each category of cards on the left of a branch line.	Card-writing rules 1. Be specific. 2. Quantify if possible. 3. Write one thought per card. 4. Date the card. 5. Sign or initial the card.
(5)	• Develop analysis cards: Team members analyze causes as needed and concisely write the results of analysis on cards. (If not needed, this step may be skipped.) • The team leader collects the analysis cards and places each card next to the respective problem card on the branch line.	Apply the same card-writing rules as for Step (4).
(6)	• Develop improvement cards: Team members generate ideas they feel will improve the problem and write them down on cards. • The team leader collects the improvement cards and places each card next to its respective problem (and analysis) cards on the right of the branch line.	Apply the same card-writing rules as for Step (4).

Table 3-1. (cont.)
Steps for Building a SEDAC

	Description	Remarks
⑦	• The team leader marks the top right corner of the improvement cards according to the following rules and tests the cards considered effective: A. Of No Interest — no mark Cards that are considered inappropriate or ineffective for improving the problem. B. Of Interest — one red dot Cards that are considered effective. These cards may include ideas that require large investment or that cannot be adopted immediately. C. Under Preparation — two red dots Cards that are selected for implementation with the following preparations under way: remodeling/adjusting tools and equipment; obtaining necessary budgets and human resources; and planning for training. D. Under Test — three red dots Cards that are currently tested, with test results evaluated on the effect side.	As the team leader judges the improvement cards effective, they are put to the test. Multiple ideas that are considered effective may be tested at the same time.
⑧	• Standardize good practices. E. Successful Test — three red dots boxed with green lines Improvement cards that produced good results on the effect side become standard cards. F. Unsuccessful Test — three red dots with a crossing line Improvement cards that are tested but failed to produce good results.	The contents of improvement cards that are confirmed effective are standardized for continued practice. Standard cards are working documents and therefore should be incorporated into official documents such as standards, work procedures, manuals, work regulations, etc.
⑨	G. First-Class Card — standard cards with a green border Contents are unique and excellent ideas.	As shown in Table 1-1, one of the purposes of companywide improvement activities is to strengthen improvement capability. The first-class (excellent) cards created through implementation serve as an indicator for how much improvement capability has been strengthened.
⑩	Adhere to the standards developed through improvement activities and maintain good results.	

of which is explained in Table 3-1. The SEDAC leader collects these cards and places them on the left side of the branches of the fishbone diagram.

Step 5 is analysis. After reviewing the problem cards, when necessary, the SEDAC team leader assigns members to conduct an analysis for each card. These members, in turn, post their results right next to the corresponding problem cards. Step 6 involves generating ideas for improvement in the form of *improvement cards*. Next, the leader follows the rules of step 7 to communicate to team members the need for refining and testing improvement cards. Then, when improvement cards have been tested successfully, they move to step 8 and become *standard cards*.

Among the standard cards, improvement ideas that are unique and excellent are called *first-class* (or excellent) cards in step 9. The contents of these *first-class* cards constitute valuable know-how based on first-hand experience and, as such, are saved for use in reproducing improvement success in the future. Finally, step 10 ensures adherence to standard cards, including *first-class* cards, to maintain positive improvement results.

SPEED AND POWER

How long does it take to complete a SEDAC project? It's hard to generalize because it all depends on the scope and difficulty of the selected improvement themes and targets. However, on average, as indicated in the actual examples that will be introduced later in Tables 3-3 and 3-4, it takes about three months from the start of a project to the achievement of its target. The main reason such a quick turnaround time is possible is because SEDAC teams start their improvement activities within four hours and conduct them as part of daily work. Speed is power. Nevertheless, I'm not suggesting we hurry at all costs. Rather, I'm simply proposing that because we are professionals, we should carry out our improvement activities purposively and in a way that takes full advantage of our strengths.

Purposiveness

A manager who was promoting improvement through SEDAC once said, "It used to take us three months before we could even begin an improvement project. But this time with SEDAC, we started in just four hours." This is not an exaggeration. When readers understand how SEDAC works, I'm sure they will agree with this manager.

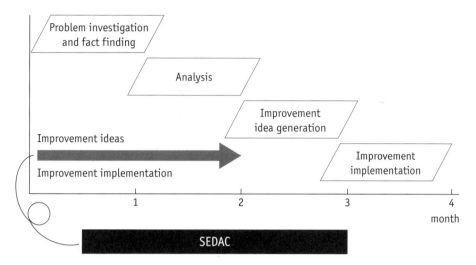

Figure 3-4.
Speeding Up Improvement

Objectives established in the P/O Matrix become SEDAC projects as they are, or after they have been further broken down. (See Figure 3-7 on page 83.) This starts things off quicker than in traditional approaches. In the past, we began actual improvement activities only after we passed through a number of milestones. First, we established improvement themes. As shown in Figure 3-4, the first step is problem investigation. In general, an employee with two to three years of service tackled this task. This person finished problem investigation in about one month and reported the findings. Senior employees then often said, "Your investigation is fine, but such-and-such aspects have not been addressed," or "Different scenarios should be considered regarding such-and-such data." Sometimes, the step of problem investigation was completed by conducting these additional tasks. In other cases, a kind section manager might say, "I will give you another month." Thus, another month went by while they were still investigating the problem.

The next step is analysis. Without clearly understanding why or to what extent the analysis should be conducted, in the past we applied all the analytical tools we learned for data analysis! In this way, we gave more than ample time to new employees so they could learn at their leisure. Although this was a good thing, the problem was that other people waited, doing nothing, while these new employees learned.

After another month went by, we held yet another reporting meeting. And when the analysis stage was finally over, we moved on to the next step, developing improvement ideas. It was at this point, much to our surprise, that in spite of the findings of our various analyses, new and different improvement ideas were often proposed and adopted. Sometimes we also found that in spite of our efforts, the whole problem could have been solved with one stroke of intrinsic technology.

Nevertheless, when we implemented improvement ideas and achieved good results, the project had a happy ending. It was not unusual, though, for the analysis and idea generation phase to take three months and for the implementation phase to take an additional two to five months.

Having learned these lessons from past experience, I wanted SEDAC team members to approach their tasks with a heightened sense of purpose. This meant that when members knew enough to point out the weaknesses and omissions of someone's problem investigation, they could write these observations on index cards or Post-its—a task that takes only an hour or so at the outset of a project. In this way, all the people concerned with a problem can integrate their knowledge quickly and efficiently.

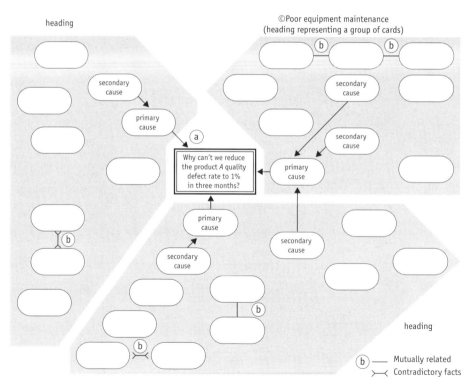

Figure 3-5.
Affinity/Relations Diagram on Improvement Theme

On the P/O Matrix, the objective, target, due date, project leader, and members are already established. In the beginning, the leader should hold at least one meeting with all project members. (If members include line people or if it is impossible to get all members together at the same time, the line leader of each group may represent the group at the meeting.)

When members are from multiple departments or sections, participation from these organizations is necessary. After all members are assembled, the SEDAC leader explains why the objective or project was selected, what approach will be followed, what the targets are, and when they should be accomplished. Then the leader gives members an hour or so to write problem cards. As shown in Figure 3-5, the question "Why can't we achieve our target?" is placed in the center. Based on their everyday experience and observations, all members write down the reasons, situations, and obstacles they feel are inhibiting them from achieving their target. SEDAC members write their cards according to the rules laid out in Table 3-1.

After an hour of card writing, each member shares his or her cards with the team. Using the affinity diagram process (or KJ method)* (one of the seven new QC tools), cards with similar content are grouped together. During this process, it's important to approach the information on each card with an open mind. The key is to start by making a number of small groups of cards and then consolidate these into fewer larger groups. In addition, if the causal relationship between cards is clear, it's helpful to designate these relationships by drawing arrows as indicated at (a) in Figure 3-5. This part of the process is derived from the relations dia-

---

*The affinity diagram has its origin in the KJ method developed by Dr. Jiro Kawakita, whose work is further described in Chapter 4. The name *affinity diagram* reflects its function well. In SEDAC, the affinity technique is used to review and group individual cards contributed by team members. Specifically, the team categorizes cards by reviewing their content affinity: if they are saying the same thing, addressing similar matters, or are related. The team then develops a heading for each affinity grouping that is representative of its contents. (Since SEDAC entails a series of steps, it does not follow exactly every detail of the affinity diagram but rather employs only parts of the overall method.)

** By asking *why* repeatedly, the relations diagram explores causes from primary to secondary, and even further upstream. For SEDAC, as indicated in (a) of Figure 3-5, an arrow from cause to effect is drawn when the causal relationship is known. In this figure, the cause that is most upstream is the root cause. When going through the process depicted by Figure 3-5, it's not uncommon for members to write down root causes from the very beginning. In such a case, there is no need to follow through with the entire process.

gram,** also one of the new QC tools. Other mutual relationships, indicated by (b) in Figure 3-5, are also designated when appropriate.

After all groupings have been completed, each group is assigned a heading that captures the essence of the information shared on its cards. These headings are indicated at (c) in Figure 3-5. All in all, it should take no more than two hours to complete the development of an affinity diagram like Figure 3-5. Although it's possible to continue this affinity process indefinitely, the team should strive to capture the important information within the prescribed time limit. Of course, during this two-hour period, active interactions among members and between the leader and members should take place. The time limit does not mean that the team has to conclude all its activities—discussions, fact-finding activities, investigation, and analysis—at this stage. These activities should and must continue as needed until the improvement project is completed. This is why it's not necessary to try and capture all information right away.

The cards gathered in the affinity diagram are then placed in the SEDAC format as shown in Figure 3-6. Information about the project, such as what to improve and the target value and date, is written on the right side of Figure 3-6, the effect side. The heading for each group of cards becomes the title of the category placed on each branch, as indicated at (d) of Figure 3-6. The individual cards developed for the affinity diagram are removed and placed on the left side of their respective branches as indicated at (e) in Figure 3-6. Also, it's important to note that when the relations diagram process identifies the casual relationships between certain cards, only the most upstream card (the root cause) should be included.

During the affinity diagram process, cards that contain the same information may be consolidated. When different cards contain conflicting information, however, they should be retained for further investigation. Also, don't bother arguing at the initial meeting about which cards are right and which are wrong. In some cases, more than one may be right. In any event, proper investigation will reveal the truth.

Part of the beauty of SEDAC is that, through the use of cards, the opinions of a single individual or very small group can survive and even prevail. This prevents the common phenomenon that occurs in meeting-room discussions: the opinions of less powerful or first-line employees (ironically, those who are closest to the facts) are overshadowed by the discussion of more powerful or higher ranking members.

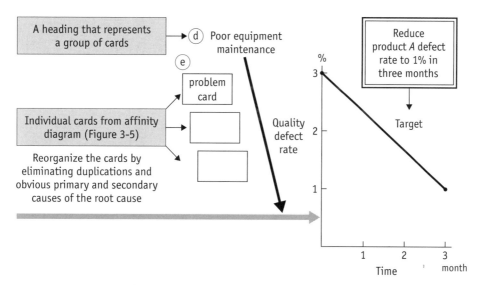

Figure 3-6.
Shaping SEDAC

In this vein, it's not uncommon for a single card to contain extremely valuable information for the project. Remember, the common information written on many cards is not necessarily the most important or useful. SEDAC is neither a survey nor a forum for majority rule; it simply ensures, by virtue of its rules, that problem and improvement cards with the correct information prevail. With this in mind, we encourage everyone to participate based on their unique strengths. In this way, first-line employees gain a better understanding of daily operations and staffers deepen their professional knowledge.

The advantage of using cards over meeting-room discussions is that cards make information more concrete and easier to grasp. In meetings, people often express themselves in an abstract manner, or one individual may express contradicting information in consecutive discussions. If such information is documented in written form, it's easier to understand, follow, and correct if necessary.

In any event, by integrating the experience of team members and the everyday data related to the improvement theme, the SEDAC team makes problems clearer and more concrete. Thus, an initially vague and confusing situation becomes more organized. Incidentally, if the team spends one hour on the process involved in generating a SEDAC, the total time spent on the project up to that point should be no more than four hours.

The reason why SEDAC-driven improvement activities begin in such a short time is because SEDAC problem cards can be addressed immediately, without elaborate investigation. In such cases, members readily suggest improvement ideas, and the SEDAC leader applies the improvement card rules and moves the project forward. In many situations, then, improvement activities begin just four hours after the project is first initiated!

Generally speaking, SEDAC concurrently addresses multiple improvement ideas for multiple problems as they are generated, one after another, and this activity continues until the project target is met. Although it's rare, some SEDAC projects achieve their target after they have developed only one to three standard cards. However, usually a SEDAC team generates at least seven standard cards before achieving its target.

After the initial information-gathering meeting, team members continue adding problem cards to SEDAC as they learn new facts from their newly experienced problems. While some problem cards contain numerical data, they often take the form of sentences that record or describe observed facts. Especially when cards contain information about intrinsic technologies, they are often written in an unquantifiable form.

The reason card-writing rules require the inclusion of the date as well as the writer's initials is because this is a basic rule of observation. Let's suppose, for example, that a team detects a specific quality defect or a minor stoppage of certain equipment, both symptoms of deeper root causes. To get a solid grasp on such symptoms, it's vital to find out how they change when observed at different times by different team members.

Step 7 of the SEDAC process is the red-dot system, which allows the leader to evaluate and respond to team members' card contributions (see Table 3-1 for how the dots are used). A busy work environment does not always permit the leader to communicate with members individually. By using the red-dot system instead, the leader communicates the following to each card contributor: how the card has been evaluated and where it stands in the implementation queue. When members disagree with the leader's decision, they communicate with the leader and resolve any differences through discussion.

The traditional set of problem-solving steps mentioned earlier—grasping the facts, analyzing problems, developing improvement ideas, and implementing ideas—is not wrong, of course. These are the basic steps of improvement. In fact, SEDAC follows the same steps, only much more quickly. It seems the confusion set in when, somehow, we began to allocate time frames in sequence for each step of the improvement process as shown in Figure 3-4.

Professionalism

Rather than blindly following the steps of improvement, we as knowledgeable people and professionals should be able to garner our strengths to achieve improvement objectives. In grasping the facts of a problem or improvement objective, team members usually possess all the information they currently need based on subject knowledge derived from their individual daily work experience. The role of SEDAC is to tap and integrate such knowledge through the steps just described. As mentioned, an output of this process is the identification of primary and secondary causal relationships among the generated problem cards.

If analysis of certain problem cards is necessary, such an analysis is encouraged only after clarifying its purpose, while simultaneously continuing progress on other cards. All improvement cards are nevertheless studied for their potential effect and tested accordingly. Based on the test results, the team determines whether they should be adopted for continued attention.

My suggestion is to conduct improvement activities in a professional manner, according to the following characteristics of the SEDAC approach:

- Staying purpose-oriented

- Encouraging interdepartmental cooperation and integration of diversity

- Sharing information through visual management

- Making concurrent improvements

Putting these key words into practice requires team members to cultivate a high level of professionalism—something they do by using SEDAC and by sharpening their job-related skills. There is no doubt that companies with excellent specialized intrinsic technologies (not just in manufacturing and R&D, but in banking, distribution, service, and other fields as well) will survive and continue to prosper. Nevertheless, it's important for all companies, including these, to strengthen their professional characteristics through daily practice, even if this practice sometimes means failure. Clearly, nothing is developed by simply wishing and waiting.

As these sections have described, SEDAC is key to materializing the fast-track conditions laid out in Chapter 1, in Table 1-3, such as condition 6, "Enabling structures to promote improvement in daily work," and condition 7, "Enabling structures that encourage creative improvement by integrating knowledge and experience."

LINKAGE BETWEEN THE P/O MATRIX AND SEDAC

Breaking Down the P/O Matrix with a Systematic Diagram

Hopefully by now you've developed at least a cursory understanding of SEDAC and how it works. Next we'll discuss the very important linkage between SEDAC and the P/O Matrix.

As shown in Figure 3-7, the P/O Matrix is segmented into various levels, from the president to the business unit head to the department head and, finally, to the section manager level. Let's suppose a section manager's P/O Matrix includes the policy *reduce process quality defects by 75 percent*. Let's suppose further that achieving the following two objectives and targets will lead to the fulfillment of this policy:

A. Reduce operations-related defects to 0.3 percent

B. Reduce equipment-related defects to 0.1 percent

Objective *B* can be addressed by SEDAC at its present level of detail. However, objective *A* is too broad to be addressed by SEDAC—"operations" is a big area. Therefore a systematic diagram is used to break it down further. The systematic diagram has a sideways tree shape, as shown in Figure 3-7. In this case, three specific section-level objectives are identified:

a. Reduce interior carbon defects

b. Reduce screen process defects

c. Reduce dust-related performance deficiency

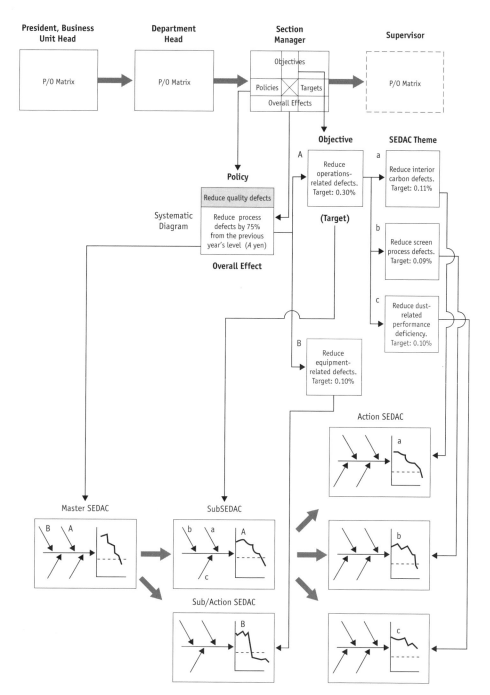

Figure 3-7.
The Link Between the P/O Matrix and SEDAC

SEDAC at Each Level

At the section manager or policy level, a SEDAC is called a *master* SEDAC. At the objective level as with objectives *A* and *B*, it's called a *sub-*SEDAC. When the objectives are broken down further, as in *a, b,* and *c* above, these are called *action* SEDACs. In the case of objective *B*, *reduce equipment-related defects*, the sub-SEDAC and action SEDAC are one and the same.

Actually, improvement activities take place every day at the action SEDAC level, and it's quite rare for master and sub-SEDACs to exist in the absence of an action SEDAC. When this happens, improvement activities are usually meaningless.

Section managers or SEDAC leaders should consider the following points in deciding whether to further break down objectives into SEDAC improvement themes, as shown for objective *A* above, or to use objectives directly as improvement themes, as in objective *B* above:

- The scope of improvement required

- The number of people involved (if more than 30, better to break it down)

If an objective is broken down, it's important to link and coordinate targets. Basically, action SEDAC targets should be set so that the master SEDAC target is achieved when the results of all action SEDACs are obtained and combined. Likewise, when all the section manager's master SEDACs are achieved, her P/O Matrix is achieved. Further, the results of each section manager's P/O Matrices are rolled up to the department head level, which are, in turn, rolled into top management's P/O Matrix. In this upwardly cascading fashion, a company's objectives are achieved. Figure 3-7 is helpful in showing mutual SEDAC relationships and in understanding how one SEDAC impacts other SEDACs, especially those at higher levels.

TYPES OF SEDAC

Depending on its purpose, or what needs to be improved, SEDAC takes on the most suitable form for revealing the structure of and addressing the problem. As shown in Table 3-2, there are several different types of SEDACs.

Table 3-2.
Various Types of SEDAC

Types (to visualize the structure of problems — Q7, N7, etc.)	Focus	Applications
Cause-and-Effect Diagram (Q7)	Diverse causes and countermeasures	• Quality defects • Stockless production (work-in-process, setup time, etc.) • Overall equipment effectiveness (equipment failures and minor stoppages) • Profit margin
Flowchart	Operations in time sequence	• Administrative work processes • Quality throughput rate
Arrow Diagram (N7)	Projects with time limits	• Staff work (planning, human resources, accounting, design, engineering, development, etc.) • Construction • Deadline-driven marketing activities
FMEA (failure mode and effects analysis)	Technologies and operations that require prediction	• Reliability engineering • New designs, equipment, and processes • To speed up improvements
PDPC (process decision program chart) (N7)	New subjects with many unknown factors	• Research and development jobs • Marketing (new market development), etc.

Q7 = 7 QC tools   N7 = 7 new QC tools

Expandable Cause-and-Effect SEDAC

In the form of the cause-and-effect diagram, SEDAC is used in the situations outlined in Table 3-2, when causes (and therefore countermeasures) are diverse. With this approach, the number of branches can be increased to fit the number of necessary cause categories. Also, as indicated by Figure 3-7, when a branch grows too big, it can be separated from the trunk and developed as a new, separate SEDAC.

Arrow Diagram SEDAC for Staff Function Improvement

SEDAC in the form of an arrow diagram, one of the seven new QC tools (see page 33 footnote), is used for staff-oriented tasks that must be carried out within a specific time frame. By developing a task or project schedule on an arrow diagram, the critical path—which contains no slack time against the required due date—is identified. Because due dates given to staff functions are often aggressive and unachievable without significant improvements, SEDAC is applied to activities along the critical path. By doing this, the quality of work is assured and projects are finished on time.

FMEA SEDAC for Prevention by Prediction

FMEA (failure mode and effects analysis) is a reliability technique segmented into two main categories: design FMEA and process FMEA. The difference between these is simply that the former is applied during the design stage, while the latter is applied during new production process development. In both cases, the idea is to predict potential failures and deficiencies during the initial review stage so as to develop countermeasures and prevent accidents, before new products and equipment are designed or new production processes are initiated.

Generally speaking, prediction requires engineering sensitivity supported by knowledge and experience. Using SEDAC, such sensitivity is sharpened through the development of unique and effective countermeasures that prevent the occurrence of predicted undesirable events.

PDPC and SEDAC Side by Side

Tasks that include many unknown factors, such as research and development and new product sales, are good candidates for the use of both SEDAC and PDPC (process decision program chart), another of the seven new QC tools. Dr. Jiro Kondo (professor emeritus at Tokyo University), the inventor of PDPC, defines it as "a chart that lays out the plan for implementing a series of measures, which are designed to move toward the final solution of a problem when the information at hand is insufficient and when the situation is fluid and uncertain." When we proceed with a project and implement plans using PDPC, we often encounter bottlenecks that must be resolved before we advance. SEDAC functions as a drill that penetrates such bottleneck problems and solves them while using PDPC to guide and carry out the project.

Specific examples of applications of the different types of SEDAC just described are given in Chapter 5. Different SEDAC methods are applied, depending on the structure of the problem or need for improvement. In each case, it's important to select the most suitable form that reveals the problem in an easy-to-understand manner. Even though SEDAC takes different forms, the essential characteristics of all SEDACs are the same: They create an enabling structure for integrating everyone's knowledge and experience and for carrying out improvements with new, unique, and creative ideas.

CASE EXAMPLES OF RESULTS FROM SEDAC IMPLEMENTATION

The results of improvement activities in two sections of the manufacturing department of Sendai Nikon, a Nikon group company that produces cameras, are shown in Tables 3-3 and 3-4. Readers who work in a manufacturing environment may find the listed improvement themes similar to those you are tackling in your organizations. In brief, Tables 3-3 and 3-4 list improvement themes, indicator values before improvement, targets, and achievement levels obtained after implementation.

Calculating target achievement levels is a matter of comparing indicator values before and after improvement. The resulting "gap" tells you how much you've improved. When 100 percent of the target is met, then improvement has been achieved as planned. When more than 100 percent of the target has been achieved, then improvement is greater than planned.

Fortunately for this company, all themes in Table 3-3, and all but one theme in Table 3-4, met or surpassed their targets. From these tables, we can determine that the average time required to achieve an improvement theme was three months. Perhaps you too would like to acquire such strong improvement power.

As listed in the two tables, the main themes for improvement are quality, productivity, equipment availability, and setup time reduction—all of which were selected in an effort to shorten production lead time. Based on this objective, then, targets for each theme were chosen. In the case of setup time, for instance, Sendai Nikon's manufacturing department team did not unnecessarily pursue a "single-minute" (nine minutes or less)

Table 3-3.
SEDAC Completion List (Sendai Nikon, Manufacturing Department, Product 1 Section)

(6/18/90 ~ 3/29/93)

No.	Themes	Targets	Problem cards	Improve- ment cards	Standard cards	Results	Achieve- ment rate	Duration	Months
90-1	Shorten RAM1-2 cycle time	16 → 14 seconds	33	42	15	12.9 seconds	155	6/18 ~ 9/29	3.0
2	Reduce adhesive process inspection errors of S-series cameras	5 → 2%	60	46	7	1.31%	123	6/18 ~ 9/29	3.0
3	Eliminate back-screen SW chattering defects of unit shutters	8 → 0/week	47	33	8	0	100	6/18 ~ 10/18	4.0
4	Improve RAM1-2 performance efficiency	89 → 95%	42	36	9	95.3%	105	10/5 ~ 12/28	2.5
5	Reduce over-counting errors of adhesive process inspection	6 → 1%	81	39	9	0.99%	100	10/13 ~ 12/28	2.5
6	Shorten precision adjustment time	110 → 70 seconds	79	50	12	66.0 seconds	110	12/10 ~ 3/09	3.0
7	Shorten RAM1-3 cycle time	14 → 12.7 seconds	16	21	6	12.5 seconds	115	1/23 ~ 3/26	2.0
91-1	Halve 0B-induced defects	108 → 90/week	60	46	13	81/week	110	1/21 ~ 4/27	3.0
2	Shorten MA-1 line cycle time	7.8 → 7.0 seconds	11	10	7	6.9 seconds	113	4/8 ~ 5/11	1.5
3	Shorten RAM1-1 cycle time	12.6 → 12 seconds	9	9	6	12.0 seconds	100	6/19 ~ 7/26	1.5
4	Halve adhesive process defect rate	10 → 5%	65	37	13	3.4%	132	6/3 ~ 8/30	3.0
5	Shorten MA-AF-L line cycle time	7.0 → 6.3 seconds	21	21	10	6.3 seconds	100	7/16 ~ 9/28	2.5
6	Improve #100 throughput rate	89.6 → 92%	84	32	10	96.1%	270	9/17 ~ 12/13	3.0
7	Improve MA-AF-L line's OEE	82 → 85%	38	34	4	90.5%	283	11/11 ~ 2/19	3.0
8	Eliminate AF-L infrared soldering defects	12 → 0/week	61	31	7	0	100	1/6 ~ 3/28	3.0
92-1	Improve #101 throughput rate	91 → 95%	69	50	13	95.8%	120	4/16 ~ 8/31	4.5
2	Shorten RAM1-1/B100 setup time	50 → 25 minutes	63	46	21	18 minutes	128	4/21 ~ 9/29	5.0
3	Improve #103 throughput rate (1)	82 → 85%	44	34	13	85.2%	107	7/6 ~ 10/3	3.0
4	Shorten RAM1-1/B70 setup time	50 → 25 minutes	63	46	21	18 minutes	128	7/13 ~ 9/29	2.5
5	Improve #103 throughput rate (2)	85 → 90%	40	32	9	91.5%	130	10/5 ~ 12/29	2.5
6	Shorten RAM1-2 (A) setup time	22 → 15 minutes	32	29	5	14.5 minutes	107	10/12 ~ 12/29	2.5
7	Shorten RAM1-2 (B) setup time	15 → 11 minutes	31	31	13	9 minutes	150	1/5 ~ 3/29	2.5

Table 3-4.
SEDAC Completion List (Sendai Nikon, Manufacturing Department, Machinery Section)

(2/13/91 ~ 10/13/92)

No.	Themes	Targets	Problem cards	Improvement cards	Standard cards	Results	Achievement rate	Duration	Months
91-1	Shorten progressive press setup time	3 → 2 H	64	40	13	1.9 H	110.0	2/13 ~ 5/31	3.5
2	Halve L, By, As1, 2 line defect rate	0.7 → 0.3%	26	29	8	0.19%	127.5	3/12 ~ 5/31	2.5
3	Shorten B, By, As, FH line cycle time	15 → 13.5 seconds	27	19	5	13.1 seconds	126.7	4/24 ~ 7/1	3.0
4	Reduce #21 scratch defects	9 → 3%	78	59	6	0.9%	270.0	6/11 ~ 8/30	3.0
5	Halve L, By, FH process defect rate	0.6 → 0.3%	62	35	15	0.19%	136.7	6/10 ~ 9/10	3.0
6	Reduce L, By, As line minor stoppages	82 → 87%	55	23	7	87.6%	112.0	7/16 ~ 10/29	3.5
7	Reduce L, By, FH process minor stoppages	78 → 88%	73	34	10	92.1%	141.0	6/17 ~ 11/2	4.5
8	Shorten P combined line cycle time	6 → 5.4 seconds	55	45	8	3.9 seconds	350.0	9/17 ~ 11/29	2.5
9	Shorten L, By, milling machine setup time	60 → 10 minutes	35	25	5	10 minutes	100.0	6/17 ~ 12/10	5.5
10	Reduce L, By, M line minor stoppages	82 → 92%	54	52	10	93.5%	115.0	11/11 ~ 3/28	4.5
11	Reduce punch fracture defects	2 → 1 month	60	50	5	1 month	100.0	12/2 ~ 3/28	4.0
92-1	Reduce B, By, As, FH process minor stoppages	78 → 88%	61	22	18	92.0%	140.0	4/13 ~ 6/24	2.5
2	Shorten P, #21F dedicated machine cycle time	20 → 18 seconds	58	53	7	15.6 seconds	220.0	4/14 ~ 7/9	3.0
3	Reduce L, By drilling machine S minor stoppages	77 → 93%	85	70	10	94.8%	111.3	4/15 ~ 7/17	3.0
4	Reduce NP-16 minor stoppages	79 → 89%	39	45	8	96.7%	177.0	4/16 ~ 7/6	3.0
5	Shorten L, By drilling machine S cycle time	32 → 29 seconds	33	10	4	30.0 seconds	66.7	6/29 ~ 9/29	3.0
6	Shorten L, By drilling machine D cycle time	1431 → 1288 seconds	64	42	36	1286 seconds	101.4	7/1 ~ 9/29	3.0
7	Reduce gear cutting machine minor stoppages	82 → 92%	55	42	8	99.2%	172.0	7/13 ~ 10/13	3.0
8	Improve P, #21F dedicated equipment's OEE	78 → 85%	100	87	10	88.7%	152.9	7/20 ~ 9/29	2.5
9	Shorten L, As1, 2 machine 2 setup time	120 → 90 minutes	31	32	20	83.0 minutes	123.3	7/21 ~ 9/29	2.5

setup. Based on identified needs, the teams set their own targets. They measured setup time improvements primarily with averages and reviewed the distribution of data to confirm dispersion improvement as well.

All in all, Tables 3-3 and 3-4 show us that the individual improvement themes of quality, productivity, and equipment availability support the overall objective of lead time reduction, even though each of these themes is meaningful in and of itself (see Chapter 7).

Now let's turn to several other SEDAC case examples. The first example is from the Kashima Works, the main steel mill of Sumitomo Metal Industries. It produces various iron and steel products, including seamless pipes and thin plates. It is one of the largest steel mills in the world and is known for its high level of quality and productivity supported by the latest technology. Table 3-5 shows the number of improvement projects and the number of related SEDAC applications at the Kashima Works from October 1986 to March 1987, during which time the company saved ¥3.5 billion ($35 million) as a result of improvement projects. After raising monetary targets for the period from April to November 1987, the company went on to save an additional ¥3.3 billion ($33 million) for a total savings of ¥6.8 billion ($68 million).

One day, I visited Kashima Works' hot-rolling plant with a group of foreign visitors. In contrast with the dynamic movement of a steel plate running through hot rollers outside a glass window, we stood inside a completely quiet, darkened control room laced with instrument panels

Table 3-5.
SEDAC Improvement Applications
(Sumitomo Metal, Kashima Works)

(10/86 – 3/87)

Shops	Improvement projects	SEDAC applications
Pig iron raw materials	18	18
Pig iron	32	32
Steel No. 1	4	4
Steel No. 2	43	43
Plate	14	8
Hot strip mill	40	35
Cold strip mill	19	17
Pickling	3	3
Large diameter pipe shop	23	11
Small diameter pipe shop	24	18
Large frame	20	17
Steel shape	9	5
Total	249	211

Table 3-6.
SEDAC Application Results (Sony Hamamatsu, 1990–1992)

Overall quality improvement		
Year \ Category	Process defect rate	Defective return rate
1990	−47%	−61%
1991	−35%	−66%
1992	−50%	−51%

Defective return rate: returned defective units/total units shipped

(1) Examples of quality improvement (1992)

Optomagnetic pickup process defect rate	−73%
Industrial optical device pickup process defect rate	−69%
VTR drum (A) defective return rate	−43%
VTR drum (B) defective return rate	−62%

(2) Examples of productivity improvement (1992)

CD pickup (A) labor productivity	+35%
CD pickup (B) labor productivity	+31%
CD mechanical deck equipment productivity	+57%

and TV monitors. It reminded me of a jet cockpit. In the room, around shift-change time, two operators were at work. The two operators about to begin the next shift stood quietly behind the working operators and observed the situation. When shift-change time came, the two new operators replaced the ones just leaving, without a word. Although a nonverbal exchange of notes and SEDAC information was typical for this plant at shift change, the foreign observers were very impressed by this impeccable transition. They observed a plant where the technology was so superior and the equipment and operations so stable that verbal communications were not required to ensure a smooth shift change!

In another case, shown in Table 3-6, the Sony Hamamatsu plant achieved remarkable quality improvements during a three-year period beginning in 1990. By 1992, they had achieved significant productivity improvements. Sony Hamamatsu manufactures key precision devices for Sony products.

In accomplishing these good results, Sony Hamamatsu relied on many joint SEDAC projects between staff and line departments. Depending on the theme, the plant also worked closely with the electronics division of Sony Components Company, a group company responsible for product design. Through the sharing of SEDAC diagrams, and through the close

Table 3-7.
SEDAC Application Results (Sony Inazawa, 1991–1992)

Overall quality improvement	
Product defect rate	−43%
Process defect rate	−26%
Defective return rate	−54%
(returned defective units/total units shipped)	
Examples of quality improvement	
Coating process defect rate	−31%
Equipment failure rate	−22%
Electron beam defect rate	−38%
Color purity defect rate	−59%
Color purity defect rate during TV set assembly	−65%

cross-functional cooperation of responsible parties identified in Section IV of the P/O Matrix, the plant was able to achieve its common themes and objectives quickly. Even where responsible parties were physically separated, they communicated with each other by sending SEDAC cards via fax to minimize meetings and project time requirements. In this way, multiple teams in different locations cooperated to achieve SEDAC aims.

Another example, shown in Table 3-7, is Sony Inazawa, maker of Trinitron CRTs for high resolution TV screens. During 1991 and 1992, Sony Inazawa saved ¥4 billion ($40 million) just as a result of process defect improvements. While monetary savings were important, these improvements yielded an even more significant result for the company: They represented a strategic move to enhance value for customers (TV set manufacturers) in the form of improved delivery reliability, ease of assembly, and customer trust in CRT quality.

Figure 3-8 illustrates the structure of staff-line cooperation for SEDAC projects in Sony Inazawa's manufacturing department. The black dots indicate participation, showing that manufacturing sections 1, 2, and 4 all impact a particular quality defect characteristic. Each section, therefore, takes up this problem on its P/O Matrix and action SEDAC. At the same time, two different staff functions participate in the same problem. These functions—the manufacturing engineering process zero defects (ZD) team and the machinery section's equipment ZD team—contribute to each of the three action SEDACs as shown also with black dots in Figure 3-8.

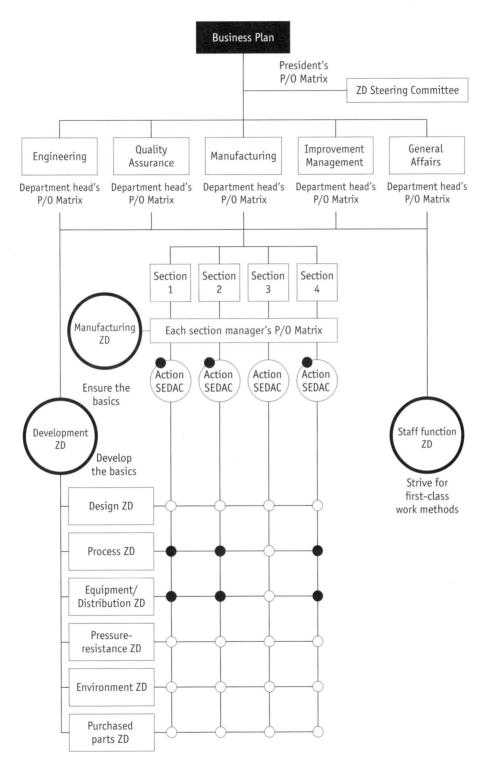

Figure 3-8.
Promotion System for Improvement Activities (Sony Inazawa)

Table 3-8.
SEDAC Application Results (Michelin Italiana, Fossano Plant, 1989–1992)

Overall effects	
Product defect loss	−94%
Process defect loss	−48%
Productivity	+20%
Equipment maintenance cost	−10%
Examples of quality improvement	
• Reduced wire-drawing process defects	−63%
• Reduced rework (time) due to coil winding defects	−85%
• Reduced cable-wrapping process defects	−14%
• Reduced rework (time) due to cable defects	
Type A	−68%
Type B	−55%
• Reduced rework (time) due to coiling defects during heat treatment	−60%
• Reduced cable-stranding defects	−71%
Examples of equipment and tool reliability improvement	
• Reduced downtime of automatic disc edging machine	−64%
• Reduced stoppages of cable stranding machines	
Machine A	−52%
Machine B	−66%
• Reduced stoppages of the bobbin remover attached to the wire drawer	−54%
• Reduced electrical part failures of wire drawers, heat treatment units, and surface treatment units	−59%
• Reduced stoppages of automatic packaging machines	−40%
Examples of productivity improvement	
• Increased output due to reduced random equipment failures in the welding shop	+15%
• Increased operational efficiency due to replacement of electric batteries on elevator forks	+36%
• Shortened average setup time	−75%

Still another SEDAC improvement example is found in Table 3-8, which covers the Fossano, Italy, plant of the tire manufacturer Michelin. The plant achieved significant results in various areas, such as improved quality, equipment reliability, and productivity. In particular, through the use of 47 SEDACs for improving process quality, the plant achieved almost zero quality defects at final inspection, as well as remarkable cost savings.

Continuing, we find Alfa-Lancia and Ferrari, two Fiat group companies. Table 3-9 lists the accomplishments of Alfa-Lancia, which achieved noteworthy results by implementing a well-run joint SEDAC with its manufacturing and design departments. Ferrari also implemented a well-coordinated joint SEDAC project with its production floor operations and its production engineering department, in addition to applying SEDAC to a painting process that requires a high level of technological know-how.

Other SEDAC application examples include Italy's Montefibre, a synthetic fiber manufacturer, which implemented various quality improvements using SEDAC that resulted in a $780,000 cost reduction in a short period of time. And Brazil's Pirelli Cables, a cable manufacturer, reported a 20 percent productivity increase by improving bottlenecks through the SEDAC process.

Furthermore, one major U.S. automobile manufacturer reported a monthly cost saving of $46,716 resulting from a dramatic reduction of quality defects on the solenoids line (May 1993). This effort entailed developing nine new standard procedures based on SEDAC cards generated from team members' original ideas—three standards for autonomous operator maintenance, four for preventive maintenance, and two for vendor management.

Service companies also have reported positive results through SEDAC. In addition to the Rome Airport mentioned in Chapter 1, the Cremona Hospital, near Milan, applied SEDAC with such themes as improving medicine management and hospital services. Two banks (Banca Antoniana and Cassa di Risparmio di Puglia S.P.A) and an insurance

Table 3-9.
SEDAC Application Results (Alfa-Lancia and Ferrari, 1989–1992)

Alfa-Lancia (Arese Plant)	
• Reduced defects as result of Alfa 164 engine assembly processes (6 SEDACs)	−75%
• Reduced defects as result of Alfa 164 body finishing process (7 SEDACs)	−78%
• Currently trying to halve defects resulting from all body assembly processes (70 SEDACs)	(−50%)
Ferrari	
• 348 TB/TS model cars	
Reduced finishing coat flaws	−60%
Reduced sheet metal dents for car bodies	−55%
Reduced painting rework	−75%
• Reduced parts that are not kept in warehouse (servicing parts)	−90%
• Reduced excess spare parts for F119 engine mechanical adjustments	−98%
• Reduced car stock in finishing operations department	−60%

company (Reale Mutua Assicurazioni) have also reported successful SEDAC applications.*

As a final note, you may have noticed that most P/O Matrix and SEDAC case examples in this book are from companies in North America and Europe. This is because these countries have had the most opportunity to introduce the P/O Matrix and SEDAC techniques. Applications in Asian and South American countries have only just begun.

*Although Table 1-1 mentions the importance of measuring SEDAC success in terms of "processes" and "results," the exact processes involved in achieving the results detailed above and in other places throughout this book are not revealed due to confidentiality.

Fundamentals of
Improvement Through SEDAC

THOUGHTS ON THE IMPROVEMENT PROCESS

Chapter 3 introduced some interesting improvement case examples of results attained by using SEDAC. In this section, we will explore why these companies achieved such good results, beginning with Table 4-1, which contains the main details of my analysis based on experience. Table 4-1 describes the main effective actions of SEDAC and the P/O Matrix, and suggests the reasons why these methods are effective in these actions.

Idea Generation

In Table 4-1, item 1 in the "Effective Actions" column refers to the use of SEDAC in promoting improvement activities and generating ideas effectively and efficiently. As this item states, the actions required to generate ideas and inspirations eventually boil down to *continuous wholehearted thinking,* which means to be constantly and passionately devoted to finding a better way.

There are, of course, many idea-generation techniques available in the marketplace. Table 4-2 compares some of these techniques for conceiving and generating ideas. Because I was involved for a long time in researching intrinsic technologies, I'm very interested in this subject and have read many books on idea generation. Once I encountered a book subtitled *Win with the Front Brain.* Since the front part of the brain is considered responsible for creativity, I read the book eagerly, hoping to find out how

Table 4-1.
Reasons for SEDAC and P/O Matrix Effectiveness

Effective Actions	Technique	Reasons for Effectiveness
1. Promote improvement activities effectively and efficiently	SEDAC	• Orients team members and directs their actions by graphically presenting the project and maximizing the organization's wholehearted thinking efforts • Shares necessary information with all members • Encourages all individuals to use their strengths and keep thinking • Integrates the team's wisdom with external knowledge for new idea generation • Standardizes favorable test results and accumulates them as intrinsic and management technology
2. Detect obstacles to the improvement process and remove them	SEDAC	• Shares necessary information with all members • No alternative techniques available for learning from failures
3. A. Manage the improvement activity B. Make the improvement process smoother by anticipating obstacles and preventing their occurrence	P/O Matrix	• Gives tangible form to top management commitment • Facilitates a systematic approach to improvement rather than just relying on the hard work of individuals • Encourages cross-functional cooperation

to use my front brain! Unfortunately, I was disappointed to find no such instructions.

However, I did learn one important fact. If I work my brain very hard, I will naturally work the front part. I also figured out that it's relatively easy for any person to exercise his or her brain as individuals. In translating this principle further, it occurred to me that for organizations to think wholeheartedly—or use the full power of their "collective brain"— they must develop a methodology that enables everyone to think together. Such wholehearted thinking implies that people muster their full potential and apply an inspired passion to their work and improvement efforts.

Another book on this subject had a very interesting table that listed famous inventors and scientists and described what they were doing when they conceived their breakthrough ideas. The descriptions were very detailed. For example, a certain chemist got a great inspiration while disembarking a carriage at four o'clock in the morning. Should we expect to receive similar inspirations by climbing out of carriages at four in the

Table 4-2.
Techniques for Conceiving and Generating Ideas

Technique	Description	Major applications	Participation	Remarks
Brainstorming	Participants freely think and express their thoughts while getting stimulated by others' opinions. To generate ideas, it is best to assemble free and unrestrained thinkers with diverse backgrounds.	Many fields, including product development and marketing	Group (5 to 7 people)	
Brainwriting	Participants freely think and write their thoughts on cards while getting stimulated by others' opinions. This garners the participation of quiet people and thus provides all participants an equal opportunity to express themselves.	Many fields, including product development, and marketing	Group (5 to 7 people)	Silent brainstorming suitable for logical thinkers
CBS method	This is brainstorming with cards. It follows and repeats the steps of individual and group brainstorming.	Problem solving in marketing, product development, and other areas	Group (5 to 7 people) Individual	Repeat steps of brainwriting and brainstorming
Fault-listing method Wish-listing method	Participants generate ideas limited to faults with or wishes for the subject. After this, they go on to develop methods for improving faults and realizing wishes.	Product improvement	Group Individual	Faults to improve the status quo Wishes for fundamental improvement
In-out method	The status quo is considered "in," while the improved situation "out." This method analyzes the steps between the "in" and the "out" and connects them by repeating idea divergence and convergence for each step.	Automatic machinery development	Group Individual	People with technological knowledge are required
Attribute-listing method	This method dissects the subject by attribute. By focusing on each attribute, participants generate new ideas for improvement.	Product improvement	Group Individual	
Checklist method	Participants think by following a prepared list of viewpoints and directions to assist in conceiving ideas. Various lists are used depending on the purpose.	Product improvement Ideas for new products	Group Individual	A suitable list must be developed that fulfills the improvement aim and covers all aspects of the project
Shape-analysis method	This method develops the combinations of all axes of the shape (of any object under study) and analyzes each combination, thereby avoiding omission.	Technology development Marketing	Group Individual	Ensures consideration of all combinations
Catalog method	Participants randomly open a catalog and think about the ideas and terminology presented on the opened page. This facilitates random thinking.	Product improvement Ideas for new products	Group Individual	
Focusing method	By forcing themselves to think and connect unrelated items, participants generate new ideas.	Product improvement Ideas for new products	Group Individual	
Synectics	By finding items that are intrinsically similar to the subject under analysis, and by gleaning inspiration from them, participants generate ideas for improvement.	Product development	Group (5 to 7 people) Individual	Specialists from each field are desirable
Gordon method	By identifying a concept a level higher than the subject for analysis, participants generate new ideas by association based on the concept.	Ideas for new products	Group (5 to 12 people)	Specialists from each field are desirable
NM method	By finding items similar to the subject under investigation, and by gleaning inspiration from them, participants generate new ideas. Steps for creative thinking are provided by this method.	Ideas for new products	Group (5 to 7 people) Individual	The clear steps make it easy to use

Source: Yoshiaki Tanaka and Yuji Nakazono, *Sozoryoku Kakushin no Kenkyu (A Study of Creativity Development),*
Japan Management Association. 1988. 124.

morning? I think our chances would be slim, in spite of our efforts. Nevertheless, I learned an important lesson from reading these examples: we must think all the time, constantly. If we keep thinking and stick to it, we will become inspired.

Some time ago, I watched a TV program about Thomas Edison. It included episodes that depicted his commitment to thought and study. I learned that even Edison, a great genius, fought hard for new ideas, and I was moved by his efforts to keep thinking with his full power and potential. Actually, the idea-generation techniques available on the market are simply ways of encouraging the act of thinking with a whole heart. It's interesting that SEDAC, as we have seen, also encourages wholehearted thinking. Now you can understand that SEDAC is a product of my desire to develop an effective and efficient way for groups of people *to keep thinking with passion* while they improve their daily work.

Using the Full Power of an Organization

The "Reasons for Effectiveness" listed in section 1 of Table 4-1 are the aspects of SEDAC that encourage teams to keep thinking wholeheartedly and generating new ideas. Because today's problems can rarely be solved by any one individual, it's necessary for groups of people to combine their full creative problem-solving abilities. To facilitate such information sharing and cooperation, and to apply individual strengths to a common goal, people need an easy and effective way of visualizing the entire structure of a problem. The various types of SEDAC introduced in Chapter 3 are effective means of attaining this visualization. Through SEDAC, all people understand the structure of a problem and are encouraged to participate in finding a solution by always thinking wholeheartedly and bringing their individual strengths into full play. As Figure 4-1 outlines, different roles within an organization have different strengths to bring problem solving and idea generation. In actuality, each individual has more specific strengths that should be tapped for the improvement process.

An interesting story that illustrates my point comes from Sony U.K., located in a village called Brigend in Wales. The village is a quiet, restful place with hotels converted from old mansions and flocks of sheep that sometimes block the road. An excellent company, Sony U.K. has been recognized with many awards, including the Queen's Award and the 1988 British Quality Award. Once I attended one of the company's disco parties for all employees. A woman who happened to be standing beside me

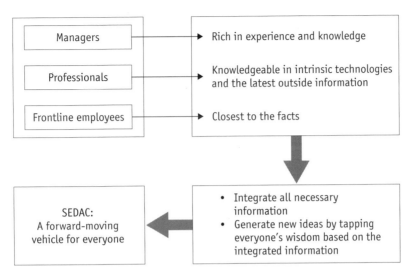

Figure 4-1.
Relying on Each Person's Strengths

told me, "I've been working for Sony for three years now, and had many different jobs before I came here. I must say, however, that this is the first time I've ever been involved in something as exciting as our SEDAC project. We're allowed to share our opinions and come up with suggestions for our jobs! In the past, I was told this was only the manager's job or the engineer's job and to keep my comments to myself." Remember that those who work in operations sites, like this woman, have the advantage of being closest to the company's products and equipment, and their ideas are as important as anyone else's, if not more important.

SEDAC as a Vehicle for Moving Forward

The description of SEDAC in Figure 4-1 as a *forward-moving vehicle for everyone* is one of my favorite points about this improvement methodology. If you follow the steps of building a SEDAC as laid out in Table 3-1 (pages 72–73), I'm certain that you will share my feeling that SEDAC is a vehicle everyone can ride on.

To move something forward, we often hold a meeting, but a meeting by itself cannot ensure progress. After a meeting, a project may move forward for a while, but as we've all experienced, it also may stall. The typical response? Have another meeting to jump-start and move the project to the next stage. This process, of course, can become exhausting. It is not desirable to implement a project in which tasks don't proceed without being pushed through meetings, or when information stops flowing at each stage. A much more desirable option is to engage in important improvement projects, such as those identified on the P/O Matrix, and then to keep everyone well informed and involved in the project at all times. For me, SEDAC is the answer to my longtime search for a mechanism capable of moving projects forward constantly and concretely.

The Leader's Role in Constant Thinking

The way SEDAC necessitates idea generation through constant thinking is one of the reasons for its effectiveness, as described in section 1 of Table 4-1. As I said, there are many idea-generation techniques on the market, and SEDAC was developed after I learned such techniques. One of the features I wanted to include in SEDAC that I felt was lacking in other techniques was a way for users to think on an ongoing basis, not just during meeting times.

Such ongoing idea generation is one of the aspects of SEDAC that the leader is expected to perpetuate. In drawing out new improvement ideas, the SEDAC leader points out specific cards on the SEDAC chart and encourages individual team members to offer their thoughts and contributions. For example, the leader may say to operators A and B, "This problem card is directly related to what you do. We have an improvement card for this problem, but it's still weak. Can you think about this problem this week and come up with a more effective improvement idea?" For another problem, the leader may determine that it requires further analysis and, consequently, direct engineer C to spend time during the week digging up its root cause from the viewpoint of intrinsic technology.

After considering their unique strengths and assigning specific tasks to members A, B, and C, the SEDAC leader ensures they will pay closer attention to the problem, investigate the situation, or think harder about the problem during the week. Of course, their efforts don't have to be perfect. Suppose each of the three members consciously thinks about the problem off and on for 6 hours during the week. That's 18 hours of brain time! Compare this to a 3-hour brainstorming session in which the same three members put in a total of only 9 "brain hours." A simple calculation shows that the SEDAC method allows twice as much thinking time and, therefore, twice as much possibility of conceiving new ideas.

This rule of thumb, incidentally, applies not only to manufacturing-oriented improvement projects, but to projects that require a high degree of technological knowledge as well. Such projects especially will not succeed unless members generate new ideas. For this reason, people in fields with high levels of intrinsic technology, such as engineering, design, and R&D, are also producing significant results by applying various types of SEDAC.

One example is Sony Semiconductor Kokubu, in Japan, which through SEDAC achieved remarkable improvement in its semiconductor wafer yield. Before SEDAC, wafer yields had been a long-standing technological issue for this organization. In another case, a U.S. manufacturer of aircraft engines achieved a technological improvement in the way it welds major engine parts. As a result, the company reduced its leak-test reject rate, an important checkpoint in the welding process, to almost zero. Also, by using SEDAC, an electro-optical division of another major U.S. company succeeded in improving a metal structural defect that had been a major technological problem for some time.

Improvement Should Be Enjoyable

Let's go back for a moment to operators A and B and engineer C. If it so happened that they couldn't come up with any good ideas after a week, the leader shouldn't scold them or ask them to expend excessive effort. Many case examples prove that it is perfectly possible to succeed with reasonable effort. In short, improvement should be enjoyable. The process should be exciting, characterized by great anticipation in coming up with and trying out new ideas, and punctuated along the way with disappointment as well as leaps of joy for attaining success.

Trial-and-Error Through Intrinsic Technology, Knowledge, and Experience

As mentioned in Chapter 3, SEDAC is a method that uses both numerical and verbal data. While statistical methods are very effective in processing numerical data, valuable information is often unquantifiable and expressed in the form of verbal data, such as statements like, "This may be a cause for this quality problem," or "This may help to solve the problem." SEDAC captures this kind of information for further investigation and experimentation. In general, harnessing such data enables you to accumulate intrinsic technology, knowledge, and experience.

In working effectively with both quantitative and qualitative data, practitioners often note that SEDAC makes it possible to go through a trial and error process systematically. SEDAC, enables people first to gather all information—numerical and verbal—that bears on their problem. After obtaining an overall picture of the problem through their data, they then determine where countermeasures are needed. Finally, they test their countermeasures and track results to determine whether they have been effective.

Reliable Standards Development

As SEDAC improvement cards (proposed countermeasures) are confirmed to be effective, they become standard cards. In this way, SEDAC is not only an idea-generation technique but also a tool for developing reliable standards through trial and error—a function that is extremely important for the accumulation of intrinsic and management technology. It's ironic that, although people talk about the importance of technology accumulation, most organizations lack a specific methodology for doing so that draws on the essence of everyday improvement activities.

This technology accumulation aspect of SEDAC is one of the reasons its users often say, "SEDAC allows us to experiment, and it is both creative and systematic." Comments like this remind me of my time as a line manager. Often, I was at a loss when employees told me, "If we follow our current standards, we will continue to produce defects. Must we follow the standards?" I remember feeling a strong desire at that time to find a way of systematically developing more reliable standards. SEDAC is an effective method for this.

A SYSTEM FOR LEARNING FROM FAILURE— WE HAVE NO ALTERNATIVE

Feedback

The concept of *feedback* combined with *system* is one of the most important concepts developed in the field of engineering in the twentieth century. Item 2 in Table 4-1 (page 98) notes the effectiveness of SEDAC in detecting and removing obstacles. This is because it provides a system for digesting feedback about what works and what doesn't. Using this feedback allows people to learn from failures and keep going to achieve success.

It's true that many SEDAC users encounter difficulties while proceeding through their projects, even when they adhere to the implementation steps laid out in Table 3-1. SEDAC is designed to help people recognize unfavorable conditions and also provides the means for thinking about and correcting them. This happens through frank discussions about the project status, in the presence of the data on the SEDAC. The SEDAC process gets leaders, team members, managers, and other stakeholders to address observations like the following:

- It's been three months since we started the project, but we have yet to develop one standard card. Unless we have standard cards, we cannot get results.

- We have three standard cards, but their content doesn't appear strong enough to achieve the target.

- We have only one improvement card with two red dots and one with three dots. It seems our improvement actions are progressing slowly. Our leader needs to exercise her authority to correct this situation.

- The initials on the cards indicate that staffers and managers aren't contributing ideas. Because this project requires technological problem solving, we cannot expect much success with this level of participation.

- The dates on the cards show that cards are written only during scheduled meeting times, twice a month. We must continuously keep thinking and generating new ideas between our meetings.

- All the problem cards have the same date, our initial meeting. Since then, we keep producing defects every day. By observing these fresh defects, we should be able to extract new information for problem cards. Why is such information neglected?

- There is no sign of new activities since the 10th of last month. What happened?

- All the countermeasures are for process A, which accounts for only about one-fifth of the overall problem. Why are we ignoring the other processes?

- The description on many problem cards is not specific. For example, one of the cards says, "Too many minor stoppages." Consequently, its corresponding improvement cards state, "Replace old equipment with new equipment," "Increase staff," or "We need more money for maintenance." Even worse, one improvement card says "Reduce minor stoppages." What we need is a problem card that specifies what equipment, where on the equipment, and how minor stoppages occur. Only then can we expect to come up with better improvement ideas.

- There are seven standard cards that we supposedly practice, yet our results don't show improvement. We need to figure out whether this is because the standard cards are off the mark, or because we have fallen short in adhering to standards.

- Since card-writing rules are not followed, necessary information is missing. Therefore, it is difficult to understand what is actually going on.

- Analysis is not enough. We must conduct a statistical test to determine if the difference is statistically significant. We also need to review the analysis from a technological perspective.

- Measuring instrument X may need to be examined for precision and accuracy.

- We need technology B, but we lack (or are weak in) this technology. We need to assign engineer D to study it. Meanwhile, we need to find out if we can get technological help from other departments.

- We need to work closely with design section C. However, the cards contributed by section C contain only superficial observations. The SEDAC leader and his manager need to meet with section C's manager to request their wholehearted cooperation.

Improvement activity leaders in charge of projects that are not going well often fail to grasp or report their experiences in the manner discussed above. If they had such an understanding, their improvement activities would go a lot smoother.

By studying unfavorable SEDACs, managers and the others can figure out how to help SEDAC leaders and thus prevent projects from failing. This is the crux of item 2 in Table 4-1. Taking time to interpret the raw data gathered during the project is the best approach for understanding why a particular SEDAC project failed.

Someone once made the following point: "We can't expect to succeed by simply doing the opposite of what caused us to fail. Can we expect to scale an unconquered peak of the Himalayas by just avoiding accidents?" Certainly we cannot. Therefore, it's necessary to make very good use of SEDAC's effective actions as shown in Table 4-1.

Empowerment and Failure Prevention

The person responsible for the objectives identified on the P/O Matrix functions as the leader, not only for his or her own unit, but also for the other departments involved. Furthermore, he or she also assumes the leadership role for any members from other companies that may be involved, though only after such an arrangement is agreed upon. Thus, the leader of an objective on the P/O Matrix automatically becomes the leader for promoting the objective's SEDAC project. The same is true when objectives are further broken down into several action SEDACs as indicated in Figure 3-7 (page 83).

Some people have commented that they feel the SEDAC leader assumes too much authority. Perhaps their observation grows out of the fact that the SEDAC leader is entrusted to prioritize improvement cards for implementation or, in some cases, to suspend improvement ideas.

As discussed in Chapter 2, the SEDAC leader is selected on the basis that he or she is the best possible person to lead a particular improvement initiative at that time. Because of this, the company has no option other than to fully empower this person. Even if the selected leader fails, the company should stand assured that the person selected was the best choice at the time.

However, as the previous section described, when the project does not proceed smoothly, SEDAC provides the leader's boss and other stakeholders with raw data about the conditions that stand in the way of success. In applying SEDAC to their projects, then, users should understand and take advantage of the following SEDAC functions: SEDAC empowers the leader with authority; it provides a system for stakeholders to facilitate necessary recovery from potential failure; and it provides the leader with a chance to learn and grow.

UNDERSTANDING FIELD SCIENCE

An Encounter with Dr. Jiro Kawakita

In developing SEDAC, I relied heavily on the concepts and techniques laid out by Dr. Jiro Kawakita (Kawakita 1967). In particular I was interested in his use of cards and the affinity diagram (as part of his KJ method for encouraging and enhancing idea generation) and in his application of field science. Dr. Kawakita partitioned science into three key areas: speculative science, experimental science, and field science. The following sections summarize my understanding of Dr. Kawakita's three sciences.

Speculative Science

Two features of speculative science distinguish it from the other two sciences:

- Speculative science relies on literature and past research that has been accumulated over time. In other words, speculative science is information that has already been organized and filtered through someone's mind.

- Speculative science emphasizes inference of the mind. Therefore, using literature and inference, speculative science can exist without coming in contact with any actual tangible subject.

Experimental Science

The obvious feature of experimental science is that it tests whether or not the hypothesis under study is true. Whereas speculative science uses no conclusive factors, experimental science tests the validity of hypotheses through experimentation.

Field Science

This third type of science—field science—was a new concept proposed by Dr. Kawakita in 1967. He positioned it as the science that allows researchers to generate their own hypotheses *in the field*. Although both experimental and field sciences value actual observations and experiences, one important difference is *where* such observations and experiences take place. Whereas experimental science is conducted in a laboratory, field science is carried out in the field. However, the difference between the two goes beyond mere geography.

Let me explain. Let's call the object of observation *nature*. The nature observed in a laboratory and in the field, however, are two different things. In the laboratory, a limited number of factors in nature are extracted in their purest form. In other words, laboratory experiments deal with artificially contrived nature. On the other hand, nature in the field exists as is. It is made up of a virtually uncountable number of elements and complex interrelationships. For this reason, when nature is observed in the field, findings tend to take the form of unquantifiable, verbal descriptions.

Dr. Kawakita also says that the most important difference between speculative, experimental, and field science lies in the researcher's attitude. When historians research old documents with an attitude similar to someone studying nature in the field, they are really conducting field science even though they are just reading documents. Similarly, when biologists study subjects in a controlled environment under a microscope, as long as they study with an eye toward nature as it occurs in the field, they are practicing field science. This is an extremely important viewpoint I fully support.

In Dr. Kawakita's estimate, speculative science has a long history of more than 2,000 years, while experimental science has been practiced since the eighteenth century. The conscious practice of field science, however, has just begun. It's good to keep in mind the distinctions between these approaches. The next section tells how they are used in the different stages of SEDAC.

The Three Sciences and SEDAC

The "field" for practicing SEDAC is the place where the company does its work. Of course, such a field is not limited only to production areas, but includes the areas where general affairs, marketing, engineering, R&D, and other functions take place as well. Naturally, a company's field is chaotic and complex, as an unfathomable number of factors act and interact in a changing sea of circumstances. Each individual problem or situation we encounter in an organization is unique and fresh, especially when we consider people, who in themselves represent limitless variability in motivation, behavior, and other intangible influencers. This subject will be discussed in more detail in the Window Analysis sections of Chapter 6 and in the QMDEI method described in Chapter 8.

As we said earlier, the subject of a SEDAC study is an improvement theme selected from daily business activities—extremely familiar matters. From their own strengths, SEDAC team members observe the events in front of them in accordance with field science and write their findings on cards. After these cards are grouped and organized, they are put up as problem cards. Then SEDAC team members continue to brainstorm until they come up with improvement cards, their own new hypotheses for solving the problems.

The results of trial implementation of improvement card ideas are then tracked on the effect side of the SEDAC diagram to determine whether improvement actions have been effective. This process is part of what Dr. Kawakita would call experimental science. Confirmed hypotheses become standard cards or first-class cards, which are stockpiled and studied during subsequent improvement rounds, in the tradition of speculative science. The necessity and effectiveness of constantly building new knowledge through SEDAC has been emphasized throughout this book.

As Dr. Kawakita sadly noted in 1967, a strong focus on field science was lacking in most organizations. I believe this is still true today among staff functions, especially R&D. The prevailing tendency is to think of R&D as a sanctuary of speculative and experimental science. The truth is that R&D, more than any other function, should follow the principles and practices of field science. One example of an organization that was able to practice this truth will be introduced in Chapter 5 ("PDPC and SEDAC," page 139).

Dr. Kawakita suggested the following field science techniques for a group of people:

1. Collect information and ideas through brainstorming

2. Develop a structural plan with this data using the KJ method (affinity diagram)

3. Develop the structure into a procedural plan using PERT (same as arrow diagram, see page 85)

In Chapter 5 ("SEDAC on an Arrow Diagram," page 121), we observe through a case example how an organization used SEDAC to simultaneously and continuously carry out these three techniques.

STUDY GROUP ACTIVITIES FOR COMPANYWIDE INTEGRATION

At one point I asked my client companies to start calling their cross-functional committees "study groups." I did this in hopes that they would be challenged to develop new methods, which I felt they were unlikely to do in a "committee" atmosphere. According to one P/O Matrix rule, all people concerned with a specific improvement theme automatically become members of its corresponding SEDAC project, which in many cases requires them to cross organizational boundaries. However, when it becomes necessary to integrate the experience gleaned from many improvement projects, a study group should be formed. Such a group optimizes a company's ability to manage common problems that cross organizational boundaries.

The only study group rule is that members can only talk about things they've already tried. Just as you can't develop intrinsic technology without experimental data, you can't develop management technology without information based on experience. We've all seen shrewd managers deliver beautiful presentations, taking up the allotted time, yet not talking about anything they've really done. Their presentations are full of concepts and future plans, not hard implementation experience. This type of discussion is not for the study group and should take place elsewhere.

Although this rule of talking only about what you've tried seems simple, often it's not well heeded, especially at the outset. To combat this tendency, the study group leader needs to remind members that those who have not yet done anything should not speak.

When a study group member is representing a SEDAC team, he or she usually shares the contents of standard and, especially, first-class cards at the meeting. The study group's job is to extract from the findings of each SEDAC team the common elements that are applicable on a companywide basis, and to organize these elements into new knowledge. Each study group member then takes the knowledge back to his or her respective work area and tries it out, if applicable. At the next meeting, members report their results. In this way, a study group creates and formalizes (standardizes) companywide know-how.

Staff Function Improvements

LESSONS LEARNED FROM PAST MISTAKES

Most people will agree that both the quality and quantity of staff function work in their organizations can be improved. In fact, this only stands to reason, since staff and management performance has a great impact on organizational performance. Just one glance at the performance disparity shown in Figure 1-5 (page 18) demonstrates this truth. In recent years, companies have been under pressure to take a closer look at their staff areas and in many cases have restructured them.

In general, however, two syndromes seem to impede staff function improvement: the uniform control syndrome and the measurement obsession syndrome.

The Uniform Control Syndrome

The uniform control syndrome arises when an organization tries to apply operational site-based improvement control mechanisms to staffers with different job functions. In this scenario, staffers from the same work area are required to form a team and come up with a common improvement theme.

The tendency to force staffers to come up with an improvement theme is a major reason for staff team inactivity—a point already discussed in Chapter 2. Needless to say, under this kind of artificial pressure, staff teams often come up with wrong or meaningless improvement themes.

Much of this problem, of course, is a result of forming a team before selecting an improvement theme.

The Measurement Obsession Syndrome

When people are afflicted with the measurement obsession syndrome, they get fixed on the idea that if something can't be measured, it's not scientific and objective. In general, my position is that measurement is only necessary if *not* measuring hampers improvement. When we don't adopt this position, too often we end up doing nothing, or we spend all our time trying to find the perfect measure instead of taking important actions. Don't misunderstand: I'm not denying the need for measurements. I simply believe that, if we focus first on what we need to do, we will always come up with a way to measure success.

The standard formula *output (quality and quantity of work completed) divided by input (labor-hours)* is often used to measure white-collar productivity. If we take this literally, however, it becomes impossible to measure white-collar productivity! The reason is because it's rare for an individual staffer to be assigned to just one task.

In general, staff personnel like engineers concurrently engage in multiple tasks, especially senior staffers and managers, who simultaneously think about multiple jobs and freely shift their emphasis from one subject to another. For this kind of activity, it's virtually impossible to measure by task the input labor-hours—(the denominator in the productivity formula). As for the numerator—the quality and quantity of work completed—this is almost always accomplished through the cooperation of many people. Here again, it's extremely difficult to measure each individual's separate contribution.

As long as these conditions exist, any formula we come up with for measuring white-collar productivity will be useless. Our original data is simply too complex and nebulous to capture. If we try to tackle this issue of staff productivity in a straightforward manner, therefore, we will surely come up empty-handed every time. Maybe some day a bright person will come up with a convincing solution to this problem. If this happens, of course, I will adopt it without hesitation.

Maybe you've been struck as I have by these two syndromes. And maybe, like me, you've concluded that we need a new approach for effectively and efficiently carrying out staff function activities. Instead of looking for ways to measure white-collar productivity, we might do better to increase our commitment to improving the way we carry out our staff functions.

ADVANCED TECHNIQUES

Various useful approaches have been introduced for improving staff work, and they're all achieving results. For example, OA (office automation) has been widely applied to repetitive administrative work. Also, the use of CAD (computer-aided design) has been successfully applied to design work, while CAT (computer-aided test) has been applied to the inspection function.

Still other techniques have been developed to counter one of Murphy's Laws: "Whenever you set out to do something, something else must be done first" (Bloch 1977). It was this feeling exactly that I had when I was a young staffer. I often wondered why I needed to spend so much time on trivial tasks that lay in heaps in front of more important tasks I really wanted to complete.

One technique attributes this problem to poor planning and emphasizes a planning system that covers not just scheduling work but problem solving as well. This technique uses a systematic method for diagnosing the situation from four perspectives: organizational culture, vitality, productivity, and image (Okada 1993). Other techniques approach the planning issue differently. One, for example, emphasizes individual commitment to spending more time on vital work while effectively handling trivial work. Still another proposes a way for focusing different working hours on different tasks (Kobayashi 1992, 1993).

In the next section, you will learn how to improve and transform white-collar work using the P/O Matrix and SEDAC, which complement each other and work well with specialized improvement techniques for staff functions. Readers are encouraged to combine the P/O Matrix and SEDAC with these techniques when necessary.

ASPECTS OF IMPROVEMENT

Attack the Work in Front

Table 5-1 is a list developed early in 1987 at the Takasago Works of Mitsubishi Heavy Industries. In developing this list with general manager Kazuo Hironaka and other plant managers, I focused on total and active participation in improving and transforming *work in front*, a phrase and driving force for improvement that was popular for a time. Basically,

Table 5-1.
Staff Function Improvement Activity

Improvement Opportunities	Desirable Conditions to Achieve
• Without a clear definition of "improvement" in staff functions, there is little understanding of what to do to improve. For example, what should the R&D, accounting, and general affairs departments do to improve?	• By recognizing that there are no special improvement themes suitable for staff functions, staffers clearly understand that the work in front of them is always the subject for improvement. • In addition to simply reducing losses, staff functions aggressively promote the concept of "improve the quality and quantity of work today over yesterday."
• There is little understanding of how to measure the quality and quantity of work outcomes in staff functions, which contributes to hesitation among staffers in initiating improvement activities.	• Staff functions use a comprehensive evaluation system that employs multiple indicators to measure the quality of work. • They also can evaluate how well know-how (intrinsic and management technologies) is accumulated through the improvement process and how well it is used.
• There is no external and objective controlling mechanism.	• In each job, staffers can meet the promised schedule or shorten it, if necessary. The improvement activity is managed by time schedules.

what it means is that all departments, staff included, should focus on the important work at hand as a subject for improvement activities.

Table 5-2 shows one of three major improvement themes, along with measurement methods, in the plant's engineering department for one particular year. As this table shows, improving work in front was important

Table 5-2.
Engineering Department's Improvement Themes and Targets
(Partial List, Mitsubishi Heavy Industries, Takasago Works)

Theme	Application	Target
Complete large-scale plant projects on time and secure profits. • Fully use the experience of existing units and thoroughly examine new design elements. • Establish basic plans early and adhere to design process schedules. • Secure profits by executing cost management.	Priority plants • Fossil fuel plants for domestic power producers and self-generators • Nuclear plants for domestic power producers • Plants for export	(Common targets for all projects) • Adherence to the drawing process due date • Zero nonconformances due to new designs • Zero claims and complaints filed by customers • Completion within budget

to the engineering department, as it was to many other departments. In support of this focus, the theme "Complete large-scale plant construction projects and secure profits" was identified, along with a few supporting projects and common targets. That year the department met all its improvement targets—an accomplishment that required a high level of engineering expertise. The general manager of the plant gave his highest praise to the accomplishments of the engineering department. This recognition was quite an honor and was very gratifying for the people in this department.

How did the Takasago Works obtain such good results? The answer is that they used a P/O Matrix to select improvement themes (objectives) and determine target values. The matrix was a valuable tool, because it forced staffers to select meaningful objectives. The more energy devoted to developing staff objectives, the more value-added productivity contributed by staff areas.

Finally, Table 5-3 is a list of staff function improvement themes at the Kashima Steel Mills, Sumitomo Metal. These were also selected from a focus on improving work in front. For Sumitomo Metal, as for many other companies, there are no special improvement themes for staffers; they simply elect to improve the way they accomplish the important tasks before them.

Always Find Ways to Measure

When we select staff function improvement themes from the work at hand, we can always find a way to measure results. As I have stressed already, before worrying too much about how to measure, we should focus on what we want to accomplish. Since the objective is to evaluate our achievements against our intentions, the task of measurement is really not so difficult when our purposes are clear.

As a rule, we should use numerical data as much as possible. If quantifiable data is not readily available, we should use an index or approximation. One example is the employee satisfaction survey scores developed by Sony France's human resources department (described in Chapter 2). Let's suppose, for example, our objective is to complete a necessary system by a certain date. Before we start our project, we should itemize the conditions or elements that constitute the necessary system, and on completion of the project, we should compare our achievement levels with these itemized conditions. Another project may be to improve standards.

Table 5-3.
Q-PAC Activity Plan for Staff Departments (Sumitomo Metal Industries, Kashima Works, 1989)

Departments	Priorities	Objectives
Planning	1. Establish a midterm vision and launch an activity to achieve it.	1. Establish concrete plans. 2. Establish milestones.
	2. Support and promote the total cost improvement activity.	1. Strengthen support for transportation cost reduction. 2. Provide cost information that contributes to sales planning and improvement of priority product profitability.
	3. Strengthen investment plans and improve the precision of the midterm investment plan.	1. Strengthen the 1989 plan. 2. Strengthen the advance review of the 1990/91 plan.
	4. Improve productivity.	1. Achieve the midterm labor-saving plan. 2. Expand IE technique applications.
General Affairs	1. Strengthen foundations and effectively utilize unused properties.	1. Establish the steel mill foundation according to the current base. 2. Develop a plan for future foundation build-up.
	2. Strengthen the functions of the general service section.	1. Improve the quality of work. 2. Identify core services. 3. Promote cost reductions (CR).
Labor Management	1. Reduce labor costs. (Achieve the midterm goal.) • Personnel costs • Other costs	1. Manage total labor cost. 2. Promote "allowed capacity = actual number of people who work."
	2. Promote human resources programs that build safe and lively workplaces. • Fundamental review of benefit programs	1. Promote employee vitalization programs.
	• Develop employee development programs that meet needs quickly.	1. Provide special single-subject courses that closely meet each department's needs. 2. Review the role and allocation of locally hired employees. 3. Strengthen the new employee development program. 4. Enhance participation in external education programs.
	• Promote safety programs that support the autonomous activities of employees.	1. Support special safety activities. 2. Improve the training sheets for administrative employees. 3. Provide safety upgrade education. 4. Review the practical hazard awareness program.
	• Actively promote support programs that contribute to on-loan employee morale enhancement.	1. Establish and strengthen the management system for on-loan employees. 2. Strengthen education for on-loan employees. 3. Hold periodical support events.
Plant Services	1. Reduce subcontract costs and optimize material and service procurement practices.	1. Streamline subcontractors and expand the limit for construction repair work. 2. Reduce supply expenses and reduce spare item inventories.
	2. Implement and support programs that enhance the total power and competitiveness of group companies.	1. Establish a system for efficient subcontracting. 2. Support the autonomy of vendor activities.
Process	1. Establish a direct throughput management system for upstream processes and improve the direct throughput rate.	1. Clarify the management system for direct throughput rate. 2. Promote measures for direct throughput improvement.
	2. Establish a direct throughput management system and improve the direct throughput rate.	1. Clarify the definition for direct throughput rate. 2. Establish a data collection system for direct throughput indicators. 3. Analyze and improve causes for indirect throughput events.
	3. Establish a direct throughput management system and improve on-time delivery rate.	1. Clarify due date for the rolling and storage processes indicators. 2. Analyze causes for non-direct throughput by product. 3. Promote measures to improve the on-time storage rate.

Table 5-3. (cont.)
Q-PAC Activity Plan for Staff Departments (Sumitomo Metal Industries, Kashima Works, 1989)

Departments	Priorities	Objectives
Process (continued)	4. Control excess materials.	1. Review the status of excess materials. 2. Promote measures to minimize planned excess materials. 3. Standardize methods for early disposition of excess materials.
	5. Promote efficient distribution.	1. Promote a distribution network undertaking. 2. Identify optimum product inventory levels. 3. Organize distribution management indicators.
Engineering	1. Strengthen competitiveness in order taking.	1. Strengthen technical services. 2. Upgrade the quality design level. 3. Upgrade the quality assurance system. 4. Improve competitiveness in testing.
	2. Speed up new product development.	1. Develop a highly shapeable steel plate. 2. Develop a sequential chromating process for electrical home appliance materials. 3. Develop a steel plate plated with new zinc alloy.
	3. Improve the success rate for quality consistency.	1. Reduce surface flaws and thick and thin plate quality defects due to metallurgical causes. 2. Improve the success rate of hitting the right test for thin plate materials. 3. Improve surface consistency of stainless steel coils.
Equipment	1. Product maintenance.	1. Improve manufacturing resources such as quality, yield, T/H, etc. 2. Improve availability.
	2. Streamline maintenance costs.	1. Extend MTBF and reduce construction costs. 2. Reduce parts and material purchasing costs.
	3. Streamline spare materials.	1. Promote individual reduction plans. 2. Promote the effective utilization and new application of spare materials by a dedicated team.
	4. Promote LSM (Line Stop Minimum).	1. Improve the start-up construction method and stationary machine layout. 2. Extend MTBF and reduce the contents of construction.
	5. Promote GD (Good Design) activity.	1. Improve design and technology development. 2. Improve and transfer technologies.
Environment and Energy	1. Prevent pollution and accidents by prediction.	1. Strengthen environmental safety practices. 2. Promote efficient smoke treatment measures for the sintering process. 3. Promote measures for graphite. 4. Promote reduction of waste materials.
	2. Achieve stable supply of energy.	1. Expand the application of condition-based maintenance. 2. Achieve stable supply of energy by establishing a new energy management system. 3. Promote facility fire prevention measures.
	3. Reduce energy costs.	1. Achieve the midterm streamlining goal. 2. Promote thermal technology development.
	4. Improve slag costs.	1. Improve earnings from blast furnace slag. 2. Streamline costs for blast furnace slag. 3. Develop technology to add value to blast furnace slag.
Plant Systems	1. Improve system development productivity.	1. Fundamentally revise system development standards and adhere to them. 2. Improve design productivity. 3. Improve production productivity. 4. Improve inspection productivity.
	2. Improve system maintenance productivity.	1. Improve system design documentation. 2. Reduce troubles.
	3. Achieve highly stable system performance.	1. Improve automatic operation rate. 2. Reduce software PM troubles. 3. Strengthen preventive maintenance.

In this case, one way to measure results is to check whether standards are developed. However, a more meaningful measurement is to evaluate whether we meet the primary objectives that called for the improved standards in the first place.

Suppose a company launches a project to reduce work-in-process inventory and consequently starts ordering materials in small lots. This new ordering system inevitably results in increased work load and decreased labor-hour efficiency in the purchasing department. In spite of these demerits, however, the company continues its practice of small quantity ordering, because the overall merits outweigh the demerits. There are many cases like this where the results for an individual or a single department do not accurately mirror the effects on the organization as a whole.

Remember that most of today's jobs require two or more people to work together. It's important, therefore, to understand the overall results of improvement activities and to recognize that they come from cooperation among many departments in both line and staff organizations. Compared with individual evaluation, such a broad assessment contributes more to boosting morale and avoiding wasteful costs. Many readers may share the feeling staffers and managers have when involved in improvement projects: They usually know in their guts how much they've contributed to overall project success.

"Winner take nothing" is a phrase I learned long ago. I take it to mean that winners are well rewarded with personal satisfaction. When I was a staff department manager, I often cited this phrase in a rather exaggerated manner to encourage my young staffers. In evaluating staff and management improvement results, it's best to strive for a clear-cut understanding of the overall results and not get too caught up in the details. Such an approach requires evaluators to possess and practice a high level of insight and skill.

Basically, there are three necessary conditions for success in improving staff functions:

- Select an improvement theme from among the most important work-in-front tasks.

- Clarify how to measure good results upon completion of improvement projects.

- Use multiple measures whenever possible to grasp the overall work outcome.

One company that has applied the above conditions is Sperlari, Italy, a Heinz group company involved in the health food business. Among other things, Sperlari has been successful in devising ways to measure such elusive characteristics as quality of service, speediness of service, and customer satisfaction. By developing indexes and other measures, the company has been able to consistently apply SEDAC to various improvement projects.

SEDAC ON AN ARROW DIAGRAM

SEDAC is very effective for staff-level improvement activities that require more intellectual productivity than any other functions and that must be completed within specific time frames. In cases when the most important objectives relate to a project schedule, it's more effective to create a SEDAC on an arrow diagram rather than making a conventional SEDAC on a cause-and-effect diagram.

Effective Use of Arrow Diagram Features

The arrow diagram is one of the seven new QC tools and originated in PERT (program evaluation and review technique). Developed by the U.S. Navy in 1958, PERT was responsible for shortening construction time on the Polaris submarine by two years.

Figure 5-1 illustrates how an arrow diagram is developed. The figure shows the same plan on two different charts: a type of bar chart known as a Gantt chart and an arrow diagram. Both types of charts list the project activities and tell how long they take, and when each is to begin and end. The key feature of the arrow diagram, however, is that it shows the critical path (heavier horizontal arrows) where deadlines must be met to meet the overall project schedule. The solid lines represent project activities, while the numbers under the solid lines represent time required, usually in terms of days, weeks, or months (here the unit is weeks). The circled numbers (called nodes) mark the beginning or end of an activity. The broken lines indicate activities for which time is not of the essence.

The arrow diagram method teaches us to consider time estimates for both the best-case and worst-case scenarios. In my experience, however, most of us don't have the luxury of projecting worst-case estimates. In fact, most of the time the ideal schedule is even tighter than the one we might construct with optimistic estimates. Have you ever heard the sentence, "I need it yesterday"? Even though we need an extra month or two,

(a) **Gantt Chart: "QC Room Construction"**

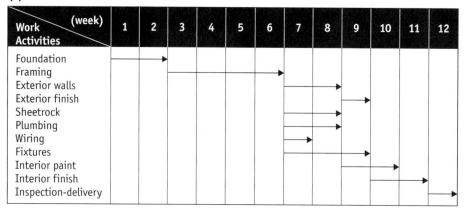

(b) **Arrow Diagram: "QC Room Construction"**

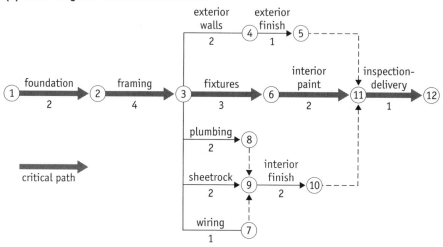

Source: Shigeru Mizuno, ed., *Management for Quality Improvement: The 7 New QC Tools,*
Portland, Ore.: Productivity Press, 1988, 251.

Figure 5-1.
Examples of a Gantt Chart and an Arrow Diagram

we start the project with the best intention of completing it on time. In this kind of time-strapped world, we usually have to develop very ambitious, tight schedules to complete our identified tasks. Truly, it's a luxury to have the time and flexibility we think we need.

Figure 5-2 shows how SEDAC would be applied along the critical path of this arrow diagram. Bear in mind that the same SEDAC rules apply to its use with the arrow diagram as to its use with the conventional cause-and-effect diagram. In this case, the critical path from node 3 to node 6 currently takes three weeks. Therefore, problem cards are collected that explore why the task takes as long as three weeks. Then,

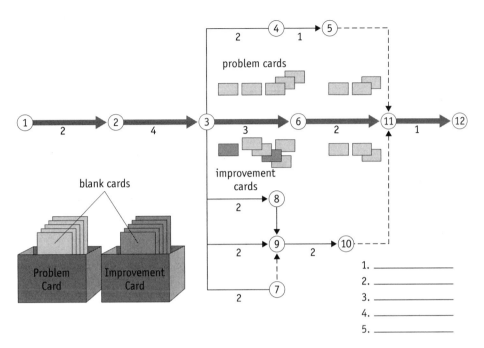

Figure 5-2.
SEDAC on an Arrow Diagram

improvement cards are generated that propose ways to shorten this path, even by just a day. On the bottom right corner of Figure 5-2, we see five blank lines. This is where expected project outcomes are listed, such as production yield, quality of work outcome, cost reduction, and so on. It's extremely important to spell out these outcomes up front. If you don't, it becomes easy to take shortcuts and consequently not make substantive improvements.

The reason this SEDAC is focused only on the critical path is because improvements on noncritical path items don't impact the due date of the project. If this SEDAC was done on the cause-and-effect diagram in the usual way, you would run the risk of spending time on wasteful improvements that do not address the most important problems.

Staff: An Engine for Improvement

Table 5-4 is a list of plantwide SEDAC projects at Takasago Works of Mitsubishi Heavy Industries in 1987. The four columns on the right side of the table show achievement rates for individual improvement projects. As the table shows, 50 percent of the projects achieved their planned targets or better. When you add in the 25 percent of the projects that achieved more than 75 percent of their targets, the overall percentage of successful

Table 5-4.
SEDAC Activity List (Mitsubishi Heavy Industries, Takasago Works, 1987)

Departments	Number of projects	Activities							
		Number of cards				Target achievement rate			
		Problem	Improvement	Trial implementation	Standard	100%	75~99%	50~74%	<49%
General Affairs	18	4,778	2,545	2,299	1,399	9	4	3	2
Purchasing	10	530	489	341	131	6	2	1	1
Marketing	8	688	421	227	66	7	1	–	–
Quality Assurance	12	643	385	290	86	7	3	1	1
Engineering	12	906	516	302	91	10	1	–	1
Manufacturing	34	2,317	1,798	1,132	787	12	8	8	6
Plant Construction	7	344	347	179	50	2	4	1	–
Nuclear Power Services	7	246	344	263	81	3	3	–	1
Hydro and Wind Power Services	3	323	258	140	42	1	2	–	–
Pumps	7	580	191	98	53	4	1	1	1
Refrigeration Equipment	4	343	315	194	17	–	1	3	–
Total	122	11,698	7,609	5,465	2,803	61 (50%)	30 (25%)	18 (15%)	13 (10%)

projects jumps to 75 percent. Of course, the true overall impact depends on the relative significance of each separate project. Also, project data represent achievement at a specified point in time and, therefore, overall achievement results are affected by how many projects are underway or completed. Even so, the numbers for Takasago Works seem reasonable, especially when compared with the experiences of three Sony group companies: Sony Inazawa, Sony Mizunami, and Sony Hamamatsu. During the period from April 1992 to March 1993, their target achievement rates were between 67 and 78 percent.

In Table 5-4, the first five departments listed, from general affairs to engineering, are staff functions. Next on the list is manufacturing, a line organization. And below this, beginning with plant construction, are the remaining departments that have both staff and line functions. Basically, under the leadership of the general manager and other plant management, the entire plant was organized in a matrix form to facilitate systematic cooperation between staff and line functions. In this matrix format, the hierarchical official organization is the warp of the SEDAC project, while the projects identified on the P/O Matrix are the weft.

Table 5-5 shows an interesting quality defect loss trend at Takasago Works, Mitsubishi Heavy Industries, from 1986 to 1988. Before 1986, the reduction of quality defect losses remained stable between 5 and 10 percent improvement each year. As the table shows, however, improvement accelerated in 1987 and 1988, when the reduction of quality defect losses were 50 percent and 36 percent, respectively. One major reason for this acceleration was the total and active involvement of staff functions. Incidentally, claim and complaint losses for the above-mentioned defects included rework costs for the further improvement of field product reliability, and parts/material and labor costs for creating additional failsafe

Table 5-5.
Reduction of Quality Defect Losses (Mitsubishi Heavy Industries, Takasago Works)

Losses	Fiscal year		
	1986	1987	1988
• Claim and complaint losses • Defect losses	73 27	43 7	26 6
Total	100	50	32
Compared to previous year	down 5%	down 50%	down 36%

Note: The 1986 total quality losses are indexed as 100.

Table 5-6.
SEDAC Projects and SEDAC Cards
(Mitsubishi Heavy Industries, Takasago Works, Hydro and Wind Power Equipment Department)

Categories	Projects
Complete priority works trouble-free	Create trouble-free production of pump hydraulic turbines
	Complete new blast furnace blower trouble-free
	Complete thermal power plant fan trouble-free
Increase orders for existing products	Increase orders for small- and medium-sized hydraulic turbines and valves
	Increase orders for renovation and servicing of hydraulic turbines
Secure profits	Promote reduction of material costs at the planning stage (hydraulic turbines)
	Promote reduction of material costs at the planning stage (wind power equipment)
	Promote overseas procurement (wind power equipment)
Develop and market new products	Expand sales of the new series of wind power equipment
	Develop marketable underwater robots

Department head's policies	Number of projects	Number of SEDAC cards			
		Problem	Improvement	Standards	First-class
Complete priority works trouble-free	3	223	209	40	9
Increase orders for existing products	2	133	76	42	1
Secure profits	3	243	172	44	8
Develop and market new products	2	199	157	48	5
Total	10	798	614	174	23

product quality assurance features. Even after these costs, the plant's overall monetary results were outstanding.

Needless to say, quality defects are reduced by the actions of the manufacturing and quality assurance departments. In addition to these, however, the design, engineering, and product development departments also play important roles in influencing results. Moreover, indirect support provided by general affairs, human resources, and accounting is an indispensable factor for success. All these departments contribute to results in both tangible and intangible ways. They teach us that, to achieve company-wide improvement, it's essential for everyone in the organization to recognize the significant role staffers play in contributing to results, even when the specific contribution of each department cannot be quantified.

The upper part of Table 5-6 lists ten improvement themes that the hydro and wind power equipment department of Takasago Works worked on from April 1989 to March 1990. The lower part of the table shows the number of SEDAC cards generated for each improvement theme category, or department head's policy. In total, they created 23 first-class cards.

Similarly, Table 5-7 (page 128) shows the improvement themes and SEDAC cards of the general affairs department of Takasago Works. Generally speaking, administrative tasks conducted by departments such as this one tend to be excluded from improvement activities. In this case, however, the general affairs department carried out its improvement activities with high morale and, as a result, produced 20 first-class cards. Such dedication and demonstrated commitment is highly commendable.

Lastly, Table 5-8 (page 129) contains data from Fincantieri, an Italian shipbuilding company. By effectively using both the P/O Matrix and SEDAC with staff participation, the company's diesel engine (for marine and industrial vehicle use) and commercial ship divisions succeeded in reducing costs by $4 million in 1992.

SEDAC ON FMEA

Use of Reliability Engineering

Whether a company provides products or services, *customer satisfaction* is gaining a renewed interest as an important management indicator. One key factor that often influences customer satisfaction is product reliability, a subject that pertains to quality assurance after products and services are transferred to the customer. The terminology of Japanese Industrial Standard JIS Z 8115 defines reliability as "The *capability* of an item to satisfy functional requirements under given conditions during a specified time," or "The *probability* that an item satisfies functional requirements under given conditions during a specified time." For the reader's information, the items referred to here are systems, subsystems, components, and parts.

Table 5-7.
SEDAC Projects and SEDAC Cards (Mitsubishi Heavy Industries, General Affairs Department)

Section	Group	Projects
Planning	N/A	Improve work performance and efficiency to achieve midterm business objectives
General Affairs	Administration	Improve administrative work performance and services
	Documentation and Public Relations	Strive for first-class performance and efficiency of documentation and public relations activities
	Environment	Prevent pollution by prediction and improve the efficiency of environmental management operations
Labor	Labor	Further promote mechanization and streamline and improve the efficiency of group performance by reorganizing operational manuals
	Personnel	Secure and develop necessary human resources for achieving midterm business plans and build up the group's day-to-day performance improvements
	Education and Training	Improve effectiveness of education and training and improve efficiency of the group's performance
	Benefits	Strongly promote priority measures for benefit plans and accelerate the plant's image enhancement efforts
Safety and Security	Safety and Health	Effectively promote safety and health management plans
	Security	Promote fire and traffic accident prevention measures and improve gate security operations
Accounting	Generators and Wind Power	Improve follow-up operations to achieve sales and profit/loss targets
	Budget	Issue construction budgets in a timely manner and promote improvement for enhanced budget management
	Pumps and Refrigeration	Improve follow-up operations to achieve sales and profit/loss targets
	Finance	Promote office automation and streamline operations
	Administration	Strengthen the management of each budget
Systems	Production	Upgrade production systems and further improve the efficiency of systems development and operations
	Administration	Upgrade administration systems and further improve the efficiency of systems development and operations
	Communication	Improve the efficiency of computer/communications related operations and further reduce communications costs.
Clinic	N/A	Review daily operations and strengthen the improvement of profit/loss performance
SGA Office	N/A	Improve the effectiveness of small group activities (SGA)

	Problem cards	Improvement cards	Standard cards	First-class cards
Planning	515	328	199	2
General Affairs	806	400	275	4
Labor	1,343	720	538	5
Safety and Security	411	227	189	2
Accounting	583	271	252	1
Systems	1,006	492	305	5
Clinic	244	142	80	1
SGA Office	135	120	51	0
Total	5,043	2,700	1,889	20

We know that products go through thorough quality control processes during manufacturing and pass a severe final inspection before they are shipped to customers. Then, products are used by customers. As

Table 5-8.
SEDAC Improvements (Fincantieri, 1990–1992)

The Diesel Engine (marine and land vehicle use) and Commercial Vessels divisions together achieved an annual savings of $4 million.	
• Diesel Engine division	
Reduced rework time by 50% in 5 months	
• Commercial Vessels division	
Reduced welding defects	
Structural parts (costs for defective nonstandard dimensions in welding)	−64%
Assembly process	−80%
Final finishing process	−60%
Cost savings due to waste reduction in the structural parts department	−30%
Labor cost reduction due to productivity improvement	
Assembly process	−21%
Final finishing process	−37%

time passes, however, the number of products that fall short of their functional requirements increases. Conversely, as time passes, the number of products that fulfill their required functions decreases and eventually reaches zero. The statement from *Hamlet* that "all that live must die" surely applies to the business of making products.

In the past, most organizations emphasized the theoretical and advanced statistical aspects of reliability engineering. Although this tendency was understandable due to the complex nature of the subject, it often delayed the practical application of reliability engineering. To combat this, Professor Tadashi Murata of the engineering department of Ryukyu University advocates that companies make effective use of techniques he calls the seven reliability tools (Koshikawa, Uekusa, and Murata 1982). By applying these tools, he says, organizations should be able to uncover helpful hints for solving 80 percent of their reliability problems. The following are the seven tools:

1. Reliability Prediction

2. FMEA (failure mode and effects analysis)

3. FTA (fault tree analysis)

4. Derating Technique

5. DR (design review)

6. Weibull Analysis

7. Reliability Cost Design Technique

Among these tools, FMEA is applied widely to:

- Identify foreseeable causes of failures and defects during the design stage and develop countermeasures for the reliability of products and in-house design equipment.

- Predict process troubles, identify causes of defects and problems, and develop countermeasures.

- Identify equipment maintenance and operations problems, list all conceivable and potential causes based on failure analysis, and solve problems.

As indicated above, the key words for FMEA are *to foresee* and *to predict*.

Table 5-9 shows a typical format for an FMEA table. Bear in mind that the format will vary slightly depending on the area of FMEA application, such as research design during product development, product design during production preparation, and process failure during production. Depending on the areas of application, the title for column 2 might refer to *Processes* or *Functions* instead of *Items*. The basic idea remains the same.

Table 5-9.
Example of FMEA Table

System _____ Subsystem _____					**FMEA Table** (Failure Mode and Effects Analysis)			Date: _____ Prepared by: _____ Approved by: _____		
(1) No.	(2) Item	(3) Function	(4) Failure mode	(5) Potential causes	(6) Effects		(7) Failure detection methods	(8) Counter-measures	(9) Failure criticality	(10) Comments
					Subsystem	System				

Source: Koshikawa, Uekusa, and Murata, *Jitsumuni Suguyakudatsu Shinraisei-gijutsu (Practical Reliability Engineering)*, Nikkan Kogyo Shimbun, 1982, 66.

The most important parts of the table are column 4, where all technically conceivable failure modes are listed, and column 5, where all potential causes for critical failures are listed. Success in applying FMEA depends on how thoroughly users identify technically conceivable and potential failure modes and their causes. Without these items, FMEA is really no different from a QC process chart.

Years ago, I occasionally prepared an FMEA when customers requested it. The scenario went like this: Three or four of us got together for a meeting and filled out what we knew on a form, without really attempting to predict anything new. Based on this experience, I didn't think FMEA was very useful; I felt it was simply a tool for organizing what we knew into a specified format.

I have since understood that our motivation and the circumstances for developing an FMEA were not right. In many cases, we were ordered to prepare FMEAs just to include them in the quality complaint response documents requested by customers. Furthermore, back in those days, our customers hardly ever questioned the contents of our FMEAs. They seemed to be satisfied as long as we presented some information in an FMEA format.

One text on practical reliability engineering instructs, "List failure modes" (Koshikawa, Uekusa, and Murata 1982). It further elaborates, "List potential failure modes by functional reliability system block. To do this, it's better to involve a group of people rather than just one designer. In such a group setting, it's best to use the brainstorming technique with two to four design engineers or a small group of people, including people representing such related but different areas as parts and materials and after-sales service. It's also effective to develop and use a checklist based on past experience." Additionally, the textbook includes the point, "List conceivable causes for critical failures" and elaborates, "Pay attention to the mechanism of failures and identify conceivable causes for critical failures—a job for which it's best to involve engineers with different specialties."

The most suitable method for conducting these tasks of FMEA is SEDAC, applied in conjunction with the integrated professional knowledge and new findings of two to four design engineers and other people from different work functions. In short, this is SEDAC performed on FMEA.

SEDAC on FMEA has been nicknamed FMEI (failure mode and effects improvement), which implies an improved version of FMEA.

FMEI is really not different from FMEA, but it offers a format for facilitating the use of FMEA in a way that is most suitable for FMEA's original purposes.

FMEI is widely used by companies that practice SEDAC, and it's producing good results. Figures 5-3 and 5-4 are examples of FMEI at Sony USA's San Diego plant, where the TV division has been applying FMEI divisionwide since 1990 with significant results.

In column 9 of Table 5-9, the criticality of each failure mode is assessed in two key aspects: effect on the system and predicted frequency of failure. Table 5-10 (page 134) provides the criteria for determining the severity level from the viewpoint of how well the system can accomplish its mission, as well as criteria related to failure frequency. To address both these failure assessments in an easy-to-understand manner, FMEI uses blue and black dots on the failure mode and cause cards as shown in Figures 5-3 and 5-4.

Figure 5-5 (page 134) is a key to the use of these dots. The number of blue dots represents the frequency of failure, while the number of black

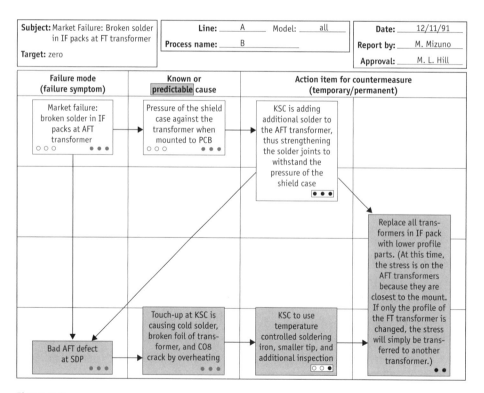

Figure 5-3.
FMEI Table (Part 1) (Sony U.S.A.)

dots indicates the severity of a particular failure mode's effect on accomplishing the system's mission—critical, significant, insignificant, or minor. As for predicted failure modes, it's not necessary to use blue dots, because the frequency of failure is unknown.

The use of an *action* column in Figures 5-3 and 5-4 is the same as the SEDAC improvement card step. In other words, improvement cards are generated for both known and predicted causes, and some of these cards become standard cards after the SEDAC red-dot evaluation process is applied. Based on an item's severity and frequency classification—the people concerned then decide whether to take strong measures on the item, even if this means spending a considerable amount of money, or to live with more moderate, cost-effective measures.

Accelerating with Prevention by Prediction

FMEI users have been successful in quickly beginning new product production by implementing preventive measures on technical problems at both the development/design and production preparation stages. Such

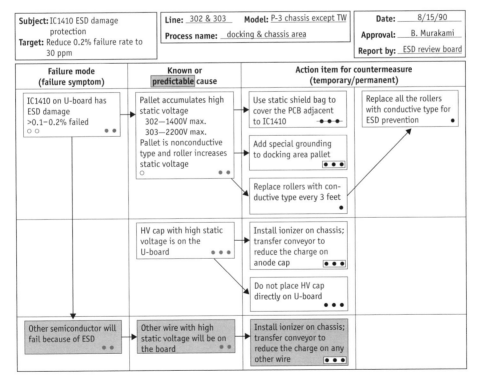

Figure 5-4.
FMEI Table (Part 2) (Sony U.S.A.)

Table 5-10.
Failure Criteria

(a) Criteria based on task achievability

Failure classification	Criteria	Remarks
(I) Critical failure	Task abandoned, loss of life	Need design change
(II) Significant failure	Unable to achieve essential part of the task	Need design review and possible design change
(III) Insignificant failure*	Unable to achieve part of the task	Need almost no design change
(IV) Minor failure*	Negligible effect	Need no design change

*No need to conduct FMEA on low-grade failures

(b) Criteria based on frequency

Failure classification	Criteria
(1)	Very frequent
(2)	Frequent
(3)	Rare, but possible
(4)	Very rare

Source: Koshikawa, Uekusa, and Murata, *Jitsumuni Suguyakudatsu Shinraisei-gijutsu (Practical Reliability Engineering),* Nikkan Kogyo Shimbun, 1982, 67.

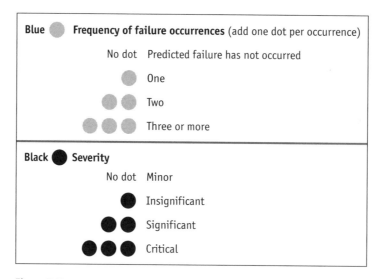

Figure 5-5.
Use of Color Dots on Failure and Cause Cards

speed is achieved by predicting failures *before they happen* and taking action to address them, rather than waiting until after the fact.

More than ever, today's companies are under pressure to introduce new products and models quickly and continuously—a task for which the prevention-by-prediction aspect of FMEI is particularly effective. Earlier in this book, for example, we introduced Sony Kokubu Semiconductor's success in dramatically increasing the production yield of its semiconductor wafer, a longtime technical problem. This plant's success was achieved through the application of FMEI.

Table 5-11 (page 136) is a list of standard cards developed for the No. 92-1 project of Sendai Nikon's SEDAC completion list, introduced earlier in Table 3-4. As noted, the circled numbers indicate that standard cards were developed for predicted symptoms and causes. In essence, Sendai Nikon's people predicted problems that might possibly occur and took measures in advance to prevent them—a task that required a high level of technological capability. In Sendai Nikon's case, they didn't necessarily use the FMEI format; they mostly used SEDAC on the cause-and-effect diagram, while incorporating FMEI principles into their SEDACs.

As these examples show, when FMEI users implement measures before problems occur, they can expect their rate of improvement to accelerate. These examples demonstrate the application of SEDAC to FMEA, *to speed up improvements* (an adaptation of the system outlined in Table 3-1).

Sharpening Engineering Sensibility

Many companies that are widely using SEDAC and FMEI are obtaining good results. Yet even using these methods, you ultimately can only "Do your best and leave the rest to providence." No matter how hard you try to predict all conceivable and potential failures, you may still miss some. Unforeseeable failures may occur even after the people implement corrective measures to their fullest capability. Although they may feel disappointed when this happens, at least they can learn better from their failures with the complete knowledge and confidence that they did their best.

As Figure 5-6 (page 137) depicts, it's our knowledge and experience—our professional sensibilities—that make our use of FMEI more effective. People who take a more relaxed approach and simply drift through their work will not encounter or recognize opportunities to sharpen their sensibilities. Many excellent engineers and designers rarely have the opportunity to learn directly from their bosses and colleagues.

Table 5-11.
Samples of SEDAC Standard Cards (Sendai Nikon)

Project: Reduce minor stoppages in B, By, AS-FH processes   **Target:** 78% → 88%
Effect: Performance efficiency   **Result:** 92.0%

Standard cards (circled numbers indicate that predicted symptoms and causes have been addressed)

No.	Description
(1)	Install a work confirmation sensor in No. 2 stamp material feeder line.
2	Change contact-type work confirmation sensors to reflection-type.
(3)	Change the location of the work passage confirmation sensor in No. 1 stamp material feeder line.
(4)	Do not use air blower while a stamp material feeder line is not in operation.
(5)	Install a switch mechanism to select stamp material feeder lines.
6	Anchor each foundation of stamp material feeder lines to prevent shifting.
7	Change the AS 2 ejection chute outlet from surface-contact type to point-contact type.
8	Change the timing of automatic chips removal after AS1 processing from while the spindle is rotating to after it has stopped.
(9)	Change the timing of work feeding and transfer for the FH-exclusive machine.
(10)	Install steel guard rails on the work slide of the ejection chute for the FH-exclusive machine.
(11)	Identify relative movements of the electromagnetic valve and cylinder (nameplate mounting).
12	Revise the program sheets for AS 1 and 2.
(13)	To prevent wear-out of the middle elevator, replace aluminum with steel.
(14)	Equip No. 1 line so that no work transfers when the inverter is not at the origin.
15	Change the work pocket width of No. 2 line elevator from 7.5 m to 6 m.
16	Change the gap between the middle elevator and the work support plate from 3 m to 1.5 m.
(17)	To induce smooth flow of work, expand the distal end taper of the ejection rod.

Therefore, they have to create their own learning opportunities and sharpen their own professional sensibilities through their work experience—including failures.

If FMEA users tackle only the known failure modes and causes, they're not meeting the key purpose of attacking potential problems. To develop a preventive orientation, people must explore the nature of problems that are currently considered unavoidable or unknowable. For this reason, the application of FMEA aims to expand the envelope of preventing recurrence to include prevention by prediction. Whatever tools they may use—FMEI, FMEA, or others—each engineer and designer should strive to come up with new hypotheses. The quality of these hypotheses, in turn, reflects how capable they are in fulfilling their respon-

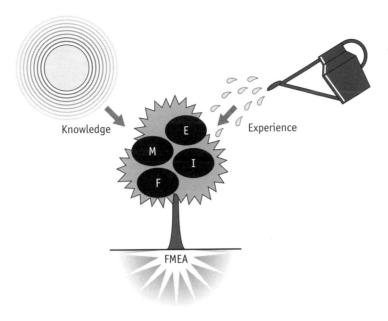

Figure 5-6.
FMEI Tree (Sony U.S.A.)

sibilities. Worn-out hypotheses only bring worn-out answers, even if they are confirmed through experimentation.

In summary, remember that "doing your best" means sharpening your sensibilities and predicting new failure modes and countermeasures for them. The opposite approach, as one Sony executive once put it, is, "Don't do your best, and leave the rest to heaven's vengeance."

Reliability Improvement and Cost

Reliability often involves some kind of trade-off. According to the JIS Z 8115 definition, for example, reliability entails seeking balance among competing factors (such as reliability, maintainability, performance, cost, and delivery) and to find optimum solutions. Generally speaking, increased cost means higher reliability. Although some costs are inevitable in assuring required reliability levels, engineers and designers nevertheless can show their skills in their efforts to assure high reliability with minimum costs. In determining how much to spend on reliability, A. V. Feigenbaum's *quality cost* is a useful measure.

In *Total Quality Control* (first published in 1951), Feigenbaum proposed that quality should be managed by assigning QC engineers to all aspects of a company from marketing, engineering, and purchasing to after-sales service (Feigenbaum 1991). The book introduced his concept of *quality cost,* defined as the sum of three costs:

Prevention cost + Appraisal cost + Failure cost = Quality cost

- *Prevention cost* includes all expenses incurred for activities related to building in quality during the process to prevent defects of finished and semifinished products.

- *Appraisal cost* includes all expenses required to inspect, test, and evaluate whether the finished and semifinished products meet the customer's requirements.

- *Failure cost* includes all expenses incurred because the finished and semifinished products do not meet the required conditions.

Contrary to the common wisdom in the 1950s and 1960s, Feigenbaum advocated that both failure and appraisal costs should be reduced by increasing prevention cost. Further, quality cost is a useful approach for rationally evaluating the impact of reductions in quality defects and failure costs. In other words, it questions how much prevention and appraisal costs are spent to reduce failure costs.

We know that quality defect losses provide a commonly used quality indicator. What's not so commonly known is that, although people often use quality defect losses as their only quality indicator, it's possible to reduce defect losses by increasing prevention and appraisal costs.

Another lesson we learn from quality cost is that we can determine what it costs to assure reliability. When a company receives a significant reliability claim or a complaint from a customer, the general practice is to issue an internal report, which often states what the company should have done—for example, "We should have conducted a tougher design review," or "We should not have cut the budget for reliability tests." These are only afterthoughts or regrets. Feigenbaum's quality cost concept, on the other hand, teaches us to worry beforehand rather than be sorry later. In other words, the application of the concept estimates potential failure costs in the event of a major claim or complaint. With this estimate in mind, the company can determine how much money it should spend on prevention and appraisal costs associated with avoiding the potential failure cost. Additionally, it's senior management's job to authorize an estimated potential failure cost. As with any improvement effort, excellence in management makes a difference.

Also, bear in mind that a potential failure may have much larger implications than problems for individual customers. It could, for example, develop into an environmental problem that affects society as a whole. In such cases, too, a company should determine the necessary investment for prevention and appraisal efforts so it can fulfill its responsibility to prevent losses to society.

PDPC AND SEDAC

Tayca, Inc., originally started as a fertilizer manufacturer in Osaka, Japan, about 80 years ago. Soon after the end of World War II, in anticipation of the future, the company drew on its technological background in the development of titanium dioxide pigment to transform itself into the fine chemical business. Since then, the company has expanded its business with a focus on technologies developed in-house and has become number two in its industry. Tayca is a unique company, led by chairman of the board and former Kyoto University engineering professor Makoto Kawane.

Tayca's R&D department has an extremely high level of intrinsic technology. Contrary to the stereotypical perception of high technology functions, the R&D department also has an interest in and passion for such management technologies as organizational vitalization and efficiency. This only confirms my observations of excellent R&D departments inside and outside Japan, including that of Sumitomo Electric where I used to work: they are enthusiastic practitioners of management technology. In fact, at Tayca, the R&D department was the first to introduce the P/O Matrix and plant its roots in the organization.

Tayca's R&D department has been using SEDAC effectively in conjunction with PDPC (Process Decision Program Chart), another of the seven new QC tools. This technique graphically maps out the possible means and methods for finding the best route to a specified goal. A PDPC is used when the goal is clear, but the means and methods are not yet established. While some possible means and methods may be foreseeable, others may be currently unknown. Figure 5-7 is an example of a PDPC that can take several different forms. A PDPC is best applied to such activities as research and development (as in Figure 5-7) and new market development, where available information is not sufficient for completing

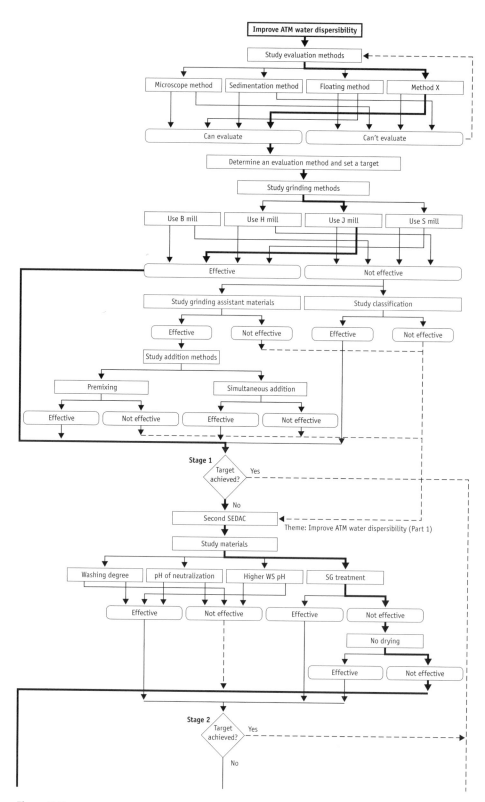

Figure 5-7.
ATM Water Dispersibility Improvement (PDPC + SEDAC) (Tayca)

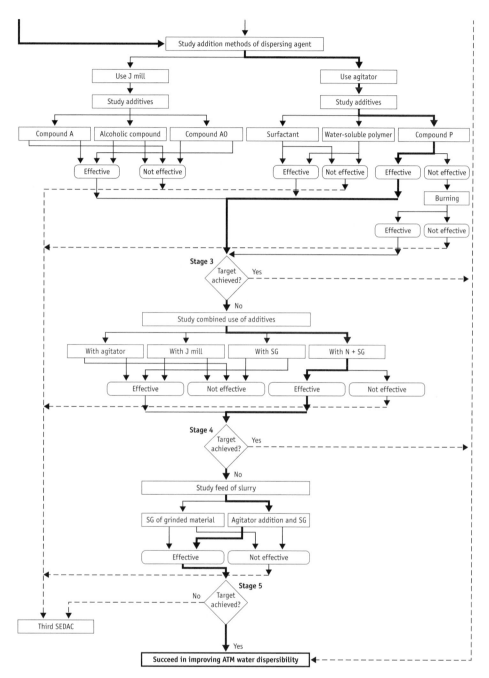

Figure 5-7. (cont.)
ATM Water Dispersibility Improvement (PDPC + SEDAC) (Tayca)

the project and where operational and business conditions are fluid and unpredictable.

The R&D department at Tayca uses a PDPC to manage the overall progress of each research theme and uses SEDAC to break through obstacles that stand in the way of progress. Table 5-12 is a TQM system flow for Tayca's Osaka laboratory that lays out specific approaches to take in the event of technology development problems and bottlenecks. The table

Table 5-12.
TQM System Flow (Tayca)

1. A project leader prepares an implementation plan from the objectives on the P/O Matrix. To develop a common understanding among members, the leader explains the contents, purposes, issues, and targets.

2. The leader draws out problems from the members by using cards.

Items	Causes	Problems	Countermeasures
What?	Why?	So what?	We will...

Each member is asked to state his or her opinion on these four aspects, although it is not necessary to address all of them.

3. The leader tallies and organizes cards by item.
Data may be input into a PC and automatically sorted whenever it is deemed helpful. During such a process, some opinions may be integrated into one, or new items may be established as the result of inference and combination.

A. If there are many problems but not so many specific suggested countermeasures, the group proceeds with SEDAC for improvement.
B. If there are plenty of countermeasures, the group proceeds with a systematic diagram for prioritization.

4. Systematic Diagram

A. The group itemizes proposed countermeasures and evaluates each item for its effects and feasibility according to a scoring method developed by the group. After each member's evaluation, the group compiles the results for prioritization.
If either effect or feasibility requires more emphasis in implementation, it may be weighted accordingly. Instead of a simple arithmetic average, the group may also use a weighted average that accounts for its current level of knowledge and experience with the problem.
B. Members are assigned to each item and progress is monitored by using a Gantt chart, arrow diagram, or other tools.

5. If the group predicts that the problem needs to be addressed by diverse countermeasures with many unknown elements, they can start building a PDPC to the best of their current knowledge, then add on to the chart as they progress. When they hit a major wall on their way, they can apply SEDAC for breakthrough improvement.

features a plan for mobilizing the entire laboratory and company through SEDAC if and when they hit a technology development wall.

The PDPC in Figure 5-7 was developed by Tayca's Okayama laboratory for their project to improve water dispersibility, one of the important quality characteristics of the ATM titanium dioxide product under development. Prior to starting this improvement project, with an aim to establish a suitable evaluation method for water dispersity, Tayca developed a quality function deployment (QFD) table with user quality requirements on one axis and Tayca product pulverulent quality characteristics on the other. As a result, they confirmed that ATM water dispersibility is better when its degree of aggregation is lower at a high slurry concentration level. After selecting the most suitable measuring method, they set an improvement target to reduce the degree of aggregation to less than 20 percent at a 45 percent slurry concentration level.

The bolded lines of the PDPC chart show the actual pathways of the Tayca experiment. At each decision point, indicated by a diamond shape, team members reviewed whether or not the target had been met and decided what additional actions they needed to take. A "no" at a decision point means that the target has not yet been achieved, even though results data show improvement over and above the starting point. Any time you encounter a "no," then, this indicates a need to continue the project according to the PDPC chart.

SEDAC is an excellent tool for breaking through technological research barriers as identified on a PDPC. In implementing SEDAC at Tayca, many people were involved, including not only the group in charge of the project, but also other laboratory members and, when necessary, other employees in the company. Since the PDPC chart alone is not powerful enough to break through technological bottlenecks, using SEDAC in this way is effective.

Figure 5-8 (pages 144–145) shows the second SEDAC Tayca developed while proceeding to stages two and three of their PDPC. As the effect side of the SEDAC shows, initial progress was made from point 1 to 2, then 2 to 3, then 3 to 4 and, finally, to 5. These results show that Tayca achieved an outstanding 9 percent degree of aggregation at the 45 percent slurry concentration level, which surpassed the target degree of aggregation of less than 20 percent at that slurry concentration level.

For this PDPC project, SEDAC was used during two bottleneck stages. In total, employees produced 31 problem cards, 78 improvement cards, 15 standard cards, and 1 first-class card. As noted in Figure 5-7, the

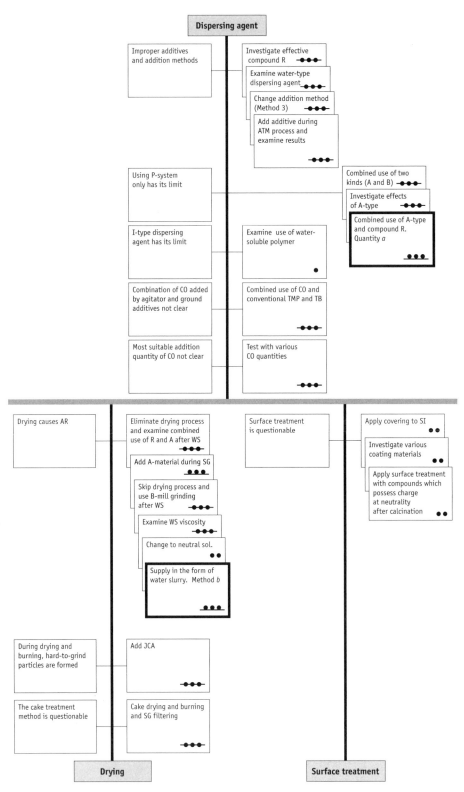

Figure 5-8.
SEDAC for ATM Water Dispersibility Improvement (Tayca)

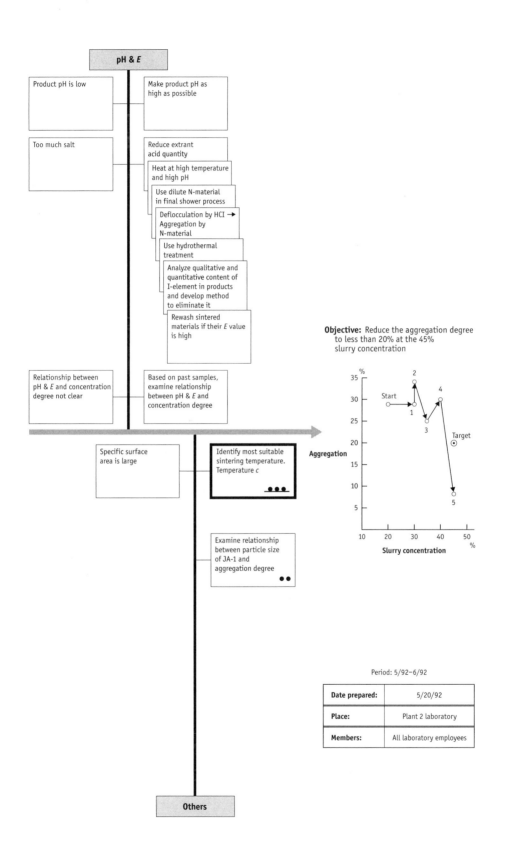

pH & *E*

Product pH is low

Make product pH as high as possible

Too much salt

Reduce extrant acid quantity

Heat at high temperature and high pH

Use dilute N-material in final shower process

Deflocculation by HCl → Aggregation by N-material

Use hydrothermal treatment

Analyze qualitative and quantitative content of I-element in products and develop method to eliminate it

Rewash sintered materials if their *E* value is high

Relationship between pH & *E* and concentration degree not clear

Based on past samples, examine relationship between pH & *E* and concentration degree

Specific surface area is large

Identify most suitable sintering temperature. Temperature *c* ● ● ●

Examine relationship between particle size of JA-1 and aggregation degree ● ●

Objective: Reduce the aggregation degree to less than 20% at the 45% slurry concentration

Aggregation

Start

Target

Slurry concentration

Others

Period: 5/92–6/92

Date prepared:	5/20/92
Place:	Plant 2 laboratory
Members:	All laboratory employees

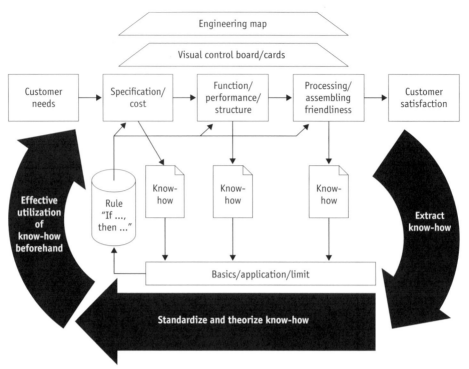

Source: *Reengineering ga wakaruhon (Easy-to-Understand Reengineering),* Japan Management Association Management Center, 1993, 213.

Figure 5-9.
Reengineering Process Model

project team originally anticipated needing a third SEDAC at the fifth PDPC stage. However, the result achieved with the second SEDAC was much greater than expected, so a third SEDAC was not necessary.

Figure 5-9 is a reengineering process model for R&D introduced by Toichiro Kamijima, director of the technology department at JMA Consulting (JMA 1993). From the perspective of SEDAC, the visual control board/cards of the model can be read as SEDAC and the process of standardizing and theorizing know-how as standard cards. Thus, through SEDAC, this model takes on a practical form and expression.

TPM AND SEDAC

Organizing Effective Measures on a Weibull Distribution

The Japan Institute of Plant Maintenance (JIPM) has widely disseminated an approach to equipment management called TPM (total productive maintenance). One of the main features of TPM is involving equipment operators in maintenance activities along with the conventional maintenance organization.

In today's production sites, robots, factory automation (FA), and computer-aided manufacturing (CAM) are in high demand, not only to improve productivity but also to build quality into products. In such an environment, it's not efficient to maintain and improve equipment using only the designated maintenance department. It's important also to involve operators in maintenance activities, since these employees are closest to equipment and work on it day in and day out.

Specific equipment failures can be classified into two broad categories: *breakdown* (loss of function) and *malfunction* (reduced function). A breakdown stops a machine completely, while with a malfunction failure a machine continues working, but produces defects. When you think about it, malfunctions are much worse than breakdowns because a malfunctioning machine makes defective products. At least a machine that stops completely can't do any harm.

In reducing both breakdown and malfunction failures, it's useful to organize necessary actions on a single sheet of paper as shown in Figure 5-10. This diagram is a Weibull distribution, developed by Swedish physicist W. Weibull, based on his experiments on the strength of a chain. It's often called a "bathtub curve" because of its shape. Essentially, this Weibull distribution is a representative distribution of reliability. The table in Figure 5-10 spells out specific activities required for reducing both breakdowns and malfunctions.

In short, the following four measures are all we must do to reduce equipment failures:

- Prevent accelerated deterioration. If for some reason the wear-out period on the Weibull distribution—where the failure rate increases—starts to occur sooner than expected, this situation must be stopped.

- Delay the onset of the wear-out period.

- Lower the random (sporadic) failure rate.

- Improve weaknesses of the equipment design. When repair or maintenance work is performed on a machine, the aim should not be simply to restore it to its previous condition, but to improve weaknesses by changing the design, if necessary.

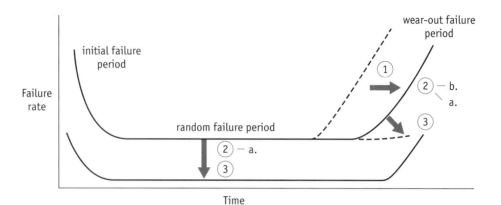

Affected areas	Purposes	Actions	Implementing departments
①	Prevent accelerated deterioration	• Correct operations and handling • Cleaning, lubrication, tightening, dust prevention, etc.	Operations
②	Detect abnormalities and correct them before equipment failures occur (preventive maintenance)	a. Condition assessment → unscheduled maintenance b. Scheduled inspection → scheduled maintenance • Discover and develop new check items and checking methods • Abolish unnecessary check items • Review inspection intervals	Operations and Maintenance
③	Instead of simply restoring to previous conditions, improve equipment while repairing (corrective [Improvement] maintenance)	• Analyze failures • Reinforce equipment weaknesses • Modify and improve equipment design	Maintenance and Equipment Design

Figure 5-10.
A Weibull Distribution and Actions Against Failures

The following sections elaborate the four effective measures discussed above. (This book does not cover the necessary actions required for the initial failure period, because, except in special cases, equipment users do not have to deal with the problems associated with this period.)

Preventing Accelerated Deterioration

If a machine is used without appropriate lubrication, with loose nuts and bolts, or in a dirty environment, it deteriorates or wears out sooner than expected. This situation is called *accelerated deterioration.* In addition to poor maintenance, improper use of equipment also triggers accelerated deterioration. Preventing this deterioration is the primary reason for involving equipment operators in maintenance activities.

Clearly, the purpose of keeping machines dust- and dirt-free is not just to make them look good. It's important to know *why* machines should be cleaned so the causes of dirty equipment can be removed. One approach is to implement actions that keep machines dust- and dirt-free and wait for a reduction of equipment failures to occur as a result. The other approach is to develop effective preventive measures for specific equipment failures by discovering through trial and error what dust or dirt must be avoided and which inspections are needed. Both approaches are necessary, but the latter is more likely to yield a sure result.

Delaying Deterioration and Wear-Out

The generic term for activities to delay deterioration is *preventive maintenance.* Preventive maintenance can take several forms. When scheduled equipment inspection uncovers an abnormality in a machine part, replacement or refurbishing should be performed before the part breaks down. If the wear-out period of a part is known, you can schedule such preventive maintenance based on the amount of time elapsed or time in use. Maintenance based on the latter is called *usage-based maintenance.*

It's also possible to delay wear-out by taking necessary actions on abnormal conditions as they are detected. This is unscheduled maintenance based on the outcome of monitoring the equipment condition.

Reducing the Random Failure Rate

Since the random failure period of a machine is usually long—most of the equipment's expected life—we should strive to reduce the failure rate during this period. Random failures occur, literally, as a result of unforeseeable or unknown causes. One way to understand the random failure period is to imagine a piece of window glass. No one knows when the glass may break, but would anyone inspect or regularly replace it because they are worried it might break? Suppose, however, some people start to play catch right outside the window. If the people inside think the ball might hit the window, they may shout, "Don't play catch here." In this case, saying something is perhaps better than doing nothing.

But what if we can't afford to watch outside constantly, and what if people play catch when no one is around to shout at them? These concerns might be resolved by installing a net in front of the window. But what if a net costs more than simply replacing the glass? Who should cover the cost in that case?

By definition, the random failure period comes after the initial failure period and before the wear-out period, and is a period when failures are unpredictable with current human knowledge. In practice, however, when the random failure period begins and ends is very hard to determine. It is the subject of an entire field called *failure analysis* or *failure physics*. Just as an ice cube starts to melt at the surface, so the predictable part of random failures is gradually revealed. Even so, it seems unlikely that all the ambiguity of random failures will eventually become clear. On the Weibull distribution curve, for instance, the random failure rate is indicated by a straight horizontal line derived from a theoretical value. The actual values, however, would form a zigzag line.

How then is it possible to reduce failure rates during the random failure period? The most reliable approach is to observe the facts carefully (e.g., monitor conditions continuously), as in the example of playing catch near the window.

Equipment operators, who are constantly closer to their machines than anyone else, are likely to observe slight changes in equipment conditions or performance. They may notice that the machine sounds somewhat different, or feel excessive heat in a certain part; they may notice slightly more play than usual in the controls. Such observations may lead to identifying causes and conducting unscheduled maintenance if necessary.

The most important point about inspection is to understand why we do it, so we don't fall into the trap of habitual inspection just for peace of mind. (Actually, habitual inspections provide little reassurance, since they quickly become routine and void of substance.) Moreover, since we don't understand causal relationships between inspection (items and intervals) and failures at first, we must repeatedly find and develop new inspection items and methods, dropping unnecessary inspection items and reviewing inspection intervals.

Corrective (Improvement) Maintenance

Whether maintenance is unscheduled, scheduled, or breakdown related, the work involves either repairing and restoring the machine to its condition before maintenance or examining its original design and correcting weaknesses. The latter activity is called *corrective* (or *improvement*) *maintenance*.

As discussed above, there are concrete and effective measures we can take for breakdown and malfunction failures using the Weibull distribution curve. SEDAC can promote and manage these measures. Whether you're working to prevent your machine from producing quality defects or from breaking down, you must build up a reservoir of know-how through trial and error. SEDAC is a highly effective way to develop and share know-how. Table 5-13 is an example of results attained using SEDAC to reduce malfunction failures.

To reduce malfunction failures, the process capability index (C_p, C_{pk})* is a leading indicator for quality defect reduction.

Doing SEDAC with Textbook in Hand

The concept of speculative science, based on literature and past research, was brought up in Chapter 4 on page 108. When the pioneers of that science document and compile their know-how, it becomes available in the form of papers and textbooks. Although it is not enough in the business world to merely memorize textbook information, neither should we ignore the work and experience that have gone on before. Value is obtained by giving life to existing knowledge and information. This means not just memorizing it, but using it in field science. SEDAC is an effective means for this. Consider the following example.

Suppose you need to cut equipment failures in half in three months. Naturally, the leader in charge of the project considers using SEDAC. He knows the basic actions he can take (measures covered in Figure 5-10). And, he has an idea of what types of failures need to be addressed and who needs to be involved. Since he's working under a three-month time constraint, he knows the measures his team comes up with must be effective and produce quick results. Fortunately, his company is implementing TPM and, therefore, he expects cooperation from the line organization.

In this case the target is to reduce failures by 50 percent, which is documented on the effect side of SEDAC. Next, the cause side must be

---

*Process capability refers to the ability of a process to repeatedly build quality into a product. The degree to which it does this is expressed in terms of a process capability index. Formulas for calculating process capability can be found in K. Ozeki and T. Asaka, *Handbook of Quality Tools* (Productivity Press, 1990), 195.

Table 5-13.
Reduction of Malfunction Failures Using SEDAC (Sendai Nikon)

No.	Items (improvement cards)	Results
1	Enhanced rigidity of supply arms (Installed ribs)	• Reduced mischuckings during feeding work • Reduced machining mistakes in subsequent processes
2	Adjusted motion timing (Revised sequence software)	• Reduced mischuckings during transferring and positioning work
3	Modified feeding hand chuck units (Installed work hold-down stoppers)	• Reduced mischuckings during feeding work
4	Improved reliability of work-detecting sensors (Replaced with environment resistant modes)	• Reduced mischuckings during feeding and transferring work
5	Modified transfer chuck claws and hold-down mechanism (Increased hold-down pressure)	• Reduced mispositionings during transferring process
6	Replaced pressure sensors for confirming open/close status of work feeding and transferring hand chucks (Mechanical type → electrical type)	• Improved reliability of open/close signals for work feeding and transferring hand chucks
7	Installed jig positioning confirmation mechanism for vertical drilling process (Air sensor)	• Completely eliminated vertical drilling defects
8	Installed jig positioning confirmation mechanism for horizontal drilling process (Air sensor)	• Completely eliminated horizontal drilling defects

developed. SEDAC branch lines are created for the three actions outlined in Figure 5-10. Then specific measures can be developed within each category. The leader uses information developed by TPM experts, shown in Figure 5-11 (pages 154–155), as a checklist to guide the team in writing SEDAC problem cards. Prepared materials like this help the leader direct the team where to observe, and also oversights and omissions in generating cards. The key is to focus on only relevant information, while skipping over information that isn't directly related to the SEDAC theme. For this purpose, it's more efficient to use the helpful guides such as Figure 5-11 than to try to develop such information from scratch. The team's activity becomes more efficient by holding the "textbook" in one hand, picking up necessary pieces of information with the other, displaying the facts for the whole team to see, and writing findings on problem cards.

Furthermore, the leader may want to steer the team towards areas he thinks are best to attack. In this scenario, it's possible to distribute necessary tasks among team members and simultaneously attack different areas. For this purpose, too, it's important to know all the possible areas where measures can be taken, so a guide like Figure 5-11 is helpful here as well.

When a SEDAC branch line (potential area of attack on the target) proves difficult, the team may leave it for a while and move on to other areas. The operative principle of SEDAC is that the objective is constant, but the means can change.

On the other hand, a workplace TPM team, for example, may take up an improvement theme separate from the SEDAC, to reduce machine failures through machine cleaning. In my experience, this kind of narrow approach tends to limit the areas of attack and, consequently, the means to achieve objectives. However, this should not be used as a reason to limit or discourage the small group activity. On the contrary, the project leader should encourage existing teams to continue tackling the problem through machine cleaning, while the remaining areas are addressed by the SEDAC team. In short, SEDAC and workplace TPM team activity can coexist.

Using TPM as an example, this section described how to use knowledge available in the form of textbooks, papers, and technical reports on SEDAC. The lesson is that valuable information should be used to its fullest, and SEDAC makes this possible. The phrase to remember is "Do SEDAC with textbook in hand." The textbooks and other technical resources should be used differently in a company than in school. SEDAC users will take full advantage of field and experimental sciences by following through with fact-finding and testing.

The discussion so far reflects results of TPM-related activities at a number of client companies. More specifically, Table 5-14 on page 155 shows results achieved through SEDAC activities at ABB Elettrocondutture, an ASEA group company in Italy that manufactures many electrical parts for home and industrial use. The Monza plant of Phillips Italy in Milan also used SEDAC to further reduce ppm-level defects due to failures of various automatic machines. They reduced defect rates by 30 to 55 percent for various product types.

The driving principle behind the TPM, P/O Matrix, and SEDAC examples in this chapter is the flexible division of labor. They illustrate the push to involve a work force that performs multiple, unstandardized jobs.

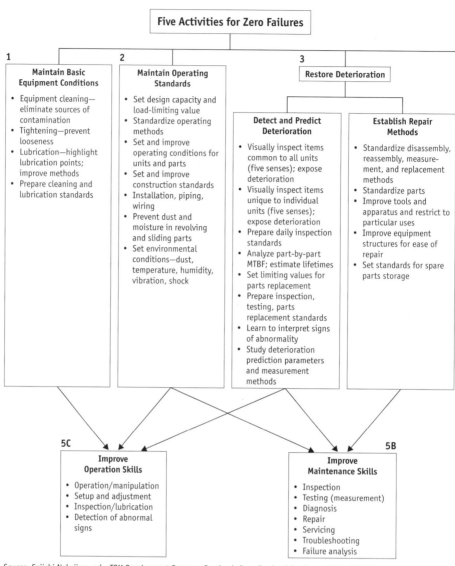

Source: Seiichi Nakajima, ed., *TPM Development Program,* Portland, Ore.: Productivity Press, 1989, 102-103.

Figure 5-11.
Failure Prevention Countermeasure Activities

This does not mean simply to develop a multifunctional work force; rather, it encourages managers, staffers, and operators to travel beyond their job boundaries.

It's often said that such a situation is impossible in Western society, and it's true that some companies in Europe and North America don't permit such open organizational practice. Nevertheless, I believe Western companies can adopt successfully many practices laid out in the preceding pages.

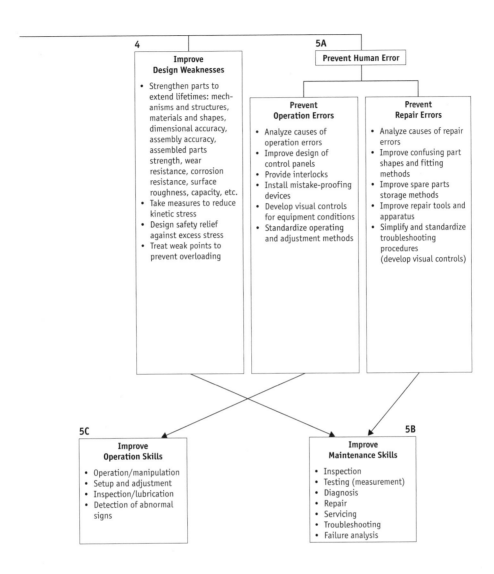

Table 5-14.
SEDAC Improvement Examples (ABB Elettrocondutture, 1990–1992)

• Overall equipment effectiveness (OEE)	
Joint process	45% → 78%
Bracket process	60% → 80%
• Setup time reduction	
Heavy press	−35%
• Process quality defect reduction (due to equipment causes)	
Four major pieces of equipment	−50%
Annual savings: $650,000	

New Equipment Development and Maintenance

Starting up new production equipment smoothly is an extremely important task for a company. In designing and manufacturing new equipment in-house, a company may find that some aspects of their current equipment, experience, and technology apply while other aspects don't apply and require research and innovation. In the latter case, the company doesn't have any previous experience and therefore foresees difficulty.

It's important to separate these two aspects of new designs and to conduct design reviews on predicted troubles so that actions can be taken to prevent them. In this way, the company can expect a better chance of smoothly running the new equipment from the beginning.

Figure 5-12 is an equipment design checklist developed by the Shiga plant of Dynic. Dynic has pioneered a wide range of products, including fabrics for bookbindings, adhesive linings for garments, and unwoven (needle-punch) carpets for residential and commercial use. The checklist in Figure 5-12 is used in conducting equipment development design reviews, which are carried out in three stages: concept, basic design, and detail design. The far left column in the figure lists the recommended TPM characteristics for the new equipment. This particular checklist is used for third-stage reviews of detail design. The legend used in Figure 5-12 is:

○ = Sufficient measures are taken based on prediction from past experience.

△ = Partial upgrades are necessary based on prediction from past experience.

✕ = Totally new design is necessary based on prediction from past experience.

As the totally new design issues (✕) are resolved by the second-stage design review, the remaining issues at the third stage design review are all partial upgrades (△). Those issues indicated with ✕ and △ symbols correspond to the predicted failure modes of FMEI. The improvement items listed in Figure 5-12 originated as improvement cards on the project SEDAC.

Table 5-15 is a P-M analysis chart used at Dynic for another piece of equipment, currently in normal operation and developed through the processes discussed above. P-M analysis is an advanced application of

Machine: DX-1   Department: A

Control items / Can consistently produce quality products	Processing speed	Tension	Cloth irregularity	Wrinkles	Pile sticking and scattering	Improvement items
Clear manufacturing conditions to build in quality (quantitative)	○	△ *1	△ *3	△ *4	△ *6	*1 Install slack detection sensors *4 Double-guider system + centering unit *6 Upgraded dust collector + enclosure (panel style) *3 Adopt double-guider system
Easy to set manufacturing conditions	○	○	○	△	△ *7	*7 Install manostat gauge on dust collector
Set conditions do not change over time	○	△ *2	○	○	△ *8	*2 Dispersion due to different cloth settings → Instruct vendors about manufacturing condition changes *8 Remove brush rolls
Easy to detect changes when they occur	○	○	○	△ *5	△ *9	*5 Tension fluctuation → Use the densimeter for judgment *9 Decreased dust collector performance → Use manostat gauge warning
Easy to restore	○	○	○	○	△ *10	*10 Devise a method for removing pile from dust collector (bucket style)

Components / Hard to fail and easy to repair	Cloth guider		Dust collector		Centering unit	Guide roll
Appropriate life (simple structure, sufficient strength)	○	Rubber roll wear-out (scheduled inspection item)	△ *11	Bearing and belt wear-out (scheduled inspection items)	○ Clean only the sensing part	○ Replace every 3 years (low load)
Easy to detect failures	○	Adhere to installation standards Preconstruction meeting	△ *12	An inspection window on soundproof box	○	○
Need to take measures on unsolved root causes	○	Enclosure and dust collector	△ *13	Floor space for Assy. replacement	○	○

Ensures operator maintenance autonomy	General		Specific			Improvement items
Easy to check and oil	○		△ *16 Difficult to oil due to the soundproof box			*16 Install a window for inspection and oiling
Easy to clean	△ *14	Adhere to installation standards	△ *17 The same as above			*14 Adhere to construction standards
Need to take measures on unsolved root causes	△ *15	Enclosure impedes bucket changes	○			*15 Install an enclosure (panel style)

Provides safe environment	Few nonroutine operations	No bumps and hooks	Proper aisle and work area sizes	No vibration, noise, smell, and darkness	Safety equipment	Improvement items
Safe, untiring, and pleasant to operate	△ *19	○	○	△ *18 Soundproof box around dust collector 85 dB → 70 dB	○	*18 Structure of soundproof box soundproof sheet + 100 mm sponge

User friendly	Easy changeover and adjustment	Proper buttons (location and size)	Operations procedure manuals	Improvement items
Ensures correct and speedy operations and changeovers	△ *19 Enclosure impedes bucket changes	○	△ *20	*19 Confirm the enclosure size *20 Develop an F-0265 operational manual

Others / Cost	Resources and energy saving	Specification and inspection list development	Improvement items
Effective utilization of idle equipment	○	△ *20	*20 Facilities section develops an inspection list

Figure 5-12.
Equipment Design Checklist (Dynic, Shiga Plant)

TPM that is effective in solving recurring problems that stem from complex causes (Shirose, Kimura, and Kaneda 1995). At this plant, a P-M analysis chart is developed for each piece of equipment. Naturally, the plant implements measures against most predicted failure modes and their causes identified during equipment development. Dynic's P-M analysis chart illustrates the extent to which the company conducts detailed reviews of unsolved design issues on an ongoing basis.

AN ORGANIZATION FOR COMPANYWIDE IMPROVEMENT

Finally, Sony Inazawa's companywide improvement system chart (Figure 5-13) shows how Sony is incorporating many of the staff function improvement techniques discussed in this book into its network organization for improvement.

Table 5-15.
P-M Analysis for Coating Equipment (Dynic, Shiga Plant)

(TPM Group, 7/21/93)

Overall symptom	Specific symptoms	Conditions	Primary causes	Secondary causes	Investigation		Counter-measures	Effects
Shape variability	The exact shape of the roller is not transferred	1. Roller is not completely filled with resin	1-1 Weak scraper filling	1-1-1 Worn-out scraper	1-1-1-1 Physical property evaluation, no evidence	○		
				1-1-2 Scraper edge angle and type	1-1-2-1 Scraper position experiment	×	1-1-2-1-1 Changed the existing setting conditions	○
			1-2 Improper resin fluidity	1-2-1 Insufficient solvent		○		
				1-2-2 Bank resin clogging	1-2-2-1 Resin sets during process, but no problem	○		
			1-3 Clogged roller	1-3-1 High roller temperature	1-3-1-1 Proper temperature: 80°–90° C	○		
				1-3-2 Infrequently used parts	1-3-2-1 Clogging at the bottom of the mat	○		
				1-3-3 Worn-out roller shape	1-3-3-1 No roller abnormality	○		
			1-4 Low bank quantity	1-4-1 At beginning and end of operation	1-4-1-1 Bank quantity comparison	△		
				1-4-2 At time of bag replacement		○		
		2. Resin on the roller is not transferred 100%	2-1 Improper resin shape	2-1-1 Roller temperature variability	2-1-1-1 No right/left difference (surface temperature)	○		
				2-1-2 Improper roller temperature setting	2-1-2-1 Roller temperature experiment (Proper temperature: 80°–90° C)	○	2-1-2-1-1 Reinforced the current processing conditions	
				2-1-3 Resin fluidity	2-1-3-1 No clogging during process	○		
			2-2 Weak bond strength between basecloth and resin	2-2-1 Low basecloth surface temperature	2-2-1-1 No significant temperature difference due to speed	○		
				2-2-2 Temperature difference due to basecloth thickness	2-2-2-1 Studied	inc.		
				2-2-3 Difference due to speed	2-2-3-1 Experiment in the plant, more than 50 m/minute improper	×	2-2-3-1-1 Standardized the processing speed at 50 m/minute	○
				2-2-4 Preheating	2-2-4-1 With/without preheating comparison	inc.		
				2-2-5 Weak tension strength	2-2-5-1 Bond strength and shape confirmation (shape variability detected)	△		
		3. Resin is left on the roller aside from the shaped part	3-1 Improper scraping	3-1-1 Gap under the scraper edge	3-1-1-1 No evidence of gap	○		
		4. Shape is not retained after transferring	4-1 Improper shape	4-1-1 Roller temperature variability	4-1-1-1 No right/left roller temperature difference	○		
			4-2 Weak bond strength between basecloth and resin	4-2-1 Low basecloth preheating temperature	4-2-1-1 Surface temperature varies by 6° C due to speed	○		
			4-3 Vibration	4-3-1 Vibration due to the bar	4-3-1-1 Shape evaluation, no problem	○		
			4-4 Variability of basecloth smoothness	4-4-1 Basecloth surface	4-4-1-1 Basecloth type comparison (surface conditions differed)	×	4-4-1-1-1 Reviewed processing conditions	○

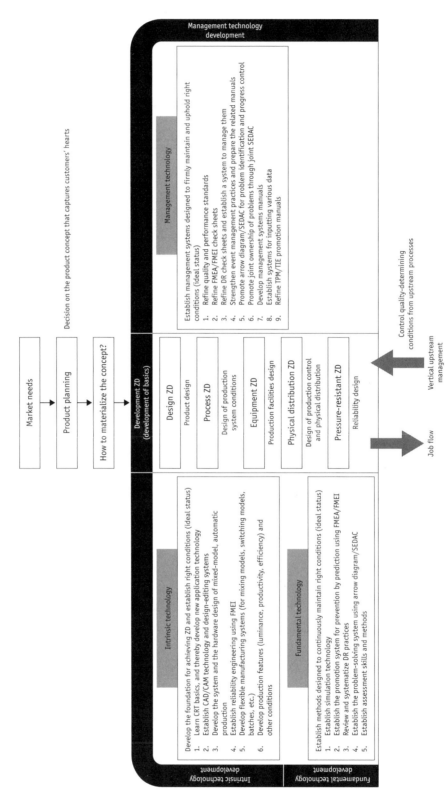

Figure 5-13.
Management System for Improvement (Sony Inazawa)

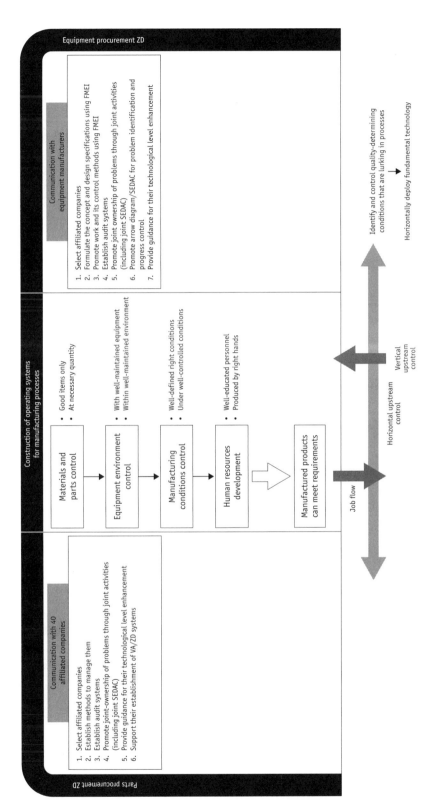

Figure 5-13. (cont.)
Management System for Improvement (Sony, Inazawa Plant)

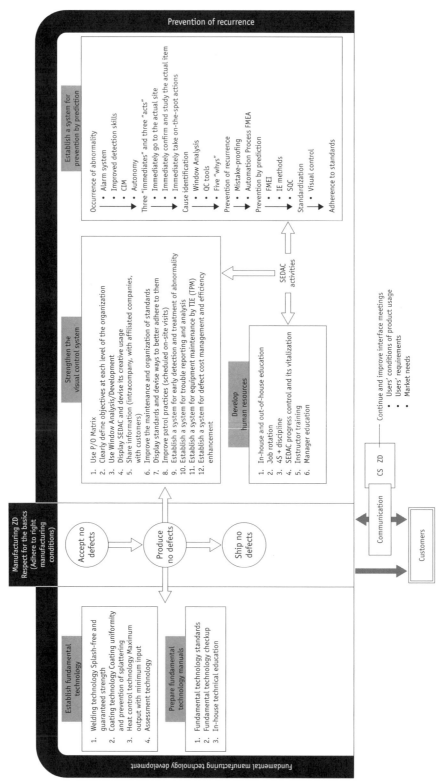

Figure 5-13. (cont.)
Management System for Improvement (Sony, Inazawa Plant)

Using Window Analysis for Accurate Fact Finding and Effective Countermeasures

AIMS OF WINDOW ANALYSIS

Whatever problem may arise, there is no way to solve it without first understanding the facts. Since each person sees things differently, correctly understanding the facts can be difficult, even though it may seem easy. In business, when we approach each problem individually and consider it separately from other problems, we often do well in understanding that particular problem. We run into trouble, however, when other problems arise while we are busily fixing the one at hand; we run around putting out one fire after another. In my desire to take organizations beyond mere fire fighting, I wanted to develop a method by which people can accurately grasp and understand the true causes of the many problems occurring around them every day. I began my efforts on this method while serving as general manager at a factory.

Like many managers, I tried to take care of each day's problems during the same day they occurred. As you can imagine, this kept me and my five supervisors very busy. We became engrossed in day-to-day quality, equipment, and other problems. In the end, I learned that all our running around didn't make things better or worse: we just maintained the status quo.

This firefighting approach can be compared to giving medicine to a group of children with colds. While the medicine cures one child's cold, another gets sick, and so we stay busy administering medicine every day.

Similarly, it's easy for managers to run around, thinking they're doing a good job. In retrospect, I now realize that management by running around is really not so honorable or effective. It's much better to improve the organizational constitution so problems don't occur in the first place—much like improving children's immune systems to prevent them from catching colds.

But how do we do this? Essentially, we need a means for analyzing raw data and for identifying what part of the organizational constitution is weak. *Window Analysis* is such a means. Window Analysis is an action-oriented technique for analyzing deficiencies from a management perspective. In short, Window Analysis is an objective method for letting data speak.

Before exploring the details of Window Analysis, it's important to understand the following types of organizational weaknesses from a management perspective:

1. Weakness in adhering to standards (manuals, documents)

2. Weakness in communicating and teaching standards and other information

3. Weakness in creating the right standards

Before we try to strengthen these weaknesses, it's necessary to understand them concretely and quantitatively and to allocate necessary resources (people, technologies, money, information, time, etc.) according to the objectives we want to achieve.

ORIGINS OF WINDOW ANALYSIS

The format of Window Analysis was inspired by Joharry's Window, shown in Figure 6-1. Joharry's Window was used by Joseph Luft and Harry Ingram to describe communication between two people. Category I in Joharry's Window is the state in which both *you* and *I* know, and Category IV is the state in which neither of us know. Categories II and III refer to the state in which either *you* or *I* do not know.

At an internal meeting, Masao Kamei, then president of Sumitomo Electric Industries, drew Joharry's Window on the blackboard to make a point about removing the walls between departments to improve company communications. Masayoshi Fuse, then a young staffer of the IE

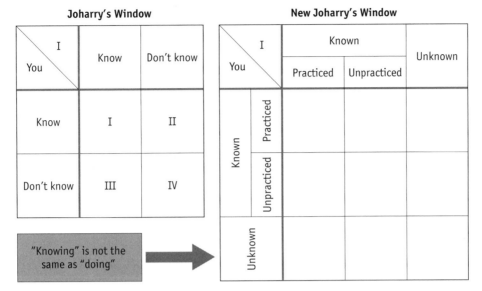

Figure 6-1.
Joharry's Window and New Joharry's Window

department where I was director, was studying the reasons for the effectiveness of SEDAC (then called CEDAC). Inspired by his comment that *knowing* is not the same as as *doing,* we subdivided the *known* category in Joharry's Window into *practiced* and *unpracticed,* thus expanding the number of panes from four to nine. We named this window the "New Joharry's Window." Later, I developed it into the Window Analysis technique as shown in Figure 6-2.

HOW TO USE WINDOW ANALYSIS

Figure 6-2 shows the basic structure of Window Analysis. Parties X and Y are the work groups or individuals who interact with each other while doing their jobs. Table 6-1 lists sample combinations of parties X and Y in various horizontal relationships, or in vertical relationships within work units. In either case, it's important to identify two work groups or individuals who can take corrective actions on a problem.

As Figure 6-2 indicates, Window Analysis has changed the names of the main divisions of the window to serve the business management function. In Window Analysis, the two major divisions are called *right methods established* and *right methods not established. Right methods* refer to work procedures and techniques (some companies call them standards or manuals) that are sufficient for maintaining work outcomes at currently

	X	Right methods established		Right methods not established
Y		Practiced 100%	Not practiced 100%	
Right methods established	Practiced 100%	A	B	C
	Not practiced 100%	B	B	C
Right methods not established		C	C	D

Figure 6-2.
Window Analysis

desired levels. Examples of right methods include procedures and techniques for maintaining quality, productivity, and equipment conditions. *Established* means the company has sufficient methods, while *not established* means it doesn't.

Right methods established is further broken down into two subdivisions: *practiced 100 percent* and *not practiced 100 percent*. When these divisions and subdivisions are placed in a matrix format, they create nine cells, or windowpanes. The conditions these cells represent can be grouped into four categories, which we will call A, B, C, and D (see Figure 6-2).

Table 6-1.
Parties X and Y—Horizontal and Vertical Relationships

Sample Horizontal Relationships				
X	Current process	Design	Production	Our company
Y	Previous process	Manufacturing	Marketing	Customer

Sample Vertical Relationships				
X	Group leader	Supervisor	Managers	Department manager
Y	Members	Employees	Group leaders	Section manager

Category A, as indicated in Figure 6-2, represents the ideal condition in which the right methods to prevent defects are established and both parties X and Y, in any combination, understand the methods and practice them 100 percent.

Category B, on the other hand, is the state in which the right methods to prevent defects are established and understood by the involved parties, but are not practiced 100 percent. From the viewpoint of management, category B deficiencies can be generalized as indicating *weakness in adherence*. More specifically, this state occurs under the following conditions:

1. Parties understand the right methods, but fail to practice them due to careless mistakes.

2. Parties understand the right methods, but cannot practice them due to lack of skills (both physical and mental) necessary to perform the job.

3. Parties understand the right methods, but take shortcuts due to lack of time, human resources, and money. (Shortcuts do not always mean negligence. Existing work structures and systems often encourage people to take shortcuts.)

On the surface, category C may be a little confusing because either party X or party Y says, "The right methods are established," while the other party says, "They are not established." This situation can be interpreted as follows. The right methods are established (or the right information is available); however, either party X or party Y, who should have been informed of the right methods, was not properly taught or did not receive the necessary communication. In terms of management, category C represents a *weakness in teaching standards and communicating information.*

Category D is the state where the right methods have not been established for any combination of parties X and Y. In terms of management, this indicates a *weakness in establishing the right methods (improvement and standardization).* More specifically, category D represents the deficiencies resulting from a lack of technological know-how. In the case of office work, category D includes deficiencies that occur because the right procedures for doing the job are not yet developed.

The actions required to correct work deficiencies entail improving problems in all categories (B, C, and D) and turning them into category A—an activity for which the following two approaches are necessary:

1. Category C → Category B → Category A: The right work procedures and the technical standards must be correctly communicated to all people concerned and their thorough adherence to these methods must be ensured.

2. Category D → (Category C → Category B →) Category A: If the current work procedures and the technical standards are not appropriate or adequate, they must be improved and methods must be changed. Then the new methods must be correctly communicated to all people concerned and thoroughly implemented.

WINDOW ANALYSIS CASE STUDIES

All work outcome deficiencies can be plotted somewhere in the window-panes of Figure 6-2. In the case studies that follow, the information in the panes from Figure 6-2 is simplified, as shown in Figure 6-3.

The five simple case studies that follow are meant to be used as exercises for correctly applying the Window Analysis technique to problems in the workplace. My hope is that, by going through these case studies, readers will learn Window Analysis and apply it to their work problems (not only quality defect problems, but also any other deficiencies). After analyzing their own problems using the window, readers might want to compile the results according to the category of management weakness (category B, C, or D). I sincerely hope that readers understand where their organizations' weaknesses are, take actions to prevent them from recurring, and eventually predict them and take action *before they occur*.

Case 1: The Coffee That No One Drank

Situation

Three concurrent sessions of a management seminar were held at a hotel, and a break was scheduled at 10:00 a.m. for 20 minutes. Arrangements were made to serve beverages and snacks to participants during the break in the lobby outside the seminar rooms. Unfortunately, the person organizing the seminar failed to inform speaker F, one of the lecturers, of the break schedule. Consequently, speaker F took breaks at nonscheduled times and participants in her session didn't receive refreshments.

Plotting on the Window

Let's consider the combination of parties X and Y as follows:

- Party X: Speaker F

- Party Y: Seminar organizer

Although the break schedule was determined in advance, the seminar organizer made a careless mistake by not telling speaker F about the break. The Window Analysis method tells us that the organizer's act of omission represents the *right method established, but not practiced*. From speaker F's perspective, the right method was not established, since she was not provided the right information. Therefore, this case is a category C problem and should be plotted on the window in pane 8, as shown in Figure 6-3.

The above situation can be interpreted in another way. Speaker F, using common sense, could have asked the organizer if he was forgetting to tell her about the break schedule. Taking this into consideration, speaker F's action (or lack of action) could be considered *unpracticed* from his perspective as well, and plotted in pane 5.

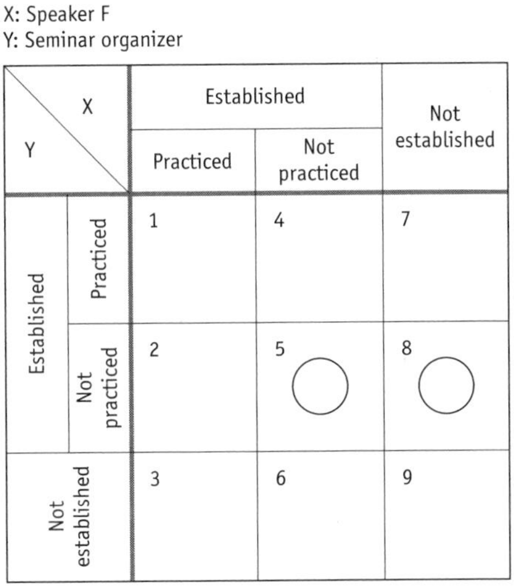

X: Speaker F
Y: Seminar organizer

Y \ X		Established		Not established
		Practiced	Not practiced	
Established	Practiced	1	4	7
	Not practiced	2	5 ◯	8 ◯
Not established		3	6	9

Figure 6-3.
Case 1: The Coffee That No One Drank

In work situations, this kind of scenario happens all the time. Our challenge is to determine where to draw the line on common sense. When we do this, we question the validity of distinguishing between *established* and *not established* on the window. In the case cited above, two possible viewpoints exist. One, you can take the viewpoint that it's common sense to have a break in the morning; in such a case, you would plot the situation in pane 5. Two, you can take the viewpoint that the practice of having a break differs by lecturer and by local custom, and that the organizer is therefore responsible to inform all lecturers of the break time. In such a case, you would plot the situation in pane 8. When problems like this occur in the workplace, you need to use your judgment to decide what viewpoint to adopt now and in the future.

Case 2: A Mistake-Proofing Mistake

Situation

Defective parts were found mixed in the parts bin for product A. Since these parts didn't have holes where they were needed, the assembly process couldn't complete three of the 200 products scheduled for the day. Producing replacement parts took a whole day and caused delays in the assembly process, as well as in the reliability testing and inspection processes. Since product A had a very tight delivery schedule, the company wasn't able to meet the customer's delivery requirement—a problem that resulted in a damaged business relationship.

An investigation revealed a flaw in the drilling process that precedes the assembly process. On the day when the defective parts were produced, the mistake-proofing device for detecting drilling omissions happened to break down. Thinking it would take too long to fix the mistake-proofing device, the drilling machine operator continued the operation without the device and produced the defective parts.

Plotting on the Window

Let's consider the combination of parties X and Y as follows:

- Party X: This process (assembly)

- Party Y: The previous process (drilling)

The machine operator of the previous process knew that he should do his job only with the mistake-proofing device in place. Nevertheless, he detached it, creating the condition of an *established and unpracticed* standard for the drilling process. Assembly process personnel, on the other hand, performed their job according to standards; from their perspectives, the standard was *established and practiced* for the assembly process. Therefore, this case is plotted in pane 2 as indicated by the circle in Figure 6-4, Part 1.

In this company, whether or not the drilling process was operating with the mistake-proofing device is not something the assembly process is required to know to do its job. As the "next process," assembly is only required to watch for defective parts and if they find them, to not assemble them. It would be incorrect in this case to consider whether people in the assembly process knew or didn't know that the drilling process operator had detached the mistake-proofing device. The problem, therefore, is not an *unestablished* standard on the part of the assembly process and should not be plotted in pane 8 as indicated by the ✕ in Figure 6-4. (Pane 8 is in category C—deficiencies that occur as a result of one of the parties not knowing what it should have known.) Here, the party that should take necessary actions to prevent the problem from recurring is the previous process—drilling. Since the assembly process can't do anything to solve the problem, it is not responsible for preventing it.

Part 1
X: Assembly process (current)
Y: Drilling process (previous)

Y \ X		Established		Not established
		Practiced	Not practiced	
Established	Practiced	1	4	7
	Not practiced	2 ⃝	5	8 ✕
Not established		3	6	9

Part 2
X: Drilling process supervisor
Y: Drilling process operator

Y \ X		Established		Not established
		Practiced	Not practiced	
Established	Practiced	1	4	7
	Not practiced	2 ⃝	5 ⃝	8 ✕
Not established		3	6	9

Figure 6-4.
Case 2: A Mistake-Proofing Mistake

Next, let's consider the combination of parties involved in the drilling process as follows:

- Party X: The supervisor of the drilling process

- Party Y: The operator of the drilling process

Since the operator ignored the requirement of doing his job with the mistake-proofing device, the condition is *established and unpracticed* on his part. As for the supervisor, the following two situations are possible:

1. It was the supervisor's responsibility to oversee how the operators were conducting their jobs. Regardless of why the operator detached the mistake-proofing device, the supervisor should have checked the operator's action. Thus, the supervisor's insufficient checking is *unpracticed* on her part. Therefore, this case should be plotted in pane 5 of the window, as shown in Part 2 of Figure 6-4.

2. Knowing the importance of the mistake-proofing device, the supervisor had been constantly coaching the operators on this point. Therefore, she couldn't imagine that the operator would run the machine without the device under any circumstances. If the supervisor felt she did everything she could do, the condition is *established and practiced* on her part. Therefore, this case should be plotted in pane 2 (see Figure 6-4, Part 2).

In any case, pane 8 is never the correct place to plot this work situation. In this example, a pane 8 condition would indicate that the supervisor did not know what she was supposed to know (that to prevent the drilling omission, the machine must be operated with the mistake-proofing device). It's inconceivable that the supervisor wouldn't know about the device.

Essentially, this case highlights the *practiced or unpracticed* dimension for a manager or supervisor as compared with an employee directed by that manager. The "practiced" of the supervisor refers to the education and guidance she provides for employees. This helps them eliminate defects and learn correct methods. Therefore, the key question in this case is how well the supervisor fulfilled his responsibility to coach and check his employees' work.

Case 3: Too Busy to Remember

Situation

A manufacturing manager and six design group members met to discuss specifications for a unique, made-to-order product. After the meeting, the designer in charge forgot to include one of the specification items in the design drawing. Although the manufacturing manager knew about the specification item, she didn't remember to share this information with the group leader in charge of production of the product. Consequently, the group manufactured the product exactly as specified in the drawing and ended up making a defective product. Since the product was relatively complicated, it took considerable time and effort to rework it.

Plotting on the Window

Figure 6-5 shows three possible combinations of parties X and Y for this case. From a corrective-action viewpoint, the combination in Part 3 is the most effective:

- Party X: The manufacturing manager

- Party Y: The designer

Since the designer failed to include one of the meeting discussion items in his drawing, for him the work condition is *established and unpracticed*. Likewise, since the manufacturing manager failed to communicate the known and important information to the production group leader, for her the work condition is also *established and unpracticed*. This case is plotted in pane 5 in Part 3, because the problem occurred as a result of both parties' fitting into the *established and unpracticed* category.

The case for the production group leader should be plotted in pane 6, category C, as shown in Parts 1 and 2 of Figure 6-5. In both instances, the leader was not informed of what he should have known. Part 1 represents the scenario in which he did not receive the necessary information in the design drawing, while Part 2 represents the scenario in which he did not receive the necessary information from the manufacturing manager.

Part 1
X: Designer
Y: Production group leader

X \ Y	Established		Not established
	Practiced	Not practiced	
Established — Practiced	1	4	7
Established — Not practiced	2	5	8
Not established	3	6 ◯	9

Part 2
X: Manufacturing manager
Y: Production group leader

X \ Y	Established		Not established
	Practiced	Not practiced	
Established — Practiced	1	4	7
Established — Not practiced	2	5	8
Not established	3	6 ◯	9

Part 3
X: Manufacturing manager
Y: Designer

X \ Y	Established		Not established
	Practiced	Not practiced	
Established — Practiced	1	4	7
Established — Not practiced	2	5 ◯	8
Not established	3	6	9

Figure 6-5.
Case 3: Too Busy to Remember

Case 4: A Ten-Day Wait

Situation

An engine-driven generator for civil engineering construction work was transported from the manufacturer to the customer's site. To prevent damage during transportation, the manufacturer placed a vibration-damping rubber sheet between the generator and its foundation. The instruction sheet that came with the generator clearly said to remove the rubber sheet and fix the generator firmly on its foundation before using the generator. Since the people at the construction site thought they knew how to use the generator, they didn't read the instruction sheet. They went ahead and ran the machine with the rubber sheet in place, not knowing what would happen. As a result, the lead wire broke into pieces, and the machine became unusable. Since the site was in a remote mountain area, it took ten days for a replacement generator to arrive, and the construction project was much delayed.

Plotting on the Window

The involved parties are:

- Party X: Manufacturer

- Party Y: Customer's employees

The manufacturer included the instruction that specifically mentioned the rubber sheet must be removed before use. For this reason, the condition of *established and practiced* applies to the manufacturer. The customer's employees, on the other hand, didn't know what would happen to the generator if the rubber sheet was not removed. For this reason, the condition of *not established* applies to the customer's employees, and the case is plotted in pane 3 as indicated by Figure 6-6.

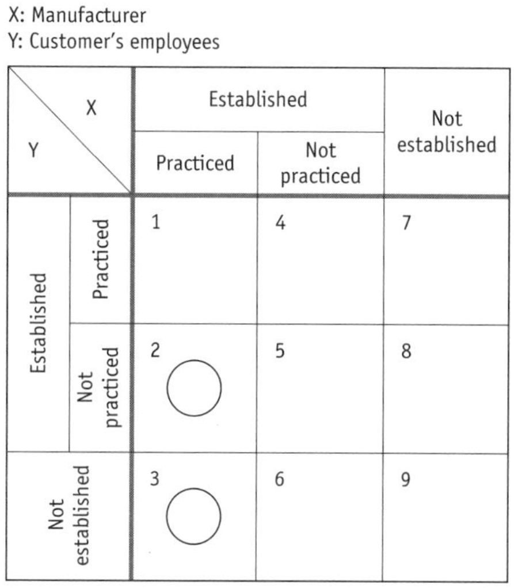

X: Manufacturer
Y: Customer's employees

Y \ X		Established		Not established
		Practiced	Not practiced	
Established	Practiced	1	4	7
	Not practiced	2 ◯	5	8
Not established		3 ◯	6	9

Figure 6-6.
Case 4: A Ten-Day Wait

USING WINDOW ANALYSIS

Of course, the incident could have been avoided if the customer's employees had read the instructions. Another feasible analysis, therefore, is that the customer's employees knew they should read the instructions before using the generator, but failed to do so. In other words, the condition is *established and unpracticed* on the part of the civil engineering company's employees. In this scenario, the case would be plotted in pane 2 as also shown in Figure 6-6.

In actuality, we should decide where to plot the problem by considering the proper course of action for preventing the problem. In this example, for the case plotted in pane 3, the solution might be to educate the customer's site employees in the removal of the rubber sheet before using the machine. For the case in pane 2, the response might be to ensure they read the instructions before using any new equipment.

Supplemental Explanation

While going through this exercise, some of my client companies took a different stance. They said that if the step to remove the rubber sheet before running the generator was so important, the manufacturer should have emphasized this more strongly. For example, to get the user's attention, the manufacturer could have highlighted that part of the instruction sheet by marking it in red. Or, anticipating the possibility that the user might not read the instructions, the manufacturer could have attached tags on each corner of the rubber sheet warning the user to remove it before use. Further, the machine could have been mistake-proofed so it wouldn't run with the rubber sheet. Since the manufacturer failed to take such precautions, the condition is *established and unpracticed* and is plotted in pane 5.

In similar situations, Window Analysis users may decide whether the problem should be plotted in pane 2 or pane 5 based on their own unique circumstances, such as the type of product, the severity of the problem, and the loss incurred as a result of the problem.

Case 5: An Accident Six Years Later

Situation

An equipment manufacturer designed and manufactured a large-scale cable stranding machine. Both the design and manufacturing departments were confident they were thorough in using the necessary technology and know-how and in building quality into the product before it was shipped to the customer. After using the machine for six years, the customer suffered a major accident when the machine's shaft broke. An investigation revealed that metal fatigue was the cause of the accident, and, consequently, the customer filed a complaint against the manufacturer.

By way of comparison, the same customer had been using a similar machine made by the manufacturer's competitor; after eight years, the competitor's machine was still running.

Plotting on the Window

Let's consider the following combination of parties X and Y:

- Party X: Design department

- Party Y: Manufacturing department

Until the company received the complaint from the customer, both the design and manufacturing departments thought their case fell into category A, pane 1 in Figure 6-7. However, after the machine failed, they conducted an investigation. Comparing their machine to the competitor's, they found that the shaft material lacked strength and that the shaft fitting was improper. They determined that when they designed and manu-

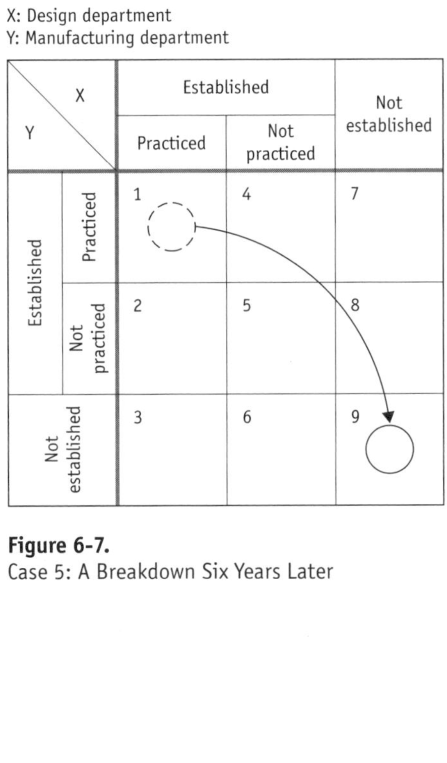

Figure 6-7.
Case 5: A Breakdown Six Years Later

factured their machine, their technological knowledge was insufficient. For this reason, the case should be plotted in category D, pane 9. In short, the case was at first considered to be category A and later, due to an investigation, fell into category D.

The converse could have happened: the competitor's machine could have failed after six years, while this company's machine could have still been running after eight. In such a scenario, the company would, of course, have received no complaint. The point is that, to keep category A products continuously in category A, companies should use reliability engineering.

In this example, after investigating the complaint, the company determined that the cause of the problem belonged in category D, pane 9. Of course, depending on investigative findings, it's possible to classify this problem in any one of panes 2 to 9. For this reason, an investigation that finds no conclusive cause should be avoided if at all possible. Don't give up until you find the cause.

LESSONS LEARNED FROM WINDOW ANALYSIS

Table 6-2 is a breakdown of quality defects by category (B, C, and D) at a sample of Japanese and non-Japanese companies for a certain period of time. The ratio of defects by category differs depending on the company or type of industry. Furthermore, the ratio of defects by category differs by department or by different product groups within a company. The point is that there is no "right" ratio of category B, C, and D problems. The key is to understand where weaknesses lie in one's own organization in terms of these categories by using Window Analysis to plot actual problems.

When quality defects occur, people often say, "These defects were caused by such-and-such technological reasons that we were unaware of before." Often, they compile a very detailed technical report on the problem. People rarely say, "Our department is very weak in adhering to standards and, as a result, we had these quality problems." This is ironic because, regardless of the company or industry, there are generally more problems in categories B and C—nonadherence by one or both parties, or ignorance of one party—than in category D—ignorance of both parties.

When a problem results in a big claim or complaint, people respond to the case specifically and learn various facts. Naturally, such an investi-

Table 6-2.
Window Analysis Results

Category	Company S (cable, wire)	Company M (heavy electric)	Company V (auto)	Company T (semi-conductors)	Company F (steel)
B	50	45	50	35	50
C	40	30	35	30	45
D	10	25	15	35	5
Total %	100	100	100	100	100

S, M: Japanese companies
V, T, F: Non-Japanese companies

gation often finds causes in categories B and C, but these tend to be treated lightly compared with the technical causes of category D cases. People might say, "This problem resulted in a big claim case, but the cause was simple human error," or "After our investigation, we found the problem was caused by foolishly not teaching the necessary procedures." No one likes to reveal problems in categories B and C, yet they are excellent candidates for major cost reductions. To reduce quality defects and losses due to claims, it's necessary to tackle not only category D, but also category B and C problems. This is done by enacting the improvement cycle:

1. Develop reliable standards using SEDAC or other methods

2. Teach the people involved about the standards to ensure adherence

3. Further improve existing standards as needed

4. Teach to ensure adherence to the revised standards

It's also important to see whether the necessary resources, such as technology, human resources, and money, are properly allocated in accordance with the content and frequency of problems in the three categories. To ensure proper resource allocation, results obtained through Window Analysis should be rolled into a P/O Matrix. This will help companies match their corporate or departmental objectives with their current management weaknesses. In line with this thinking on resources, the data in Table 6-3 can be compiled and calculated in terms of monetary losses by category.

Difficulty in Fact-Finding

The idea for Window Analysis began with common sense: One cannot take correct actions to resolve a problem without first understanding the facts. One important advantage of Window Analysis is that it will not allow you to plot a problem in a pane unless you have a firm grip on it. In other words, the objective of Window Analysis is not simply to plot the problem; rather, it is to trigger the people involved to engage in fact-finding. Such new actions are what count in making a company's organizational constitution stronger tomorrow than it is today.

An Advantage of Window Analysis: Prevention by Prediction

Another advantage of Window Analysis is that it enables the user to understand the organization's weaknesses from the perspective of management by compiling obtained data. This allows the user to go beyond conventional problem solving, where each individual problem is viewed separately and separate solutions are built each time. When such solutions are implemented, invariably, similar problems occur elsewhere, and the organization falls into a mode of constant fire fighting. Understanding overall management weaknesses, on the other hand, is the starting point for preventing recurring problems, as well as for predicting and solving potential problems before they occur.

The most important point to remember in applying Window Analysis is *not to use it to blame people*. Rather, Window Analysis should encourage a positive atmosphere in which the involved parties tackle problems and move on to a mode of prevention and prediction. While Window Analysis is not a tool for finger-pointing, sometimes it requires people to squarely face the facts and own up to weaknesses. The hope and intention here is that user organizations will foster the attitude and culture for encouraging such courageous behavior.

ORIENTING ACTION

Here are the key features of Window Analysis:

1. It triggers the actions necessary for identifying the root cause(s) of individual problems. Without correct fact-finding, correct actions cannot be taken.

2. By compiling data collected for Window Analysis, problems can be categorized in terms of management weaknesses. As shown in Figure 6-8, these are:

- Weakness in adhering to standards

- Weakness in communicating and teaching standards

- Weakness in developing standards

By quantitatively understanding organizational weaknesses, it becomes possible to take actions that prevent problem recurrence and to predict and prevent new problems, thus ending ceaseless fire fighting.

3. By understanding management weaknesses, it becomes possible to allocate necessary resources for improvement, such as technology, human resources, or money, depending on the type of weaknesses identified. These resource allocations and their results should be reflected on the P/O Matrix.

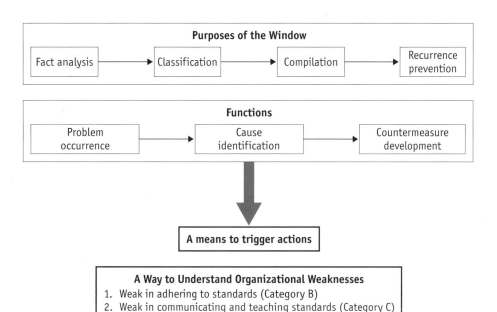

Figure 6-8.
Using Window Analysis to Understand Weakness

Figure 6-9 summarizes the corrective actions that should be taken for Window Analysis results in the different categories:

- For category D *(right methods not established)*, improve and develop the right methods using SEDAC, for example.

- For category C *(right methods established, but some people do not know)*, strengthen education and training as well as information management.

- For category B *(right methods established, but not thoroughly practiced)*, depending on the specific area of weakness, review and improve current supervising and coaching practices, conduct skills training, and develop countermeasures for human errors (mistakes).

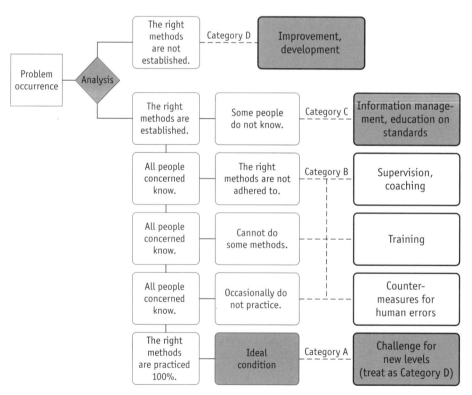

Figure 6-9.
Countermeasure Paths

DRAMATIC RESULTS

Chapter 1 included an improvement example from Sony Senmaya, where the quality improvement of car CD players using SEDAC resulted in the opportunity to become Nissan's OEM manufacturer. Figures 6-10 and 6-11 are the stratified data from Figure 1-7, showing product defect rates by type of defect. Figure 6-10 shows the dipping defect rate, while Figure 6-11 the operational defect rate. While the reduction of the dipping defects progressed smoothly using SEDAC and the experimental design method, it was very difficult to surmount the hurdle of operational defects through these means alone.

During the period from October 1985 to February 1986, as shown in Figure 6-11, the reduction of operational defects did progress smoothly, even though the rate of reduction gradually slowed. By March and April, however, defects were not continuing to decrease and, in fact, turned slightly upward. With an October 1986 deadline for project success, managers and team members were getting eager to achieve the target. Up until February 1986, the measures they had taken were effective. These measures, however, were based on their knowledge and experience, and they had simply run out of ideas.

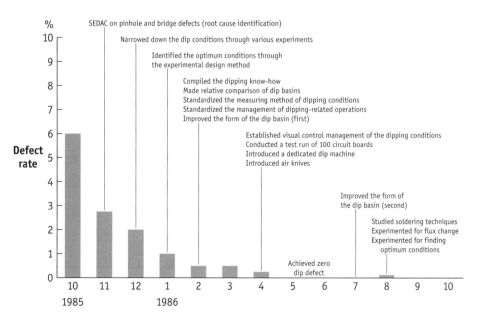

Figure 6-10.
Dipping Defects (Sony Senmaya)

To meet their deadline, managers applied Window Analysis to operational defect raw data for the months of February, March, and April. In addition to their existing knowledge and experience, they attempted to let the data speak to uncover problems from a management perspective. The analysis results revealed weaknesses in their manual for soldering and in the method for checking outcome quality. With these findings, managers were able to develop additional countermeasures for stabilizing operations. Such countermeasures included basic soldering technique education and training, skill enhancement training, and jig and tool improvement. As a result of these actions, dramatic drops in operational defects were achieved as shown in Figure 6-11.

By studying the five case studies introduced earlier in this chapter, it's hoped that readers will learn to correctly apply Window Analysis to problems in their own companies or departments. Of course, accurate fact-finding and correct analysis require considerable energy. Remember, though, that information obtained through Window Analysis at the right moment will lead to sound and effective actions such as those discussed in relation to the Sony example. Further, as you let the data speak for itself, you will find that you can go beyond the limitation of people's knowledge and experience to achieve tangible results.

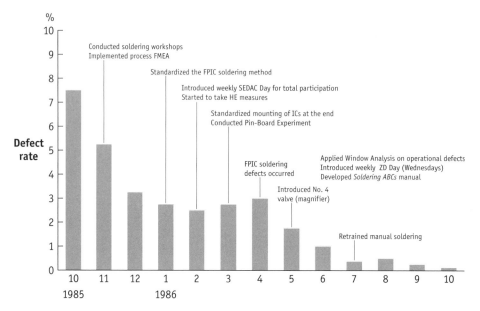

Figure 6-11.
Operational Defects (Sony Senmaya)

The key is to use Window Analysis when it's most needed. If you put great effort into the analysis, it pays off. Since the analysis requires a considerable amount of energy, however, it's not recommended to apply it extensively, especially when the problem is insignificant. Although accurately grasping the facts sounds natural and simple, doing it is much more difficult than saying it, as many people who have tried will attest.

In applying Window Analysis readers should beware of the following mistake. Sometimes people say, "We did Window Analysis, but we still don't understand the facts." If you could find the facts by using the Window, I suppose Agatha Christie would have made Hercule Poirot use Window Analysis! The point is, Window Analysis is a tool for analysis, not for learning the facts in the first place. Facts can be found only through investigation, not through Window Analysis. After the facts are uncovered and understood, then you apply the window to them.

Finally, Window Analysis users sometimes fall into the trap of endlessly pursuing the logic of *what if*. What if we had done this, or what if we had done that. This makes Window Analysis unnecessarily complicated. Remember that the window is not a tool for organizing all possible solutions; it only helps analyze facts that have occurred, have been investigated, and are understood. After Window Analysis, make an improvement plan on a P/O Matrix, then use SEDAC to test solutions and standardize successful ones.

Stockless Production and SEDAC

ORIGINS OF STOCKLESS PRODUCTION

Stockless Production is an approach that aims to transform a company's production system. Research and development in the Stockless Production approach began in the industrial engineering (IE) department of Sumitomo Electric Industries. Later, the Kansai Industrial Engineering and Management Systems Society continued the development through an industrial engineering application study group guided by Akihisa Fujita, an IE authority and professor in the commerce department of Kansai University.

Through these activities, many people contributed and integrated their wisdom and efforts eventually to what eventually became the Stockless Production system. Precisely speaking, *less stock* production is a more accurate name for this system, but the term "stockless" has become popular because it is easier to say.

Through my function as director of IE for Sumitomo Electric Industries from 1975 to 1981, and three-term chairman of the IE application study group mentioned above, I was involved in publishing the book *Stockless Production* (IE Application Study Group 1986). Professor Yukinobu Kimura (currently teaching at Takaoka Junior College) and I supervised the book's compilation by the IE application study group.

Various production system methodologies, such as JIT (just-in-time), have been applied at many companies and have achieved good results. In essence, Stockless Production is not different from these methodologies. But many companies have failed in improving their production systems. Our observations reveal that most reasons for failure boil down to an inconsistency in the way systems are implemented within a company. Such companies often push partial practices developed at other companies in selected areas while leaving other areas untouched.

For this reason, the IE study group decided to weigh and absorb the existing knowledge and excellent practices of many advanced companies, both in Japan and elsewhere, and to systematically organize findings. In doing this, we followed the basic IE approach: analysis and integration. In a nutshell, we learned that the key feature of Stockless Production is its scientific approach.

In 1986, the year *Stockless Production* was published, the IE study group added new members and evolved into a new study group called SIGMA (Strategic Integration for Greater Market Adaptability), also part of the Kansai Industrial Engineering and Management Systems Society. SIGMA developed a methodology that features two main principles: *strategy* to provide value to customers and *integration* to totally optimize the production system. The SIGMA methodology combines two sets of techniques: those of Stockless Production for developing fast material flows, and those of Computer Integrated Manufacturing for integrating information flows. The SIGMA group was led by Professor Fujita, Shinroku Tsuji (currently a professor at Distribution Science University), and Masayoshi Fuse (chief engineer of the production engineering department of Sumitomo Electric Industries). In 1993, the study group published *SIGMA*, a sequel to *Stockless Production*. *SIGMA* further refined Stockless Production with a contemporary thrust. Some aspects of the group's research were described in Chapter 2.

The intention of this book is not to cover the details of Stockless Production and SIGMA, but to present an overview that introduces the use of Stockless Production in relation to the P/O Matrix and SEDAC.

STOCKLESS PRODUCTION: EIGHT MEASURES

To implement Stockless Production, it's essential for managers, staffers, and work group leaders to become equally knowledgeable about the fundamentals of production control. To facilitate necessary education and training, these fundamentals have been compiled into 13 principles of Stockless Production, as shown in Table 7-1.

Table 7-1.
Thirteen Principles of Stockless Production

> 1. Production has two interrelated dimensions: process and operation.
> 2. Delay occurs as the result of division of labor, and transport occurs when a process is divided into subprocesses.
> 3. There are two kinds of delays: lot delay and process delay.
> 4. Delays constitute the largest portion of production lead time.
> 5. Process delay is considerably reduced by balancing the line and diminishing bottlenecks.
> 6. Lot delay is reduced by making lot size smaller.
> 7. Limiting work-in-process to smaller quantities is an effective means for shortening production lead time.
> 8. Synchronizing the line is effective in shortening production lead time and, at the same time, in raising efficiency.
> 9. Whether a line is well synchronized or not, efficiency plunges to a much lower level if work-in-process is totally eliminated.
> 10. Capacity should be immediately adjusted to match load fluctuation, thus avoiding increased process delay.
> 11. Waiting time before production begins should be adjusted by controlling backlog.
> 12. Shortening the production planning cycle leads to the reduction of waiting time.
> 13. Maintaining stock of semifinished products is an effective means to shorten made-to-order product production lead time. However, stock should be kept at a minimum.

The objective of a Stockless Production training course is to teach enough basics so participants can apply their knowledge in the workplace and act on constantly changing realities. Its aim is to grow out of the traditional practice whereby a handful of process controllers and managers walk around and talk themselves hoarse telling people what to do when they notice things they think need to be done.

The eight measures for shortening production lead time (throughput time), shown in Figure 7-1, were developed by integrating the 13 principles of Stockless Production. Later in this chapter we will see how these eight measures are addressed by SEDAC for the comprehensive implementation of Stockless Production. However, before getting into the details of using SEDAC in this context, one of the eight measures, "establish standards," needs more explanation about what it is and how it is used.

Production Is a Network of Processes and Operations

There are two dimensions of production: *processes* and *operations* (Shingo 1965, 1988). Processes relate to the conversion of raw materials

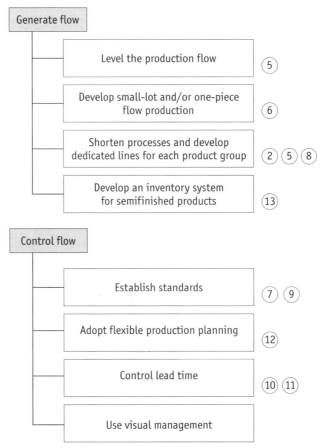

Note: The circled numbers correspond to the principles listed in Table 7-1.

Figure 7-1.
Eight Measures for Shortening Lead Time (Stockless Production)

to finished products. Processes are concerned with making products as fast as possible, with a short lead time. Operations relate to the actual work done by people or machines. The focus of an operation is to add value to the product in an efficient way; this often boils down to making as many units as possible in a given time. These two dimensions are like intersecting axes, as shown in Figure 7-2. Although it may not seem so at first glance, by nature the process and operation dimensions have mutually conflicting interests.

Years ago, I worked in a plant that manufactured large, intricately shaped gears by pressing and sintering iron powder. Naturally, the dies used for pressing these gears also possessed very intricate shapes. Basically, it was a pain in the neck to change these dies.

Production seeks harmony between operations (focusing on people and machines) and processes (focusing on flow of materials from raw materials to finished goods).

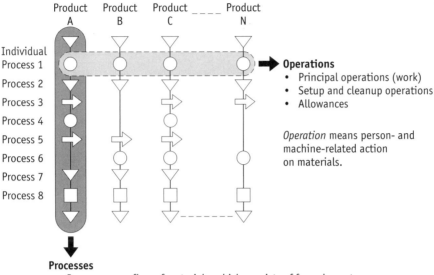

Product A   Product B   Product C _ _ _ _ Product N

Operations
- Principal operations (work)
- Setup and cleanup operations
- Allowances

Operation means person- and machine-related action on materials.

Processes
- *Process* means flow of materials, which consists of four elements: ○ processing, □ inspection, ⇨ transport, and ▽ delays. Materials flow from process 1 through process 8.

Figure 7-2.
A Network of Production: Processes and Operations

From the operation-oriented viewpoint of *making many,* it was understandable in this situation that once a die was set, people wanted to make the gears with that particular shape in large quantity—not only for this month, but also for the next month, the following month, or even half a year's worth, if possible. As far as each operation is concerned, this style of batch production increases production efficiency.

On the other hand, from the process-oriented viewpoint of *making fast,* people didn't want to have one die occupy the machine for too long. In this scenario, when the press operation finishes making the month's supply of one gear model, the die is then changed to make a supply of another gear model that is more urgently needed. Intrinsically, neither viewpoint is more important than the other. The balance between process and operation considerations is a management decision that should be made based on the company's market demand and competition. How important it is to *make fast* relative to *making many* is the fundamental decision senior and middle managers must make and communicate before implementing Stockless Production.

Of course, the contradictory interests of the two viewpoints described in the example above can be managed by shortening setup times and stabilizing changeover operations. Nevertheless, the contradictory nature of the two viewpoints remains.

What Levels of Product Availability Do Your Customers Want?

If a company implements Stockless Production without management vision and clear thinking on the optimum balance between process (making fast) and operation (making many), its effort lacks purpose. When this is the case, and when the business environment changes, the company often stops implementation, and consequently results are compromised and only temporary. In making decisions on the optimum balance between process and operation, then, management should consider both customers and production strategies.

Figure 7-3 shows three production schedules. In all cases, 100 units of model X, 60 units of model Y, and 40 units of model Z are produced in a month. The left column depicts one-piece flow production where only one model is produced at a time in the following sequence: X–Y–X–Z–Y–X–Z and so on. The middle column depicts small-lot production, where five units of X, then three units of Y, and finally, two units of Z are produced every day. Finally, the right column in Figure 7-3 shows the batch production schedule, where all 100 units of X are produced at the beginning of the month, 60 units of Y after this, and 40 units of Z at the end of the month.

Strictly speaking, from an operations point of view, batch production is the easiest production operation. In deciding what production schedule to use, however, the easiest way is not always the best way; it's important to base your decision on a number of factors, including what kind of production system your company has and your customer's required delivery time. Also bear in mind that many production possibilities exist—there can be many variations between pure one-piece flow and pure batch production. Different production schedules represent varying degrees of "levelization," or averaging out production models and quantities.

Determining the appropriate production schedule requires a strategic judgment about the relationship between product availability and customer satisfaction. Keeping in mind the market demand and the company's relative competitive position, management needs to decide how fast its products should be available for the customer. As its original name

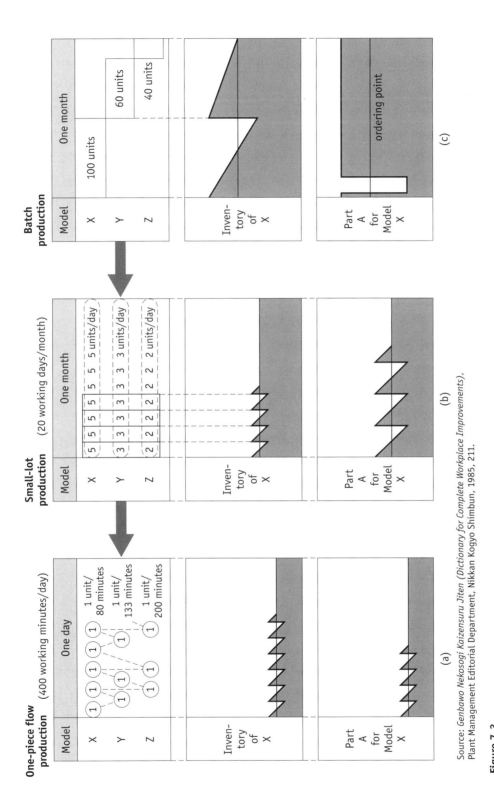

Source: *Genbawo Nekosogi Kaizensuru Jiten (Dictionary for Complete Workplace Improvements),* Plant Management Editorial Department, Nikkan Kogyo Shimbun, 1985, 211.

Figure 7-3.
Comparison of Production Schedule Leveling

less stock suggests, Stockless Production aims to reduce stock levels to their optimum in light of the company's unique set of circumstances and current situation. As we will see, the quantity of stock produced and the length of lead time are directly related.

The following examples provide an interesting perspective on the balance between customer needs and an economic production strategy. Around 1989, I had the following conversation with executives at Ferrari, the Italian car manufacturer. I asked them, "You said your customers don't mind waiting even two years for their Ferraris. But don't you think if you shortened the waiting time to three months you could sell more?" They said, "We don't want to sell any more than we do now." I was quite surprised to hear such an answer, but later I learned that this attitude was typical among traditional European manufacturers.

According to German examples cited by Professor Kazuo Yoshida of the Kyoto University economics department, many traditional European manufacturers handle economic boom—when market demand exceeds manufacturing capacity—by making customers wait. Professor Yoshida also notes that, since the market is so well segmented, it's unlikely that other manufacturers will cut into it and win waiting customers. During a slow economy, this phenomenon is offset by shorter customer waiting times. Because of this situation, it wasn't necessary for these European manufacturers to increase their production capacity beyond the point at which demand exceeded capacity. So many countries, so many practices!

What Indicators for Managing Production?

To make products as fast as possible, or to shorten lead (throughput) time, it's vital to notice and reduce delays. Figure 7-4 shows an indicator that in Stockless Production terms is called *flow value* or *F value*. While materials move through processes to become products, they are either processed, inspected, transported, or delayed. Flow value is an index where the numerator is the total time consumed by these four activities (the average production lead time) and the denominator is the net processing time. As indicated by several cases in Figure 7-4, three-digit *F* values are not as rare as one might expect.

A simple case of a three-digit *F* value is as follows. Suppose a laundry service picks up your shirt at home and says it will be returned in three days (72 hours). What will happen to your shirt in this time span? In this case, the net processing time for washing, drying, and ironing is probably

$$\text{Flow Value } F = \frac{S}{T} = \frac{\text{Average production lead time}}{\text{Net processing time}}$$

$$= \frac{\bigcirc + \square + \Rightarrow + \triangledown}{\bigcirc} \quad \text{(See Figure 7-2 for symbols.)}$$

F Value Examples

Plant	Net processing time (T)	Average production lead time (S)	F Value
A	100.0 h	800 h	8
B	10.0 h	250 h	25
C	0.5 h	72 h	144

Figure 7-4.
Flow Value

less than 30 minutes. The *F* value then becomes a whopping three-digit 144. What happened to your shirt, you ask, during the balance of the 72 hours? Transport? The laundry isn't far from your home. Inspection? Unlikely. The only reasonable answer is delays or stoppages.

This example is the rule rather than the exception. In fact, the bulk of the so-called production period is often riddled with delays. It is on delays, therefore, that we should focus in shortening lead time. Suppose, for example, an advanced washing machine that can wash twice as fast becomes available. If the laundry purchases and uses this machine without changing anything else in the way it does business, lead time will be shortened from 72 hours to only 71 hours and 45 minutes—an insignificant decrease from the customer's point of view.

The *F* value is an important indicator for office work as well. When people discuss increasing the speed of office work, they tend to focus on speeding up processing time. This, again, is the same as a laundry focusing on a new washing machine. Instead, both organizations should focus on delays, not processing time. How often, for example, does a document sit in the in-box before it's read and processed? It's not unusual for a document to sit for three days, even though it takes only three minutes to process.

As expected, office delays are further amplified when work is divided and many people are involved. It shouldn't be surprising, then, that many office work improvement successes I've witnessed in Western companies resulted from more than just reducing lead time by focusing on delays or stoppages; they resulted from also removing delays due to the division of work among people as well as between people and computers.

Lead Time and Work-in-Process Quantity

The graph shown in Figure 7-5 is called an input/output (I/O) chart, which has great significance. Basically, the input curve represents the cumulative workload of a given process (or the quantity of work finished in the previous process), while the output curve represents the cumulative work completed by a given process. The horizontal gap between these two curves shows process throughput time, while the vertical gap shows the quantity of work-in-process at a given time. Figure 7-5 also includes a line graph that shows a daily quantity of work-in-process trend, or the vertical gap between input and output each day. If a line graph showing the horizontal gap for each day was made instead, this would reflect the trend of throughput time.

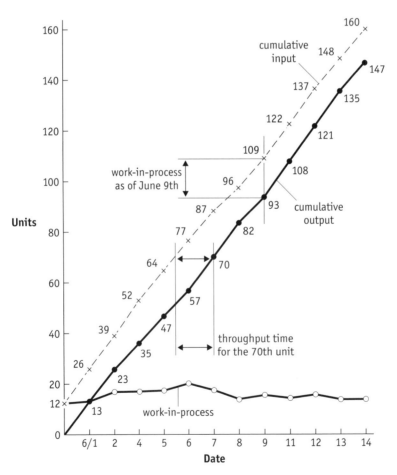

Figure 7-5.
Interpretation of Input/Output Curves

As Figure 7-5 clearly shows, there is a positive correlation between throughput time and work-in-process quantity. Figure 7-6 shows this another way. As the dotted lines indicate, when the gap between the input (workload) and output (capacity) curves widens for some reason, this reflects an increase in both throughput time and work-in-process quantity. Therefore, you can manage or control production by using either throughput time (standard flow time) or work-in-process (standard stock quantity) as production indicators.

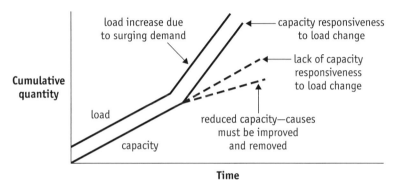

Figure 7-6.
Relationship Between Load and Capacity

Figure 7-7 shows the standard flow time for a process. This is the amount of time that should elapse from delivery of workpieces from the previous process to completion of the current process. Generally

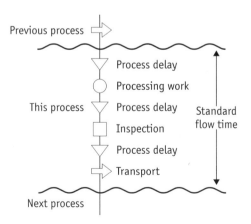

Figure 7-7.
Elements of Standard Flow Time (Example)

speaking, if your production environment is continuous make-to-order or make-to-stock, you can manage production by controlling either standard flow time or stock quantity. On the other hand, if production is a one-of-a-kind product or project (for example, construction, shipbuilding, manufacturing of large-scale equipment, etc.), you'll want to manage by standard flow time.

HOW TO PROMOTE STOCKLESS PRODUCTION

When work-in-process inventories accumulate, they extend production lead time and weaken organizational fitness for production. Why does work-in-process accumulate? Table 7-2 lists some typical reasons. Figure 7-8 puts these in a graphic perspective, showing what needs to be done to lower work-in-process inventories. The altitude of the "production plane" represents established standards such as work-in-process quantity or production lead time. The objective of the plane is to fly as low as possible without hitting obstacles, which represent accumulated work-in-process inventories, or prolonged throughput time, resulting from the reasons listed in Table 7-2. The higher the obstacles, the bigger the problems. Figure 7-8, then, illustrates the following key aspects of implementing Stockless Production.

1. Determine the altitude of the plane (in this example, at level 1) by setting standard stock quantities (or standard flow time). Next, lower the altitude to level 2, then to level 3. The point to remem-

Table 7-2.
Reasons for Work-in-Process Accumulation

Reasons	Identifiable Problems
1. Not obvious	1. Standard work-in-process quantities are not determined
2. Imbalance in capacity	2. Capacity is not balanced between two processes
3. Batch production with large lot sizes	3. Setup operations take a long time
4. Frequent quality defects and equipment failures	4. Safety stock is kept in fear of material shortage due to defects and failures in the previous process
5. Shortage or absence of skilled workers	5. Safety stock is kept for the same reason cited in 4
6. Production instructions given too early	6. Poor production planning and control

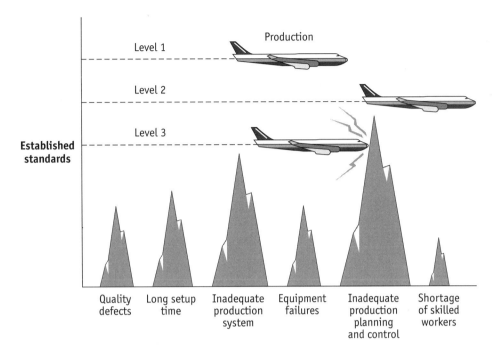

Figure 7-8.
Standards and Obstacles

ber is that the work-in-process level will never go down as a natural consequence of improvements; rather, *you have to determine the standard level and implement it.*

2. At level 2, no obstacles are in the way of the plane; therefore, lower the standard stock quantities to this level at once.

3. At level 3, the plane will hit an obstacle, which indicates that standard stock quantities are too low to smoothly operate production activities. Due to such a lack of work-in-process inventories, a serious problem is expected. Remember, obstacles in the way of the plane are problems that need to be improved at the time. By removing these obstacles, standard stock quantities can be further reduced.

4. In reality, you can't always know whether your production plane is flying safely at level 2 or if it is in danger by flying at level 3. Even though you want to aggressively lower your inventory level, you don't want to cause production confusion due to a lack of inventory. To avoid such trouble, it's effective to use a buffer

system. Suppose, for example, your current standard for work-in-process is ten pieces, and you want to find out if you can run production with eight pieces. So you adopt a temporary work-in-process standard of eight pieces and set two pieces aside as buffer. If an emergency arises, you can use the buffer and avoid delays. Furthermore, such an emergency situation lets you know what and how much you need to improve to smoothly run production with eight pieces. On the other hand, if you run production without touching the buffer for six months, common sense suggests that you can authorize a reduction of the standard work-in-process level from ten to eight. Such an approach is extremely effective in reducing standard stock quantity or flow time in a quick and safe manner.

DEVELOPING A PROMOTION SYSTEM USING THE P/O MATRIX

A P/O Matrix is useful when a company wants to systematically conduct improvement and transformation activities, including Stockless Production. In short, the P/O Matrix enables management to make necessary decisions in an organized manner.

In today's business environment, it's not sufficient for a company simply to shorten production lead time and reduce work-in-process inventories. As Figure 2-4 showed (page 36), this only improves quality, cost, and delivery from the producer's viewpoint. Instead, a company's P/O Matrix should include policies and objectives that strive to enhance the value of products from the customer's viewpoint. Such a viewpoint seeks ways to achieve customer satisfaction by taking advantage of the company's unique production lead time and process control position. (See the case examples on pages 208–15.) When the company adopts the TQM concept that *the next process is our customer,* it can expand its opportunity to improve work processes from the perspective of internal customers as well.

Once policies are set on the P/O Matrix, corresponding objectives and targets are determined. Then, the leader and cross-functional team members are identified. As discussed in previous chapters, these objectives are further broken down, if necessary, and evolved into improvement activities using SEDAC.

IMPLEMENTATION USING SEDAC

As indicated in Table 7-3, depending on the items you select as input and output for the I/O chart, you can decide what measures and central items to use as indicators for managing production. Figure 7-9 graphically presents some of these production management indicators. Further, you can set the standard value in terms of flow time or work-in-process, whichever serves you better. The relationship of these two indicators is expressed as follows:

Standard stock quantity = standard flow time × standard production quantity

As graphically presented by the I/O chart in Figure 7-5, stock quantities and flow time correspond to the vertical and horizontal gaps, respectively. Whatever final goal you may have, the practical way to implement Stockless Production is to set an interim target of 20 to 30 percent reduction from the current standard flow time or stock quantities. Figure 7-10 shows a SEDAC that uses the work-in-process quantity between two processes as an indicator.

As introduced in Figure 7-1, *establish standards* is one of the eight measures for Stockless Production. By observing the effect side of the SEDAC, you can find out how well you are currently performing against standard flow time or stock quantities. To implement another measure, *control lead time,* you can use an I/O chart. Further, *use visual management* is also one of the eight measures, and you can use SEDAC to make this happen. As we have seen, a key advantage of SEDAC is that it visually

Table 7-3.
Production Management Measures and Control Items

Measures		Control Items	
Lead time	Amount of work	Input	Output
Production period	Backlog	Orders received	Shipment
Waiting period	Amount of work waiting to start	Orders received	Input to the first process
Months in stock	Inventories	Finished products for storage	Shipment
Flow time between two processes	Work-in-process	Previous process's output	This process's output

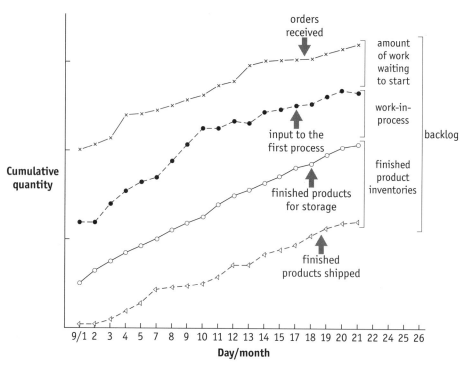

Figure 7-9.
Input/Output Control (Example)

presents the information flow regarding a given improvement project. The remaining measures, too, are addressed by placing them on the cause side of a SEDAC.

When your indicator shows that your current performance is worse than the standard, it should prompt you to look for the causes and write them down on problem cards. Then you develop countermeasures on improvement cards. In this way, you can make progress in Stockless Production through SEDAC. The key to success is to do this as part of your daily job. While you work every day, you monitor the indicator, find the causes that increase flow time or work-in-process, write them down on problem cards, and take countermeasures through the generation of improvement cards.

Such a disciplined approach allows you to take necessary actions when they're needed. In essence, you avoid making improvements that don't really count and, as a result, you improve the efficiency of your efforts and achieve quick results. After conducting improvement activities for some time, if you've maintained your indicator lower than the current target, it's time to adopt the target as your new standard. Then you set a

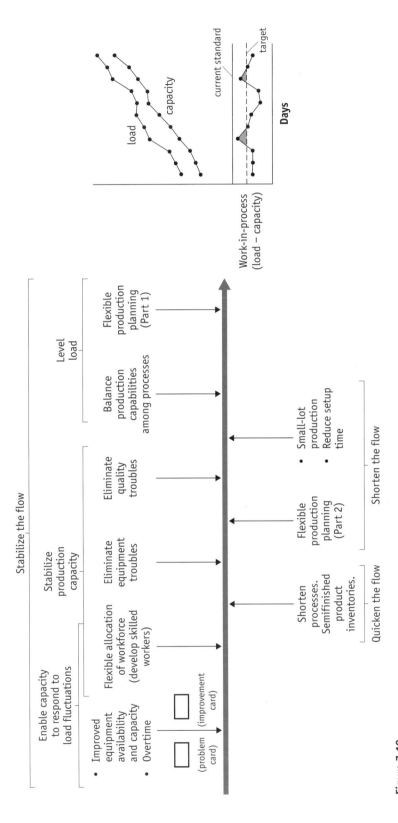

Figure 7-10.
Reduction of Work-in-Process Between Two Processes Using SEDAC

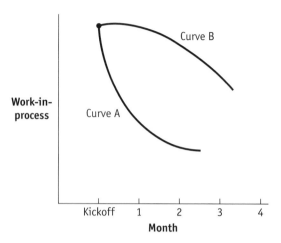

Figure 7-11.
Speed in Achieving Results

new target, continue your improvement activity until it's achieved, and so on, until you achieve your final target.

Basically, your throughput time is shortened and work-in-process is reduced at the rate you change your standards. This means using SEDAC systematically along each step of the production process. When you're finished, your aggregate results will show improvement similar to curve A in Figure 7-11.

It's important to note that, in terms of overall effect, there is an interesting distinction between quality improvement and Stockless Production. With quality improvement, the effect is derived as a natural consequence of improving the causes of quality defects. With Stockless Production, the effect comes from taking deliberate action on throughput time or work-in-process quantities—action that entails determining standards and putting them into practice. If you don't take such deliberate action—even though you've shortened setup time, balanced production line capabilities, and reduced equipment failures—you won't see the effect on production lead time and work-in-process inventories.

In short, although quality improvement activities may result in saving labor, they will not directly affect throughput time or work-in-process, as indicated in curve B of Figure 7-11. If such activities are persistently continued, curve B may eventually reach the level of curve A, but clearly the path of curve A is more efficient. By addressing throughput time or work-in-process quantities directly, you can expect to see results more quickly.

COMPUTERIZATION AFTER STABILIZING IMPROVEMENTS

While following through the steps of Stockless Production as discussed in the previous section, it's effective to formalize (standardize) improvements for computerization. The same is true for FA (factory automation). Whatever you do, don't make the mistake of introducing FA without first making IE improvements. If you do, it's likely that your FA systems will become white elephants.

Using SEDAC for three to four months to improve your production system will, in most cases, yield remarkable reductions in production lead time and work-in-process quantities. Only after this happens is your system ready for computerization. The SIGMA study group developed a software package called SPACE (Stockless Production Assisted by Computerized Environment) that can be tailored to individual production lines. Each production line's SPACE is networked with the plant's mainframe computer for the purpose of downloading order and product specification data and uploading production output data. Under this hierarchical structure, each production line's different control needs are managed by the line's SPACE, while data shared throughout the plant is managed by the mainframe.

Through this experience, Masayoshi Fuse of SIGMA prepared Table 7-4 to show the necessity of the kaizen (continuous improvement) approach. Due to recent developments in information technology, the client-server computing environment makes it possible for end users to develop their own programs based on their own specific needs and to

Table 7-4.
Kaizen Approach and Its Means

Kaizen Approach	Means
Formalize before computerization	Management technology • Stockless production
Activate line people's creativity • Quick Plan-Do-Check-Act cycle • Balance between each line's Kaizen and factorywide standardization	Information technologies • End-user computing • Network computing

Source: Kansai Industrial Engineering & Management Systems Society (ed.), *Strategic Integration for Greater Market Adaptability "SIGMA,"* Nikkan Kogyo Shimbun, 1993, 183.

improve on them, if necessary. Fuse also emphasizes that such kaizen capabilities are essential for successfully implementing Stockless Production.

SECURING RESULTS THROUGH THE SCIENTIFIC APPROACH

Chapter 1 introduced the Bucyrus, Ohio, plant of Timken which *Industry Week* named one of America's best plants in 1992 for outstanding improvements, due in part to use of the P/O Matrix and SEDAC. The plant effectively used SEDAC to improve its production system and reported many remarkable results, including reduced work-in-process inventories, shortened production lead time, shortened setup time, and improved equipment availability.

Another U.S. automotive component manufacturer used SEDAC to introduce one-piece flow production and reduced its work-in-process inventories by more than 99 percent. As a result, the company achieved a remarkable reduction in production lead time. Concurrently, the company conducted many improvement activities using SEDAC, including quality, setup time, labor-hour losses, equipment downtime, machine cycle time, and productivity—all of which contributed greatly to its profits.

A number of Italian companies have introduced Stockless Production. For example, shipbuilder Fincantieri reported success in reducing production lead time and work-in-process quantities by using the P/O Matrix and SEDAC. Further, Uno A Erre, a manufacturer of gold for rings, necklaces, bracelets, and other jewelry items, implemented Stockless Production using SEDAC and reduced its work-in-process inventories as

Table 7-5.
Examples of Improvements Using SEDAC (Uno A Erre)

Work-in-process reduction	
Department A	−45%
Department B	−32%
Department C	−35%
Processing time reduction (development of jigs and tools, mechanization, work improvement)	
Line D	−25%
Line E	−53%
Line F	−42%

shown in Table 7-5. At the same time, Uno A Erre conducted various IE improvements, which resulted in remarkable reductions in processing time. (Uno A Erre employs 900 people and is one of the largest and oldest companies in its industry.)

Also in Italy, Fatme, an Ericsson Group company that manufactures electronic parts for telephone switchboards and networks, applied SEDAC during its implementation of Stockless Production. Under this effort, the head office in Rome set out to improve on-time procurement performance and reduced delays to almost zero (a 96 percent reduction). Fatme's Avezzano plant also used SEDAC to achieve a 60 percent reduction in process defects on its robot lines.

Finally, Japan's Sendai Nikon has had a companywide focus on its work-in-process turnover rate since 1991, and has achieved significant results every year. Sony too is currently promoting LTI (lead time improvement) projects with associated companies.

CHALLENGING DELAYS IN INFORMATION FLOW WITH CIM

Now I'll introduce a case in which the principles of Stockless Production were applied to creating a smooth flow of information in addition to materials. This unique organizational transformation project was taken up by the corporate accounting department of Tayca in Japan, which basically has the same functions of a typical information systems department. The project, born out of the necessity for developing a computer-integrated manufacturing system (CIM), has been implemented under the leadership of top management since 1990.

Although the concept of computer-integrated manufacturing was introduced in the early 1970s, the concept attained its popularity in the late 1980s. According to one definition, "CIM is a flexible production system with self-regulating functions for achieving management efficiency through the utilization of computer and network technology, which enables the system to capture the flow of materials and information in a unified manner" (Research Group for Management Systems Technology 1989). In essence, CIM arms companies like Tayca with valuable information for developing company strategy.

To achieve companywide management efficiency, Tayca set the following CIM objectives:

1. Speedy and accurate response to sales opportunities

2. Systematic and efficient production activities based on future predictions

3. Customer-oriented research and development

Figure 7-12 (pages 209–212) is a systematic diagram of the production and sales information systems supported by Tayca's corporate accounting department. Note that the systems are categorized accounting to their broad objectives. Figure 7-13, developed by the SIGMA study group, shows the relationships between five strategic patterns and VALUE, the conceptual structure introduced in Chapter 2 for comparing value from the producer's and customer's point of view. It's interesting to note that Tayca's broad objective categories coincide with the five strategic patterns listed in Figure 7-13.

All over the world, truly necessary and meaningful systems have a curious resemblance, as the above example shows. In our pursuit of better methods, it's important to discover the common factors that cut across all successful organizations.

Strategy classification			Customer values				
		Strategy Patterns	V	A	L	U	E
I	A. Satisfy varied customer needs	1. Product individualization	◎	○			▲
		2. Product systematization	◎		○	○	▲
	B. Improve product availability	3. Quick delivery	▲			○	◎
		4. Product freshness	▲	○			◎
II	C. Improve internal productivity	5. Quick response	○			○	○

I: Strategies to provide new values
II: Strategy to realize internal productivity

V: Varied needs satisfaction
A: Amenity
L: Low risk
U: User costs minimum
E: Effective availability

◎ Primary objective
○ Secondary objective
▲ Minimum necessity
(◎ is often fulfilled at the expense of ▲.)

Source: Kansai Industrial Engineering and Management Systems Society, *Senryukuteki Togo Seisankanri Sisutemu "SIGMA" (Strategic Integration for Greater Market Adaptability)*, Nikkan Kogyo Shimbun, 1993, 60.

Figure 7-13.
Five Strategy Patterns

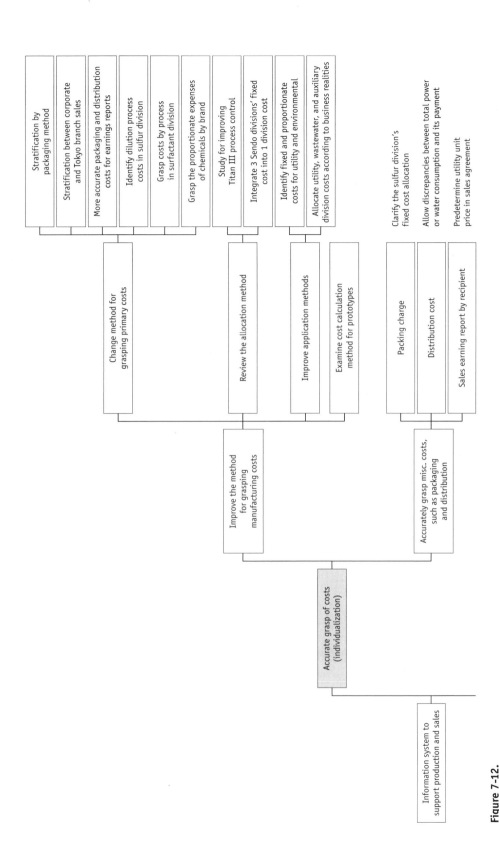

Figure 7-12.
Strategic Information Systems (Tayca)

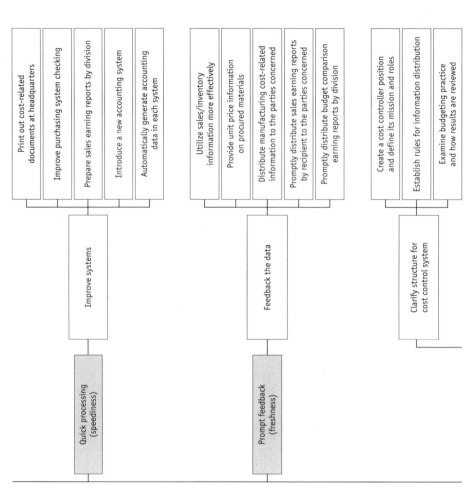

Figure 7-12. (cont.)
Strategic Information Systems (Tayca)

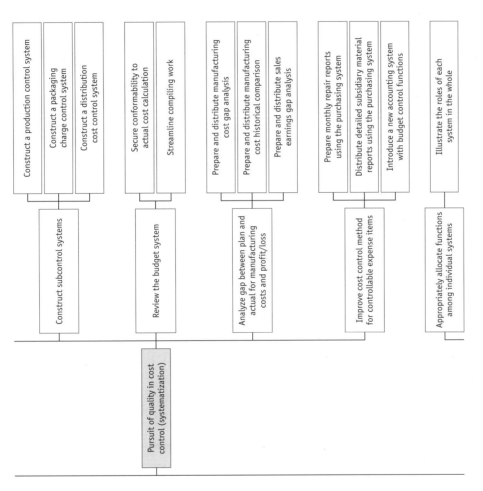

Figure 7-12. (cont.)
Strategic Information Systems (Tayca)

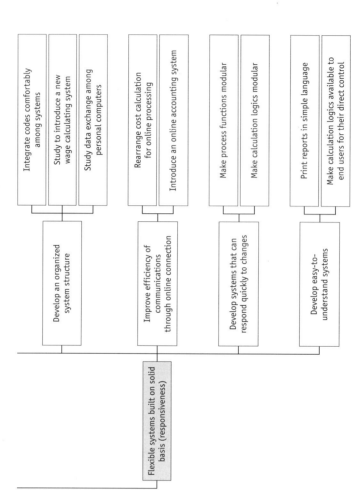

Figure 7-12. (cont.)
Strategic Information Systems (Tayca)

CAD/CAM: AN ADVANCED COMPANY'S WEAPON FOR BUSINESS STRATEGY REALIZATION

This section excerpts and presents production system improvement cases at several of the SIGMA study group member companies introduced earlier (Kansai Industrial Engineering and Management Systems Society 1993). As shown in Table 7-6, the study group analyzed cases in terms of strategy, integration, and self-organization.

Strategy here means a set of decision parameters for each customer-oriented perspective represented by the VALUE acronym (see Figure 2-4 on page 36). The idea is to develop specific measures and means for providing value to customers. In addition, *self-organization* refers to the capability of a system for organizing and evolving itself in the field of Stockless Production, TQM, automation, and so forth. Although all cases in Table 7-6 furnish much instructive information, we will focus on the first two situations here.

Case 1: Melbo Suits Company

This company developed a production system in which first-class brand suits can be made to order at prices and delivery lead times competitive with those of ready-made suit manufacturers. Orders are sent online from retail stores to factories, where suits are instantly designed for specified sizes, colors, and patterns using a special computer aided design (CAD) system developed by the company. The CAD system transforms standard designs into custom orders through a unique method that achieves a level of wearing comfort unparalleled by existing methods. Based on the CAD data, suit pieces are automatically cut by a computer aided manufacturing (CAM) system.

Sewing for Melbo isn't done by subcontractors, as is often the case in this industry in Japan. Instead, it's done in-house by integrated production lines quite similar to those in the automobile industry: different suit sizes, colors, and patterns are manufactured sequentially. To make such one-piece flow production possible, Melbo adopted various engineering approaches. For example, through the application of industrial engineering, the company shortened thread change time and improved operations and line balancing. Further, using mechanical engineering knowledge, Melbo developed various irons and sewing machines that efficiently handle different parts of suit making and automated such difficult jobs as zipper insertion. As a result of these innovations, Melbo's system enables the company to produce a mixed sequence of products (semi-custom suits) on the same line just one day after orders are received.

Table 7-6.
Advanced Production Systems: Strategy, Integration, and Self-Organization

Case	Melbo Suit	National Bicycle	Sekisui Chemical	Hewlett-Packard Japan	NSK	Takeda Chemical
STRATEGY						
Product	Suits	Sport bicycles	Prefab. houses	Electronics	Bearings	Pharmaceuticals
Market						
Status	Matured	New	Growing	Growing	Matured	Matured
Trend	Fashionable Diversified	Fashionable	Fashionable Diversified	Rapid Innovative	Diversified Reliable	Strict quality assurance (validation)
Value						
Varied needs satisfaction	Semi-order-made	Semi-order-made	Semi-order-made		Huge product lineup	
Amenity	World-class brands Just-fit	Personal design Just-fit		Cutting-edge technology		
Low risk	High quality Durability	High quality Reliability	Reliability	Reliability	Reliability	Perfect quality assurance
User costs			Cost saving by quick construction	High cost performance	Saving user design costs	
Effective availability	Delivery in two weeks	Delivery in two weeks		Short delivery lead time		
INTEGRATION						
Material flow	Integrated one-piece flow lines	Integrated one-piece flow lines	Integrated one-piece flow lines	Integrated one-piece flow lines	Flowshop lines	Continuous flow-shop lines
Information flow	Online order entry CAD/CAM	Fax order entry CAD/CAM/CAT	Design simulation CAD/CAM	CIM	CIM	FA Process control
SELF-ORGANIZATION						
Technology	Stockless production Original CAD and machines	Original information system and machines	Total productivity activities	Total quality management Original machines	Original information system and machines	Original information system and machines
Motivation	Leadership by key persons	Leadership by key persons	Leadership by key persons	Leadership by key persons	Leadership by key persons	Leadership by key persons

Case 2: National Bicycle Industries

A new production system called the Panasonic Order System (POS) was developed to create a new market for made-to-order sport bicycles, priced around ¥100,000 ($1,000). Orders are accepted at retail stores where a customer's body dimensions are measured precisely by a newly devised tool called a fitting scale. The sizes, color pattern, and customer's name are then filled in on a one-page order form and sent to the POS factory via facsimile. Finally, the order is entered into a CAD/CAM system that generates manufacturing process data.

For its POS system, this factory introduced a new one-piece flow production line separate from the existing mass production operations. The way it works is that a bar-code tag is prepared for each order. When the tag arrives at each work station, a bar-code reader scans and receives process data transmitted from the system. For example, when a bar code is scanned in the part picking area, the system activates small lamps (to assist part pickers) only on those part shelves that contain necessary parts for the order. In the pipe-cutting area, it sends tube-length data to an automatic pipe cutter. Further, in the inspection area, a three-dimensional measurement machine compares actual data with specified CAD data. When all is done, a made-to-order bicycle is manufactured and delivered within two weeks.

In closing, we can extract the following four points from the two cases just described:

1. The main strategy is to increase product value. Neither company adopted the conventional strategy of higher quality, quicker deliveries, and lower prices. Instead, they assembled their new strategies by asking their customers what functions and utilities they wanted.

2. The production system is the key and essential weapon in realizing their strategies.

3. All departments were integrated on the basis of a shared strategy.

4. Necessary technologies—managerial, informational, or industrial—were used and purposefully applied.

Improving and Maintaining Organizational Fitness

INTELLECTUAL CREATIVITY: PRACTICE IS THE KEY

So far we have discussed many aspects of building business fitness, and have looked at many improvement cases. Ultimately, the information contained between the covers of this book can be boiled down to two points:

1. *Continuous wholehearted thinking* is needed for generating new ideas. By exerting this kind of improvement effort as an organization, not just as individuals, you can accumulate new knowledge and know-how based on experience.

2. By adding such new knowledge (know-how, standards, manuals, etc.) to your existing repertoire and applying it to the next round of improvement, you can achieve good to excellent results, whether your efforts are similar to those you've made in the past or completely new and unprecedented.

Further, the idea is to continuously spiral upward through these two points. In so doing, you apply a scientific approach to your management activity. In observing client companies, I've noticed that those who do better in implementing these two points get better results.

It's important to recognize that both points require skill—skill that doesn't come automatically, but has to be developed in an organization. Wholehearted thinking, for example, calls for formalizing (standardization) or converting experience to knowledge. Unfortunately, the models developed and lessons learned from experience during standardization often do not represent anything new; they're simply the regurgitation of outdated ideas that lack originality. Even worse, sometimes organizations standardize bad experiences and failures! Of course, failure is not a bad thing if you use it to extract valuable know-how that will help you in the future. The point is that you want to develop acumen for exerting the utmost energy and creativity in your improvement activities and for capturing your newly developed improvement know-how for continued positive application.

As for enhancing and applying your new knowledge, the key is in stretching the horizon—not just applying new knowledge to the same type of situation, but applying it to entirely new areas. A good example of this is the application of principles of motion economy to developing a machining center, described in Chapter 1. In following this approach, we shouldn't expect to do well from the beginning; we need practice. Since it's virtually impossible for people who are already busy at work to find time just for practice, we need a system that allows us to practice while we get our jobs done. As we've seen, SEDAC and the P/O Matrix are just the tools for this. But like anything, the results we derive from practicing these tools are greatly influenced by the attitude and will of the people involved.

DOING THE WORK OR BEING FORCED TO DO THE WORK?

Suppose people in your company have done well not only in learning the concepts behind the P/O Matrix and SEDAC, but also in learning how to apply them. Suppose, too, they've acquired various up-to-date management technologies. Suppose even further that your company has fully built up valuable intrinsic technology.

In such a scenario, you can assume your company has excellent "offensive" and "defensive" techniques. Does this mean, however, that people understand how to use these techniques, that they are motivated and capable of using them, and that implementation is immediate and effective? Although we might be persuaded to believe this is so, the reality isn't so simple. The fact is that the accrual and use of management technology is a challenging endeavor.

Regardless of the country or the type of business or industry, people are always a big challenge; humans are complicated beings. We all know that just understanding how to use management techniques doesn't guarantee immediate and trouble-free implementation. Intrinsic technology is protected under patent because people can reproduce the same product in the same manner by obtaining its blueprint. But management technology cannot be patented. Management techniques that bring success to one company may not succeed at another. The reason for this, in a very broad sense, is simply *people*. Every company has its own unique mix and flavor of people, and therefore it's necessary for insiders to develop management technology suitable to their company's unique human profile and organizational culture.

Whether they are implementing the P/O Matrix or SEDAC, I've often observed that the attitude of senior managers makes a big difference in their success. Accomplishing almost any major undertaking, including the P/O Matrix and SEDAC, requires a fiery leader who operates out of a deep sense of mission and motivates other people to make an extra effort and surpass their previous limits.

In trying to define this special energy, a group of Sony people led by Makoto Hoshi came up with the word *passion* to characterize the company's people. The same group also began companywide education and further cultivated improvement efforts in an organized manner. The cornerstone of these education and improvement efforts is the precept that new activities are based on an understanding of human behavior and begin with the *passion* and *determination* of executives and managers. The Sony group named their model QMDEI, which stands for Quality Management through Determination, Education, and Implementation (Hoshi 1992; Sony 1992).

As Figure 8-1 shows, the purpose of QMDEI is to establish a corporate culture that continues to improve CS (customer satisfaction). For the item, "Everyone understands his/her roles and responsibilities," the Sony curriculum includes comprehensive and well-thought-out descriptions of roles, attitude, education, and implementation specifics at each level of the organization, beginning with the president. This applies not only to Sony Corporation, but also to all its group companies. In many cases, the descriptions are not new to those at a given level of the organization.

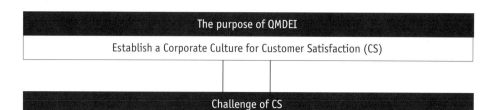

| The purpose of QMDEI |
| Establish a Corporate Culture for Customer Satisfaction (CS) |

| Challenge of CS |
| <ul><li>Work toward customer satisfaction</li><li>Everyone understands his/her roles and responsibilities</li><li>Never stop trying to achieve higher goals</li><li>Promote innovation and improvement within daily routine work to achieve CS</li><li>Prevent all defects to achieve CS</li><li>Establish a competitive and energetic organization with full employee participation</li></ul> |

Figure 8-1.
The Purpose of QMDEI (Sony Corporation)

Nevertheless, it's very significant that a large firm like Sony shares a common language with people throughout the organization.

Such common knowledge becomes effective when the DEI cycle (determination, education, implementation) is deployed, as shown in Figure 8-2. As the description of *determination* suggests, a cycle of awareness begins to turn when individuals at all levels recognize and become convinced that their actions are the key to changing the status quo of the company. At Sony, the corporate quality and reliability department is leading the transfer of QMDEI from its Japanese plants and divisions to plants and group companies in other countries. The hope is that some participants will further develop their management technology in a way that generates a passion most suitable to their own environment.

Finally, Figure 8-3 (page 222) shows how DEI fits in with the P/O Matrix and SEDAC at Sony.

GOOD MAINTENANCE AMPLIFIES IMPROVEMENT RESULTS

Table 8-1 (page 223) lists the steps of improvement implementation and relates them to roles of the P/O Matrix, SEDAC, and Window Analysis in supporting each step. Of course, this table is not an exhaustive list, as many more management techniques are available to support specific improvement efforts.

The ninth step of the table says "Maintain good results by adhering to standards." In his book *Kaizen,* Masaaki Imai writes about daily management (Imai 1988) and alludes to the need for finding out if standards exist

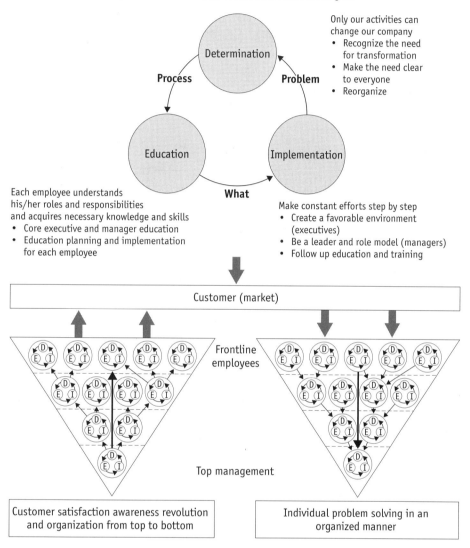

To be recognized as the worldwide standard for customer satisfaction, we must identify problems in the existing situation. We must persistently promote the DEI cycle in line with future strategies.

Only our activities can change our company
- Recognize the need for transformation
- Make the need clear to everyone
- Reorganize

Determination

Process

Problem

Education

Implementation

What

Each employee understands his/her roles and responsibilities and acquires necessary knowledge and skills
- Core executive and manager education
- Education planning and implementation for each employee

Make constant efforts step by step
- Create a favorable environment (executives)
- Be a leader and role model (managers)
- Follow up education and training

Customer (market)

Frontline employees

Top management

Customer satisfaction awareness revolution and organization from top to bottom

Individual problem solving in an organized manner

Figure 8-2.
DEI Cycle Deployment

and, if they do, reviewing them for appropriateness. If standards do not exist, you need to develop them. If they do exist, you need to find out whether people adhere to them and, if they do not, train and discipline people to do so.

While SEDAC is a specific tool that addresses the first part of this point (whether standards exist), it's equally important to address the second part of the point (whether standards are followed). As we explored

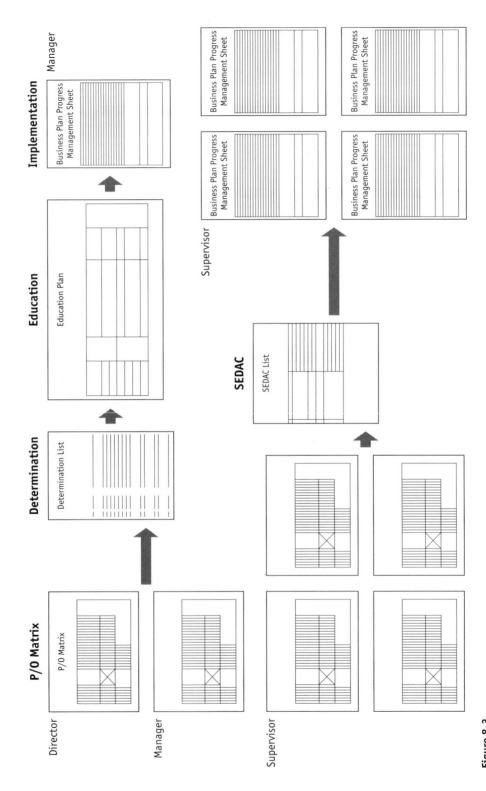

Figure 8-3.
Relationship of SEDAC and DEI

Table 8-1.
Improvement Implementation Steps and Management Techniques

Major Steps of Improvement	Management Techniques
1. Identify what to improve and clarify specifics	P/O Matrix
2. Determine how to measure improvement results	Policy/objective deployment, policy management, management by objectives
3. Decide the target, duration, leader, and members	
4. Analyze problems and data → Extract information for improvement	Seven QC tools, seven new QC tools, Window Analysis, SQC, IE
5. Generate improvement ideas	Brainstorming and other idea generation methods
6. Develop and test counter-measures to see results	SEDAC
7. Standardize contents that produce good results	
8. Expand improvement efforts into areas formerly considered "unknowable" and "unavoidable"	Reliability engineering
9. Maintain good results by adhering to standards	Daily management, supervision, control charts, visual management

in Chapter 6 on Window Analysis, you must ask whether standards are followed and look at what kind of management system you have.

To further elaborate this point, consider quality management. In Japan and elsewhere, improvements spurred by quality management are popular. At many conferences, presenters talk about how they've used a particular method to improve quality. What's interesting is how rare it is for people to share the details of how they're maintaining their good current status.

Use of Control Charts for Process Control

Many readers are familiar with the use of control charts for process control. When current standards are appropriate and consistently practiced, the control chart shows that the process is statistically in control. For this reason, this section introduces a sample SEDAC application that includes both quality improvement and maintenance through the effective utilization of control charts. Discussing this sample SEDAC application entails explaining why SEDAC has evolved to the point where it includes the features described in Table 3-1 and Figure 3-3.

When I began my search for process control methods, I had high expectations for using control charts for process control. In retrospect, I recognize that I was confused about the function of a control chart. My original confusion can be summarized as follows:

- First, a control chart is used to monitor a statistically in-control condition of individual factors (causes) within a process. However, I wanted to use the control chart as an improvement tool on a process outcome (effect). This meant that when process outcome data showed an abnormality, I attempted to improve the process by taking actions.

- Further, when I applied a control chart, I tried to use it on the process outcome (e.g., product A's quality characteristics, line B's yield, equipment C's failure rate, etc.)—even though the causal factors of the outcome were unknown.

Essentially, I learned that it was impossible to identify specific causes and take action on the process using a control chart in the manner I have just described. Because of this, I couldn't make good use of control charts. After considering their nature, I realized that their shortcomings were inherent in their original purpose. Still, I struggled with the limitations of control charts for a long time and didn't understand them while engaged in the thick of production.

Back in those days, I often wished that some higher being would highlight the exact cause on the cause-and-effect diagram among the countless possibilities that seemed scattered like stars in the universe. From the perspective of Window Analysis, discussed in Chapter 6, it becomes clear that it's logically impossible to specify the cause and take corrective action based on detection of an abnormality on a control chart.

Applying Window Analysis, suppose you determine that a quality defect is a category D problem. Since this implies finding a cause from a yet-to-be-developed method, it's impossible to find such a cause. In the case of category C, a cause has to be identified among information that has not been communicated. If it's a careless category B mistake, then it's unreasonable to expect the person who made the mistake to be aware of the cause. In each of these Window Analysis categories, then, it's difficult if not impossible to identify causes.

Once I was making these points at a seminar in Italy when a gentleman from Pirelli interrupted me. He said, "But I can think of possible causes when a control chart indicates abnormality." Indeed we can. Back then, we too thought of possible causes when out-of-control situations occurred. Although we couldn't pinpoint the specific cause that contributed to abnormality on the control chart, this didn't mean we stood with our arms folded, doing nothing. Naturally, the people involved—first-line employees, supervisors, staff, and managers—took actions based on their best estimations.

When we think of possible causes of a problem, we draw on our experience accumulated over time, judgments based on intrinsic technology and on-site observations. Since we're not amateurs at our jobs, we can usually infer several possible causes, even though we might not be able to pinpoint them scientifically. In some cases, these causes lead not only to actions for reducing control chart dispersion, but also to actions that further improve quality characteristics. In terms of SEDAC, these possible causes take the form of problem cards.

Historically, quality control in Japan has actually meant quality improvement. Although people track quality characteristics on a control chart, they are often more concerned with making changes for the better than for just keeping the chart "in control." For each estimated cause, they develop countermeasures and test them to see how they affect the control chart. Measures that bring positive results are then standardized for continued adherence and maintenance of the good situation. This process is similar to SEDAC, where improvement cards are followed by standard cards.

SEDAC on a cause-and-effect diagram, in fact, grew out of the process just described. It is important to understand that SEDAC represents a reversal of the cause-effect direction. Rather than waiting for changes to occur on the effect side and then looking for causes on the cause side, SEDAC deliberately changes causes in an effort to observe their impact on effects. Such a shift empowers people to initiate the search for knowledge on their own rather than waiting until a serious problem forces them to do so.

Living Control Charts

In Chapter 3 I mentioned that most SEDACs that were successful in achieving their targets had seven or more standard cards. Of course, the number of standard cards a SEDAC has is a function of card content and target difficulty level. For this reason, the number seven is only a general yardstick. When standard cards address operational procedures and technical standards, the standardization process concludes by revising or adding procedures and standards to existing ones. In the case of equipment and jig improvement, standardization means not only making changes to respective parts, but also developing a manual to guide future inspection and maintenance.

The content of a standard card is closely related to a control chart for process control. Suppose that through trial and error we discover that process control items such as temperature, concentration, and part quality characteristics must be kept within certain ranges to maintain a product's quality characteristics. Control charts may be used, therefore, to monitor temperature, concentration, and part quality characteristic process indicators. In such a case, the concern is to monitor the process by making sure that individual process indicator data remains within control limits and that data samples continuously indicate a statistically in-control situation. For this purpose, control charts are very effective. This is true even during activities to improve a product's outcome quality indicator; maintaining good process conditions by adhering to established standards is extremely important in maximizing the effect of new countermeasures.

Research supports this point. Figure 8-4 shows results of a study on quality defect reduction based on 86 SEDAC applications (Fukuda 1978). The SEDAC teams were stratified into two groups—one that succeeded in finding new methods (improvements to category D of Window Analysis) and one that focused their efforts only on adhering to established standards (category B and C improvements). Data showed that it was more effective to reduce quality defects by finding new methods than by simply retraining and ensuring adherence to existing standards. However, when the group that found new methods was further stratified into two subgroups—one that had always adhered closely to established standards and one that had always been weak in adherence—a significant different in the results was revealed. Another analysis in the same article revealed that the subgroup with better adherence had a higher success rate in finding new methods. Thus, while adherence to existing standards may not be as effective as finding new methods, it increases the chance of discovering new methods and contributes to maximizing their effects.

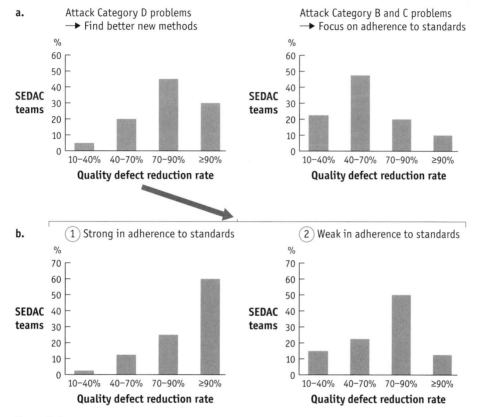

Figure 8-4.
Correlation Between Ability to Find New Methods and Strong Adherence to Standards

Figure 8-5 (page 228) is an example of the effective use of control charts for enhancing an improvement effort. The SEDAC in Figure 8-5 is an improvement project for reducing sintered alloy product height defects. The manufacturing processes are numbered from 1, pulverization, to 6, surface treatment. As you can see, this project already produced six standard cards and progressed to the status of an improvement effort before achieving its target. (In this example, standard cards have been moved to the top of the effect side for easier identification.)

One of the standard cards specifies height limits for molded workpieces before sintering, while another states treatment solution concentration limits. For each of these process indicators, data was collected and confirmed within the respective specification limits. Then a control chart was constructed for each set of data. As a result, both process indicators were monitored on control charts to make sure data points stayed within control limits.

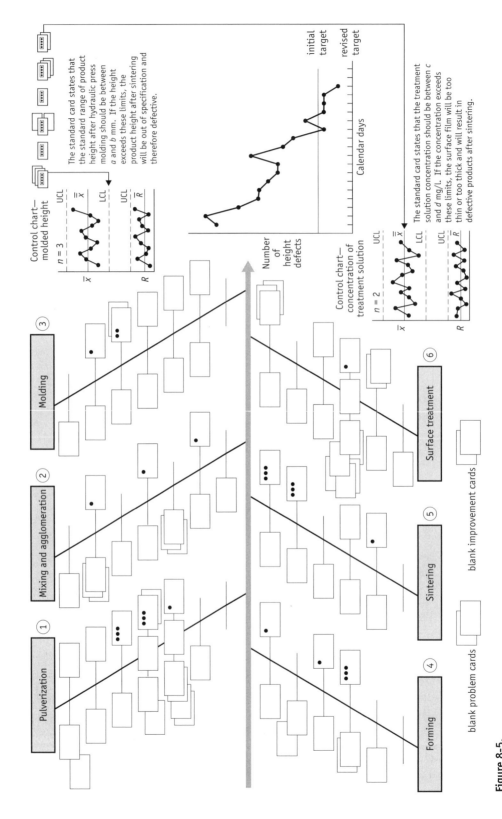

The standard card states that the standard range of product height after hydraulic press molding should be between *a* and *b* mm. If the height exceeds these limits, the product height after sintering will be out of specification and therefore defective.

The standard card states that the treatment solution concentration should be between *c* and *d* mg/L. If the concentration exceeds these limits, the surface film will be too thin or too thick and will result in defective products after sintering.

blank problem cards

blank improvement cards

Figure 8-5.
Height Defect Reduction of Sintered Alloy Products

Having made these charts, we know why the data points of molded workpieces (pre-sintering and post-hydraulic press process) fall outside control limits: the quantity of powdered metal varies when it's mechanically fed into the mold through the chute. Therefore, when this out-of-control situation occurs, we know we have to take the following corrective actions:

- Check the previous process—agglomeration—to see if the standard operations are being performed. It's likely that the particles of powdered material are not made in such a way as to form the specified distribution curve.

- Another likely cause is clogging or deformation of the automatic material feeding mechanism in the molding process. To investigate this, it's necessary to review how the equipment has been checked and maintained. By doing this, you identify the cause and restore the unit to its previously stable condition.

TRUST AND EVERYDAY CHECKING CAN GO HAND IN HAND

An increasing number of companies are applying for ISO 9000 series quality standard certification. At the time of this writing, more than 700 Japanese companies have been certified (PL Research Group 1992). It seems these companies are maturing by improving and maintaining their quality practices through institutionalizing the required ISO 9000 internal audits. At this pace, the ISO 9000 certification audit will probably become the norm in a few years, for many companies around the world. In light of this trend, this section focuses on what we can learn from ISO 9000 rather than on the certification process itself.

In 1991, the ISO 9000 series came to life as the definitive set of international standards for quality processes in various types of companies. In actuality, many companies have already achieved levels much higher than what ISO 9000 requires. Even for these companies, however, it's wise to take advantage of ISO 9000 to further strengthen quality control and assurance practices.

In light of this, I recommend that companies ask themselves the following three ISO questions:

1. Do you have an established standard for this matter? Show me.

2. Do you have evidence that the standard is correctly adhered to? Show me.

3. On a day-to-day basis, what do you use to manage and make sure the standard is reliable and adhered to? Show me.

For people who are not involved in work processes covered by ISO 9000, the same three questions can be asked in a daily management context.

For most Japanese companies, the question about adhering to standards correctly is particularly difficult; it seems many companies take considerable shortcuts in this area. The following example from several years ago should shed some light on this negative tendency. When I was a quality assurance manager for a division of Sumitomo Electric, quality was not improving, despite our wishes. When asked why, all general managers and people in charge of quality assurance at the six division plants gave us model, politically correct answers. Still, quality didn't improve.

Finally, with concurrence of the division general manger, we initiated a practice called *QA patrol,* which we conducted for a year and a half during the latter half of my three-year tenure as division quality assurance manager. We formed a QA patrol team of five people and visited a plant for five days of every month. In the spirit of helping our customers, the team would walk around the plant and point out instances in which standards were not followed.

While we were conducting the QA patrol, people sometimes confronted me, saying, "You often talk about management by trust. Why, then, are you checking on us? Don't you trust us?" My response was, "We trust your motivation to do your job right. However, human behavior is often unreliable, and we want to help you do your job right by discovering these behaviors."

What we learned from this experience is that when people say, "something must be done," often it isn't. This doesn't mean that people did nothing; rather, it means they did 80 or 90 percent of what needed to be done. If we compare this situation with catching fish in a net, it means we're trying to catch the "quality defect and complaint fish" with a net that has a 10 to 20 percent hole. Should we be surprised that some of our problem fish always escape?

Of course, we took this situation seriously: we felt that without making the hole smaller, whatever we did would be in vain. To get our feet on solid ground, then, we made it a point to develop an understanding of what we needed to do to close the hole in the net.

Since the QA patrol team was the surrogate customer, the plant was obliged to respond with countermeasures to the team's findings within one month. When the team found countermeasures to be too superficial, or beyond the plant's capability to follow through, it returned them to the plant for further refinement. With the team insisting on its status as customer, this QA patrol practice went on for a year and a half, during which time the division experienced remarkable improvements in its quality performance.

Later, Sendai Nikon and other client companies adopted this practice. Conducting the QA patrol practice in a similar manner, they too have experienced positive results. This shows that it's possible for company insiders to identify and rectify their own weaknesses. For this reason, I support a regular internal audit as a part of ISO 9000 series standards implementation, even if it differs somewhat from the QA patrol method I have described.

Some people argue that the ISO 9000 series doesn't really contribute to quality improvement. My position is that, by devising a way to conduct an effective internal audit, you can produce good results. The necessary attitude is to rely only on what you can affirm through walking the walk, not just talking the talk.

The lessons learned from my QA patrol experience also contributed to my later defining the Window Analysis subdivision of *established*—*practiced* and *unpracticed*—at the 100 percent level. Furthermore, since we're requiring people to adhere to standards at 100 percent, the content of these standards has to be worth following. The need for worthwhile and reliable standards, then, becomes a starting point for SEDAC development.

Although the element of "improvement" was not included in the initial ISO 9000 series, it was added later in ISO 9004-4, a guidance standard. Whether or not improvement is explicitly mentioned in the certification standards, I believe the improvement concept is implied there because standards do result from improvements. When adherence to standards is required, it's not hard to visualize improvement efforts in the background.

Table 8-2 is a simple comparison between management techniques discussed in this book and ISO 9002 requirements. By observing clients that have already received ISO 9000 certification, my conclusion is that they would pass the audit as long as they are doing the right things right—which means correctly implementing the P/O Matrix, SEDAC, or whatever systems they may follow.

CAUTIONS IN USING SEDAC

This book has covered the use of the P/O Matrix and SEDAC as an effective system for companywide transformation and improvement. Of course, many management techniques are available around the world, and each has its own features and strengths. By all means, these should be used as needed. Neither the P/O Matrix nor SEDAC encourages readers to discard whatever management systems or techniques you are currently using in favor of these. Rather, the P/O Matrix and SEDAC should work together with other techniques for the mutual strengthening of both. I encourage you to further improve the application of the P/O Matrix and SEDAC in any way you can. After all, this is how science and technology should evolve anyway. In anticipation of such further development, I would like to point out a few cautions in using SEDAC.

The first caution is both positive and negative. As I've said, SEDAC allows simultaneous implementation of multiple improvement ideas. This contrasts with the conventional QC approach that encourages team members to analyze a quality problem, specify the root cause, and take countermeasures against the cause. While this approach is certainly scientific, quality problems are rarely the result of a single cause. Since the SEDAC approach encourages people to take many actions concurrently, it's very effective in fixing quality problems. This is good because, often, the causes of problems get so intertwined and interdependent over time that they have to be addressed simultaneously.

On the other hand, it's often difficult to determine how much each individual SEDAC countermeasure contributes to results. In response to this, I often say, half-jokingly, "Wouldn't you rather be in the position of not knowing how you got better than not knowing how to get better?" Nevertheless, this difficulty in ascribing weight to specific SEDAC countermeasures can be a limitation.

If clients really want to find out how much each countermeasure contributes to results, I encourage them to design an in-plant experiment to

Table 8-2.
ISO 9002* and P/O Matrix, SEDAC, and Other Methods

Interpretation of ISO 9002 requirements	Useful techniques	ISO 9000
1. Top and First-line Management Responsibility, Authority, and Linkage Management defines quality policy, including objectives and responsibility to build in quality and ensure everyone understands, implements, and maintains the quality policy. (1) Initiate action to prevent the occurrence of any quality-related nonconformances, (2) Identify and record any quality problems, (3) Lead (initiate, recommend, or provide) all relevant personnel for solutions, (4) Verify the implementation of solutions and [(5) Standardize solutions that produced good results]	P/O Matrix SEDAC	4.1 Management Responsibility 4.1.1 Quality Policy 4.1.2.1 Responsibility and Authority
2. Quality Control on Processes Ensure processes that directly affect quality are carried out under controlled conditions. Controlled conditions include: (1) documented procedures defining the manner of production and where the absence of such procedures could adversely affect quality, (2) documented procedures for use of suitable equipment and suitable maintenance of equipment, (3) full everyday compliance with these procedures and (4) quality of products built in during the process meets the specified requirements.	SEDAC Window Analysis	4.9 Process Control
3. Corrective and Preventive Action Corrective and preventive action and documentation for quality nonconformance. (1) Handling of product nonconformances (2) Temporary action on the process (3) Investigation into causes and taking permanent action on the process (prevention of recurrence) (4) Preventive action on the process (prevention by prediction) (5) Actions on products in the market (recall if necessary)	SEDAC FMEA SEDAC	4.14 Corrective and Preventive Action
4. Internal Quality Audits Verify whether quality activities and related results comply with planned arrangements and determine the effectiveness of the quality system. (1) Quality audits are carried out by personnel independent of those having direct responsibility for the activity under audit. (2) Management personnel responsible for the area take timely corrective action on deficiencies found during the audit.	QA audits (QA Patrol) Window Analysis	4.17 Internal Quality Audits

*ISO 9002 is the quality systems model for quality assurance in production, installation, and servicing.

confirm their individual impacts. However, once people have achieved good results, they don't usually bother to identify the cause or figure out how much each of multiple causes contributed to the overall results. So, the concern remains that SEDAC might include unnecessary counter-measures. Before implementation, SEDAC users should develop the habit of considering each countermeasure carefully from an engineering per-spective to be sure it has a positive impact on the result.

A second caution about SEDAC I would like to point out is that, even though SEDAC is a simple method, results depend highly on how people apply it. Actually, this boils down to the third of the seven fast-track con-ditions discussed in Chapter 1: superior managing capabilities. As I have emphasized throughout the book, the commitment and understanding of executives and managers make a big difference in the results.

A third caution is the physical aspect of using SEDAC. Cards on a SEDAC wall chart tend to fall off. Space for posting a SEDAC may not be available. The contents of SEDAC cards may include confidential information that cannot be displayed where outsiders might see. Further, SEDAC cannot be brought into a cleanroom or dust-free workplace.

Other SEDAC cautions are people-related. Some employees can't write or read cards. Some speak only foreign languages. Others are reluc-tant to initial their cards for fear of being exposed or checked up on. Further, sometimes too much authority is vested in the SEDAC leader, or the organization lacks suitable SEDAC leaders.

Some of these problems can be overcome with a little creativity. If falling cards are an issue, you can write the information directly on the chart according to the rules of SEDAC card writing. For those who can't write, SEDAC leaders and subleaders can write cards for them. Even the language barrier can be overcome when people are motivated by the activity. For example, the employees of Sony Germany spoke 21 different languages. Nevertheless, as Figure 1-6 showed, Sony Germany has achieved remarkable results. If there is a will to succeed with SEDAC, there is a way.

AGENDA FOR MANAGEMENT TECHNOLOGY

Continuing to Develop Capabilities

"When I go to write something on a card, it's already in my head. Should I still be required to write it on a card?" It seems there are very smart people all over the world, because I occasionally get this question in Japan and overseas.

You get an idea in your head first, and a card is just a piece of paper to record it, of course. Since cards functions like memos, cards adopted as standards should be incorporated into existing standards by adding to them or revising them. Whether technical or administrative, the basic material for reliable standards comes from know-how (standard cards) that has been obtained through improvement activities.

Whatever the future may bring, people and companies will still be engaged in the effort to improve the quality of our work, products, and services. More specifically, these efforts exist to develop and accumulate knowledge to do our jobs better (category D improvement of Window Analysis), to create better flows of information (category C improvement), and to strengthen our will and ability to do the job right (category B improvement). Clearly, these efforts are expected to grow in importance rather than weaken.

The disposition people must have to succeed is a sense of responsibility and a proclivity for sincere work, mutual trust, integrity, and the notion that it is a virtue to work hard to be better. Also, people should maintain the habit of reaching out and showing compassion when team members need help in their work.

Whenever a system or practice might negatively affect the disposition just described, thoughtful consideration is required. Whether this impact is direct or indirect, once this positive disposition is lost, it's extremely difficult to restore.

Clearly, the reader should not think that I'm encouraging people to become extreme company devotees. Even among so-called company devotees, the above qualities are often lacking.

In this vein, I want to clarify what *total participation* really means. When I used this expression at a management conference in Italy, a listener in the audience raised his hand and said, "Italy is a free country. Therefore, it's impossible to expect total employee participation." Since the gentleman certainly brought up an understandable concern, I drew the picture shown in Figure 8-6 to illustrate my response.

From my experience in working closely with excellent companies, I've observed the following. Suppose it takes four people to row a boat. One person (or 25 percent) is working very hard on improvement activities, breaking a sweat to move things forward. Two people (50 percent) are moving along with the first person by moderately working on

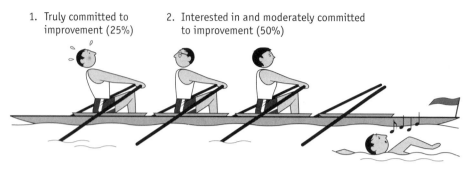

1. Truly committed to improvement (25%) 2. Interested in and moderately committed to improvement (50%)

3. Uncommitted to improvement (25%)

Figure 8-6.
A Boat and Four People

improvement activities. The other person (25 percent) isn't really working or participating in improvement activities at all. In this scenario, I stressed that the most important point is that executives and managers should be among the first 25 percent—those working up a sweat.

Please don't misunderstand. My intention is not to debunk the target of total participation. I merely point out that you don't have to have *100 percent* participation to be successful. So, using various examples, I told the man that if he could achieve a similar level of participation in his company, he too could expect great success. He responded that if that kind of total participation was okay, his company could do it.

If the perception outside Japan is that Japanese companies are doing well because all their employees are working extremely hard, this is regrettable. First of all, it's not true. Also, such a perception creates alienation with the rest of the world thinking the Japanese are too strange to work with. In any event, I don't think it's healthy for any management culture to operate in a monolithic environment that doesn't accept any differences.

Instituting Simplicity and Ease

Since management techniques are meant to be used every day, they must be as simple as possible, like a farming tool with no frills. If it's not simple, it's not practical for use. For example, one time we attempted to use different colored cards for subcategories of SEDAC problem cards: causes, symptoms, obstacles, and questions. For Window Analysis, we tried a cubic window with a Z axis in addition to the X and Y. Such innovations are typically enjoyed by those who create them and even make them feel they've made the techniques more sophisticated. Yet when we attempted to use these complicated innovations, we didn't find them helpful in making our jobs easier. If we hadn't been aware of this and instead forced people to use these complicated tools, we would have ended up arguing about minor and unessential details.

Whether it's the P/O Matrix, SEDAC, or Window Analysis, readers are welcome to further refine these techniques by using their ingenuity to add new applications and ideas. It is my hope, however, that new features will be only those that can intrinsically make the techniques better and easier, not harder to use. Further, it's especially important for staff people to avoid creating complicated, elaborate, paper-based tools and imposing them on the line organization.

Making the judgment as to whether such changes and modifications are helpful is not so difficult. If the people making the changes are the only ones who can use them, the answer should be obvious. Above all, management techniques such as QC and IE should be warm enough not to threaten the people who have to use them.

Vitalizing the Suggestion System

Many companies have systems for rewarding workplace improvement suggestions (ideas) from employees. Companies often track the number of suggestions per employee per year. SEDAC activities usually increase the number of suggestions considerably. In general, ideas contributed through the SEDAC process are subjects for reward as follows:

- Improvement cards with one red dot for idea (primary) award

- Improvement cards with green box around three red dots for result (secondary) award

In addition to providing a framework that facilitates idea generation, SEDAC also expands the range of ideas. Under a traditional suggestion system, ideas are mostly focused on improving certain parts of equipment, jigs, and so forth—what Window Analysis would call category D improvements that increase knowledge of intrinsic technologies. SEDAC, on the other hand, draws out improvement suggestions in categories B and C as well, raising ideas related to communication and adherence to standards. Thus SEDAC works not only to increase the number of suggestions, but also to meet the needs of the organization, since most companies have far more problems in categories B and C than in category D.

TOMORROW

Direction of Changes

In this book, I have introduced many examples where companies achieved remarkable results through their improvement/transformation activities. The underlying management philosophy for these activities has been respect for people.

As I defined in the preface, I have discussed technology in two broad categories: (1) intrinsic technology, which refers to the essential techniques and methods for conducting work and achieving tasks, and (2) management technology, which refers to the techniques and methods for improving the quality or quantity of tasks. Through my experience in working with many companies in their use of management technology, I learned that high morale of the people involved is the necessary prerequisite for success.

Unless people have the aspiration to make the quality or quantity of their work output better tomorrow than today, management technology can do little for them. As discussed in the previous section, people cannot succeed without a sense of responsibility and a proclivity for sincere work, mutual trust, integrity, and the notion that it is a virtue to work hard to be better. Undoubtedly, these factors will continue to be necessary conditions for a company's sustained success for many years to come. Moreover, developing this disposition is an organization does not happen overnight; it requires continued genuine efforts over time.

As introduced in this book, the P/O Matrix is an effective management methodology for improvement/transformation. The P/O Matrix enables companies to translate their priority issues into their employees' day-to-day business activities. The P/O Matrix also facilitates cross-functional cooperation beyond departmental walls, which have often been considered obstacles for improvement in the past. Furthermore, in its development process, the P/O Matrix encourages companies to examine what core competitive strengths they currently possess and to identify what competencies they should develop for their future success.

On the other hand, SEDAC is effective for idea generation through capitalizing on individual team members' diverse advantages. SEDAC also encourages companies to develop a habit of wholeheartedly thinking through problems and their causes. Furthermore, SEDAC helps them routinely extract and build up new knowledge from their improvement activities.

Both the P/O Matrix and SEDAC are simple methods that everyone can use, and one of their main features is their visibility. By looking at a P/O Matrix and SEDAC in action, the users can share necessary information for their improvement activities. Using P/O Matrix and SEDAC application examples, I also discussed how to accelerate the speed of improvement.

This book included many examples from Japanese and Western companies. While working with these companies, I have paid more attention to the commonalities between Japanese and non-Japanese companies than to their differences.

As readers have seen, the P/O Matrix and SEDAC have been successfully applied in both Japanese and non-Japanese companies with quite different management systems. As we've seen throughout this book, American as well as European (mainly Italian) companies have achieved excellent results. The data shared here about such results, by the way, have been provided and approved by participating companies, not by this author.

As mentioned earlier, Timken's Bucyrus, Ohio, plant was recognized in 1992 as one of the best plants for achievements made through the application of the P/O Matrix and SEDAC. As we know, nothing is completely impervious to exception. In the case of the P/O Matrix and SEDAC, however, data indicate that success is the rule, not the exception—especially when we add the successes of many other U.S. companies whose applications have not been published here.

Such-and-Such Management Japonica

Each nation has its own economic and social systems, and we can't really say one is right or superior. Nations are simply different. In this sense, Japan is not any more different from other countries than they are from each other. Each country is its own unique entity.

When people focus on differences, any management system developed outside one's own country doesn't seem to be relevant. This is especially true when discussions take place in a vacuum. It's like sitting at a desk and worrying about a few millimeters of difference in fittings. In hypothetical space, nothing seems to work; you have to get out there in reality and put your ideas to work.

In conclusion, I offer the following. Suppose one management technique is developed in one country, say, Japan. Based on its origin, you could call it *such-and-such management Japonica*, as one might name a species of plant. Like a plant, it's really not strange for this brand of management to flourish in other parts of the world, especially when the environment is right or when it's fostered with proper care. During this growing process, subspecies or mutant varieties may develop, as when an improved version is developed for a particular country's or company's environment. As I have demonstrated here, the necessary attitude for such development of transformative management is to constantly learn from one's own everyday reality and to create something better on one's own.

According to the laws of aerodynamics, bumblebees cannot fly, reads a plaque on the wall of one CEO. The truth is that, although we can't explain it, *bumblebees can fly.* The challenge for all of us, then, is to have an open-minded attitude that pushes us always to search for answers and find a better way—even when it seems the odds are stacked against us.

Got weary of reading *Sun Zi*** at the window,
Rain mildly knocks cherry blossoms outside the window.

— Tomosaburo Nakao

---

* *Sun Zi* is the oldest Chinese book on war tactics.

REFERENCES

Chapter 1

Dimancescu, Dan. 1994. Gekitekini Susunda America Seizogyono Seihinkakushin (Dramatic Advancement of American Manufacturers' Product Innovations). *Management* 21, 4, no. 5:20.

Fuse, Masayoshi. 1982. Kanrigijyutsu to Keieikannri Shiensisutem (Management Technology and Business Management Support Systems). *Sumitomo Denko IE Brief* 7-1:5–7.

Hasegawa, Keitaro. 1993. *Choshitugyo (Ultra-bankruptcy)*. Tokuma Shoten, 225.

Kawakita, Jiro. 1993. *Sozoto Dento (Creation and Tradition)*. Shoudensha, 51.

Kitagawa, Kazue. 1994. *Sozoteki Hakaino Seishin (The Spirit of Creative Destruction)*. Nihon Keizai Shimbun.

Kondo, Yoshio. 1993. *Zenshateki Hinshitsukanri (Total Quality Management)*. JUSE Press, 203.

Chapter 2

Akiba, Masao. 1994. *TP Manegimentono Susumekata (Implementation of Total Productivity Management)*. Japan Management Association Management Center.

Hosoyamada, Noriko. 1992. Deming 14 Points—Dr. Deming no Seminani Sankashite (Observations and Impressions of Dr. Deming's Seminar). *Hinshitsukanri* 43, no. 11:59.

Ishikawa, Kaoru. 1981. *Kanrigijutsu Poketto Jiten (A Concise Dictionary of Management Technologies)*. JUSE Press.

Kansai Industrial Engineering and Management Systems Society. 1993. *Senryakuteki Togo Seisankanri Sisutemu "SIGMA" (Strategic Integration for Greater Market Adaptability)*. Nikkan Kogyo Shimbun, 13–15.

Kondo, Shuji. 1981. *Shinseihin Shinjigyo Tansakuho (New Product, New Business: A Method for Investigation)*. Japan Management Association (JMA), 90.

Senjyu, Shizuo. 1986. *Yasashii Keizaiseikogakuno Hanashi (An Easy-to-Understand Story of Engineering Economy)*. JMA.

Tamura, Shoichi. 1987. *Ohanashi Hoshin Kanri (A Story of Policy Management)*. Japanese Standards Association (JSA), 46, 60.

Toshiba Corporation. 1977. *Mokuhyokanrino Shinko (Management by Objectives in Depth)*. Aobashuppan.

Chapter 3

Ishikawa, Kaoru. 1981. *Kanrigijutsu Poketto Jiten (A Concise Dictionary of Management Technologies)*. JUSE Press.

Chapter 4

Kawakita, Jiro. 1967. *Hassoho (A Method for Idea Generation)*. Chuokoronsha.

Tanaka, Yoshiaki, and Yuji Nakazono. 1988. *Sozoryoku Kakushin no Kenkyu (A Study of Creativity Development)*. JMA, 124.

Chapter 5

Billinton, R., and R. N. Allan. 1983. *Reliability Evaluation of Engineering Systems*. Pitman Publishing Inc.

Bloch, Arthur. 1977. *Murphy's Law*. Los Angeles: Price/Stern/Sloan Publishers, 11.

Feigenbaum, Armand V. 1991. *Total Quality Control*, third ed., revised. New York: McGraw-Hill.

JMA. 1983. *Howaitokarano Seisansei (White-collar Productivity)*. JMA.

JMA. 1993. *Reengineering ga wakaruhon (Easy-to-Understand Reengineering)*. Japan Management Association Management Center, 213.

Kapur, K. C., and L. R. Lamberson. 1977. *Reliability in Engineering Design*. New York: John Wiley & Sons.

Kobayashi, Tadashi. 1992. *Topputo Keieikanbunotameno DIPS (DIPS for Executives)*. PHP Kenkyujo.

Kobayashi, Tadashi. 1993. *DIPS towa Nanika (What Is DIPS?)*. PHP Kenkyujo.

Koshikawa, Uekusa, and Murata. 1982. *Jitsumuni Suguyakudatsu Shinraisei-gijutsu (Practical Reliability Engineering)*. Nikkan Kogyo Shimbun, 47.

Makabe, Hajime. 1966. *Weibull Kakuritsushi no Tsukaikata (How to Use the Weibull Probability Paper)*. Japan Standards Association (JSA).

Merli, Giorgio. 1991. *Total Quality Management*. ISEDI.

Nakajima, Seiichi, ed. 1989. *TPM Development Program*. Portland, Ore.: Productivity Press (based on *Seisan Kakushinno tameno TPM Tenkai Puroguramu*. JIPM, 1982).

Okada, Mikio. 1993. *Gijyutsushano Chiteki Seisansei Kojo (Intellectual Productivity Improvement for Engineers)*. Japan Management Association Management Center.

Ozeki, Kazuo, and Tetsuichi Asaka. 1990. *Handbook of Quality Tools: The Japanese Approach*. Portland, Ore.: Productivity Press, 195 et seq.

Shakespeare, William. *Hamlet*. I, ii, 72.

Shiomi, Shimaoka, and Ishiyama. 1983. *FMEA, FTA no Katsuyo (Effective Use of FMEA and FTA)*. JUSE Press.

Shirose, Kunio, Yoshifumi Kimura, and Mitsugu Kaneda. 1995. *P-M Analysis: An Advanced Step in TPM Implementation*. Portland, Ore.: Productivity Press.

Suzuki, Tokutaro, ed. 1992. *New Directions for TPM*. Portland, Ore.: Productivity Press (based on *TPM no Shintennkai*, JIPM, 1989).

Uchimaru, Kiyoshi, Susumu Okamoto, and Bunteru Kurahara. 1993. *TQM for Technical Groups: Total Quality Principles for Product Development*. Portland, Ore.: Productivity Press (based on *Gijyutsushudanno TQC*, JUSE Press, 1990).

Chapter 7

Ford, Henry. 1988. *Today and Tomorrow*. Portland, Ore.: Productivity Press (originally published by Doubleday, Page & Co., 1926).

Fukuda, Ryuji. 1983. Kannrigijyutsu sono Renshuno Susume (Management Technology Practice). *Journal of the Japanese Society for Machinery* 86, no. 775:582.

IE Application Study Group, Kansai Industrial Engineering and Management Systems Society. 1986. *Stockless Seisan (Stockless Production)*. Nikkan Kogyo Shimbun.

Kansai Industrial Engineering and Management Systems Society. 1993. *Senryakuteki Togo Seisankanri Sisutemu "SIGMA" (Strategic Integration for Greater Market Adaptability)*. Nikkan Kogyo Shimbun.

Research Group for Management Systems Technology. 1989. *CIM Keieikodokano tameni (CIM for Higher Business Management)*. Nikkan Kogyo Shimbun.

Shingo, Shigeo. 1965. *Kikaihaichi Kaizenno Giho (Improvement Techniques for Machine Layout)*. Nikkan Kogyo Shimbun.

Shingo, Shigeo. 1988. *Nonstock Production*. Portland, Ore.: Productivity Press (based on *Non-sutokku seisan hoshiki e no tenkai: Toyota seisan shisutemo no shin no igi*. Japan Management Association, 1987).

Yoshida, Kazuo. 1993. *Nihongata Keiei Shisutemuno Kozai (The Merits and Demerits of Japanese-Style Management)*. Toyo Keizai Shimbun, 3, 124, 125, 190.

Chapter 8

Kusaba, Ikuro, ed. 1986. *Kanrizu Katsuyo no Kihon to Oyo (The Fundamentals and Applications of Control Charts)*. Japan Standards Association (JSA).

Fukuda, Ryuji. 1978. The Application of the CEDAC for Standardization and Quality Control. *Hyojunkato Hinshitsukanri (Standardization and Quality Control)*. August–September, 70–71.

Hoshi, Makoto. 1992. Hinshitsuwa Keiei Sonomono Dewanaika (Quality Is Business Management Itself). *Common Future, NTT Data Communications*.

Imai, Masaaki. 1988. *Kaizen*. Kodansha, 8 (published in English by McGraw-Hill, 1986).

PL Research Group, Nakamura, Nagayoshi, and Miyazaki, compilers. 1992. *ISO 9000 Unyo Jitsumu Manuaru (Practical ISO 9000 Implementation Manual)*. Japan Management Association Management Center.

QMDEI CDI. CS Management Training Manual. Sony Reliability and Quality Assurance Department. 1992.

Sony Reliability and Quality Assurance Department. 1992. *Sony no Hinshitsu Runessansu (Sony's Quality Renaissance)*. Japan Management Association Management Center.

Sugi, Masao. 1982. Nihonjin Tsumari Watashitachino Sozoseinitsuite Kangaeru (Thought on Our Japanese Creativity). *Engineering Study Group Paper of the Sumitomo Electric Industries, 29*.

Yoshida, Kazuo. 1993. *Nihongata Keiei Shisutemuno Kozai (The Merits and Demerits of Japanese-Style Management)*. Toyo Keizai Shimbun, 3, 124, 125, 190.

ABOUT THE AUTHOR

Ryuji Fukuda graduated from the engineering department of Kyoto University in 1954 and entered Sumitomo Electric Industries Ltd. He served Sumitomo in a number of managerial positions and in 1975 was named director of the industrial engineering department at the company's head office. From 1981 through 1992, Mr. Fukuda served on the board of directors and as a general manager and advisor for Meidensha Electric Manufacturing Co., Ltd. From 1983 to the present he has been an independent management consultant and an advisor to the Japan Management Association.

Mr. Fukuda served as a part-time lecturer on reliability engineering in the system engineering department at Kobe University from 1976 through 1987. He is the author of numerous works that have been translated into many other languages, including *Managerial Engineering: Techniques for Improving Quality and Productivity in the Workplace* (Productivity Press, 1983) and CEDAC: *A Tool for Continuous Systematic Improvement* (Productivity Press, 1989).

INDEX

Books from Productivity Press

Productivity Press publishes books that empower individuals and companies to achieve excellence in quality, productivity, and the creative involvement of all employees. Through steadfast efforts to support the vision and strategy of continuous improvement, Productivity Press delivers today's leading-edge tools and techniques gathered directly from industry leaders around the world. Call toll-free 1-800-394-6868 for our free catalog.

Achieving Total Quality Management
A Program for Action
Michel Perigord

This is an outstanding book on total quality management (TQM)—a compact guide to the concepts, methods, and techniques involved in achieving total quality. It shows you how to make TQM a companywide strategy, not just in technical areas, but in marketing and administration as well. Written in an accessible, instructive style by a top European quality expert, it is methodical, logical, and thorough. Major methods and tools for total quality are spelled out and implementation strategies are reviewed.
ISBN 0-915299-60-7 / 392 pages / $50.00 / Order ACHTQM-B276

CEDAC
A Tool for Continuous Systematic Improvement
Ryuji Fukuda

CEDAC, encompasses three tools for continuous systematic improvement: window analysis (for identifying problems), the CEDAC diagram (a modification of the classic "fishbone diagram," for analyzing problems and developing standards), and window development (for ensuring adherence to standards). This manual provides directions for setting up and using CEDAC. Sample forms included.
ISBN 1-56327-140-0 / 144 pages / $30.00 / Order CEDAC-B276

Companywide Quality Management
Alberto Galgano

Companywide quality management (CWQM) leads to dramatic changes in management values and priorities, company culture, management of company operations, management and decision-making processes, techniques and methods used by employees, and more. Much has been written on this subject, but Galgano—a leading European consultant who studied with leaders of the Japanese quality movement—offers hands-on, stage-front knowledge of the monumental changes CWQC can bring.
ISBN 1-56327-038-2 / 480 pages / $45.00 / Order CWQM-B276

Corporate Diagnosis
Setting the Global Standard for Excellence
Thomas L. Jackson with Constance E. Dyer

All too often, strategic planning neglects an essential first step and final step-diagnosis of the organization's current state. What's required is a systematic review of the critical factors in organizational learning and growth, factors that require monitoring, measurement, and management to ensure that your company competes successfully. This executive workbook provides a step-by-step method for diagnosing an organization's strategic health and measuring its overall competitiveness against world class standards. With checklists, charts, and detailed explanations, *Corporate Diagnosis* is a practical instruction manual. Detailed diagnostic questions in each area are provided as guidelines for developing your own self-assessment survey.

ISBN 1-56327-086-2 / 115 pages / $65.00 / Order CDIAG-B276

Handbook for Productivity Measurement and Improvement
William F. Christopher and Carl G. Thor, eds.

An unparalleled resource! In over 100 chapters, nearly 80 front-runners in the quality movement reveal the evolving theory and specific practices of world class organizations. Spanning a wide variety of industries and business sectors, the authors discuss quality and productivity in manufacturing, service industries, profit centers, administration, nonprofit and government institutions, health care and education. Contributors include Robert C. Camp, Peter F. Drucker, Jay W. Forrester, Joseph M. Juran, Robert S. Kaplan, John W. Kendrick, Yasuhiro Monden, and Lester C. Thurow. Comprehensive in scope and organized for easy reference, this compendium belongs in every company and academic institution concerned with business and industrial viability.

ISBN 1-56327-007-2 / 1344 pages / $90.00 / Order HPM-B276

Handbook of Quality Tools
The Japanese Approach
Tetsuichi Asaka and Kazuo Ozeki (eds.)

This comprehensive teaching manual, which includes the seven traditional and five newer QC tools, explains each tool, why it's useful, and how to construct and use it. It's a perfect training aid, as well as a hands-on reference book, for supervisors, foremen, and/or team leaders. Accessible to everyone in your organization, dealing with both management and shop floor how-to's, you'll find it an indispensable tool in your quest for quality. Information is presented in easy-to-grasp language, with step-by-step instructions, illustrations, and examples of each tool.

ISBN 1-56327-138-9 / 315 pages / $30.00 / Order HQTP-B276

Implementing a Lean Management System

Thomas L. Jackson with Karen R. Jones

Does your company think and act ahead of technological change, ahead of the customer, and ahead of the competition? Thinking strategically requires a company to face these questions with a clear future image of itself. *Implementing a Lean Management System* lays out a comprehensive management system for aligning the firm's vision of the future with market realities. Based on hoshin management, the Japanese strategic planning method used by top managers for driving TQM throughout an organization, *Lean Management* is about deploying vision, strategy, and policy to all levels of daily activity. It is an eminently practical methodology emerging out of the implementation of continuous improvement methods and employee involvement.

ISBN 1-56327-085-4 / 182 pages / $65.00 / Order ILMS-B276

ISO 9000 REQUIRED
Your Worldwide Passport to Customer Confidence

Branimir Todorov

ISO 9000 certification is the required passport for suppliers who want to do global business today, and this book clearly explains the qualification process. Branimir Todorov's *ISO 90000 Required* fills the need for a compact and readable guide for managers to the basics of ISO. Avoiding confusing and unnecessary details, the book is a valuable primer for managers looking for a basic introduction to the ISO standards, as well as an accessible reference to key topics for readers already involved in ISO certification.

ISBN 1-56327-112-5 / 224 pages, illustrated / $27.00 / Order ISOREQ-B276

Learning Organizations
Developing Cultures for Tomorrow's Workplace

Sarita Chawla and John Renesch, Editors

The ability to learn faster than your competition may be the only sustainable competitive advantage! A learning organization is one where people continually expand their capacity to create results they truly desire, where new and expansive patterns of thinking are nurtured, where collective aspiration is set free, and where people continually learn how to learn together. This compilation of 34 powerful essays, written by recognized experts worldwide, is rich in concept and theory, as well as application and example. An inspiring follow-up to Peter Senge's groundbreaking bestseller *The Fifth Discipline*, these essays are grouped in four sections and address all aspects of learning organizations: the guiding ideas behind systems thinking; the theories, methods, and processes for creating a learning organization; the infrastructure of the learning model; and arenas of practice.

ISBN 1-56327-110-9 / 571 pages / $35.00 / Order LEARN-B276

Making the Numbers Count
The Management Accountant as Change Agent on the World Class Team
Brian H. Maskell

Traditional accounting systems are holding back improvement strategies and process innovation. Maskell's timely book addresses the growing phenomenon confronting managers in continuous improvement environment. It unmasks the shortcomings of a management accountant's traditional roles and shows the inadequacy of running a business based on financial reports. According to Maskell, in a world class organization, the management accountant can and should take the lead in establishing performance measures that make a difference.
ISBN: 1-56327-070-6 / 150 pages, illustrations / $29.00 / Order MNC-B276

Management for Quality Improvement
Managerial Engineering Techniques for Improving Quality and Productivity in the Workplace
Ryuji Fukuda

A proven path to managerial success, based on reliable methods developed by one of Japan's leading productivity experts and winner of the coveted Deming Prize for quality. Dr. W. Edwards Deming, world-famous consultant on quality, said that the book "provides an excellent and clear description of the devotion and methods of Japanese management to continual improvement of quality." This book lays the foundations for your most powerful and effective quality improvement efforts. Specific methods covered in the book include CEDAC (the Cause-and-Effect Diagram with the Addition of Cards), IE improvements, small group activities, and stockless production techniques. (Training programs on CEDAC, the award-winning system outlined in this book, are also available from Productivity.)
ISBN 0-915299-09-7 / 208 pages / $45.00 / Order ME-B276

A New American TQM
Four Practical Revolutions in Management
Shoji Shiba, Alan Graham, and David Walden

For TQM to succeed in America, you need to create an American-style "learning organization" with the full commitment and understanding of senior managers and executives. Written expressly for this audience, *A New American TQM* offers a comprehensive and detailed explanation of TQM and how to implement it, based on courses taught at MIT's Sloan School of Management and the Center for Quality Management, a consortium of American companies. Full of case studies and amply illustrated, the book examines major quality tools and how they are being used by the most progressive American companies today.
ISBN 1-56327-032-3 / 598 pages / $50.00 / Order NATQM-B276

Performance Measurement for World Class Manufacturing
A Model for American Companies
Brian H. Maskell

If your company is adopting world class manufacturing techniques, you'll need new methods of performance measurement to control production variables. In practical terms, this book describes the new methods of performance measurement and how they are used in a changing environment. For manufacturing managers as well as cost accountants, it provides a theoretical foundation of these innovative methods supported by extensive practical examples. The book specifically addresses performance measures for delivery, process time, production flexibility, quality, and finance.

ISBN 0-915299-99-2 / 429 pages / $55.00 / Order PERFM-B276

The Right Fit
The Power of Ergonomics as a Competitive Strategy
Clifford M. Gross

Each year, poorly designed products and workplaces account for thousands of injuries and skyrocketing costs. That's why ergonomics—the human factor in product and workplace design—is fast becoming a major concern of manufacturers. Now one of the country's top experts argues that ergonomics will become the next strategic imperative for American business, the deciding factor in which companies ultimately succeed. Here's a brilliant non-technical introduction for corporate planners and strategic decision makers.

ISBN 1-56327-111-7 / 185 pages / $24.00 / Order ERGO-B276

Secrets of a Successful Employee Recognition System
Daniel C. Boyle

As the human resource manager of a failing manufacturing plant, Dan Boyle was desperate to find a way to motivate employees and break down the barrier between management and the union. He came up with a simple idea to say thank you to your employees for doing their job. In *Secrets to a Successful Employee Recognition System,* Boyle outlines how to begin and run a 100 Club program. Filled with case studies and detailed guidelines, this book underscores the power behind thanking your employees for a job well done.

ISBN 1-56327-083-8 / 250 pages / $25.00 / Order SECRET-B276

Stepping Up to ISO 14000
Integrating Environmental Quality with ISO 9000 and TQM
Subhash C. Puri

The newest ISO standards, announced in mid-1996, require environmentally-friendly practices in every aspect of a manufacturing business, from factory design and raw material acquisition to the production, packaging, distribution, and ultimate disposal of the product. Here's a comprehensible overview and implementation guide to the standards that's also the only one to show how they fit with current ISO 9000 efforts and other companywide programs for Total Quality Management (TQM).
ISBN 1-56327-129-X / 280 pages / $39.00 / Order STPISO-B276

The Unshackled Organization
Facing the Challenge of Unpredictability Through Spontaneous Reorganization
Jeffrey Goldstein

Managers should not necessarily try to solve all the internal problems within their organizations; intervention may help in the short term, but in the long run may inhibit true problem-solving change from taking place. And change is the real goal. Through change comes real hope for improvement. Using leading-edge scientific and social theories about change, Goldstein explores how change happens within an organization and reveals that only through "self-organization" can natural, lasting change occur. This book is a pragmatic guide for managers, executives, consultants, and other change agents.
ISBN 1-56327-048-X / 202 pages / $25.00 / Order UO-B276

Visual Control Systems
Nikkan Kogyo Shimbun (ed.)

Every day, progressive companies all over the world are making manufacturing improvements that profoundly impact productivity, quality, and lead time. Case studies of the most innovative visual control systems in Japanese companies have been gathered, translated, and compiled in this notebook. No other source provides more insightful information on recent developments in Japanese manufacturing technology. Plant managers, VPs of operations, and CEOs with little spare time need a concise and timely means of staying informed. Here's a gold mine of ideas for reducing costs and delivery times and improving quality.
ISBN 1-56327-143-5 / 189 pages / $30.00 / Order VCSP- B276

To Order: Write, phone, or fax Productivity Press, Dept. BK, P.O. Box 13390, Portland, OR 97213-0390, phone 1-800-394-6868, fax 1-800-394-6286.

Outside the U.S. phone (503) 235-0600; fax (503) 235-0909

Send check or charge to your credit card (American Express, Visa, MasterCard accepted).

U.S. Orders: Add $5 shipping for first book, $2 each additional for UPS surface delivery. Add $5 for each AV program containing 1 or 2 tapes; add $12 for each AV program containing 3 or more tapes. We offer attractive quantity discounts for bulk purchases of individual titles; call for more information.

Order by E-Mail: Order 24 hours a day from anywhere in the world. Use either address:

To order: **service@ppress.com**
To view the online catalog and/or order: **http://www.ppress.com/**

Quantity Discounts: For information on quantity discounts, please contact our sales department.

International Orders: Write, phone, or fax for quote and indicate shipping method desired. For international callers, telephone number is 503-235-0600 and fax number is 503-235-0909. Prepayment in U.S. dollars must accompany your order (checks must be drawn on U.S. banks). When quote is returned with payment, your order will be shipped promptly by the method requested.

NOTE: Prices are in U.S. dollars and are subject to change without notice.

Continue Your Learning with In-House Training and Consulting from Productivity, Inc.

The Productivity Consulting Group (PCG) prides itself on delivering today's leading process improvement tools and methodologies that bring rapid, ongoing, measurable results. Through years of repeat business, an expanding and loyal client base continues to recommend Productivity to their colleagues.

The PCG offers a diverse menu of products and services tailored to fit your company's needs, from focused, results-driven training to broad, world class conversion projects. Whether you need on-site consultation for a day or assistance with long-term development, our experienced professional staff can enhance your pursuit of competitive advantage.

In concert with your employees, the PCG will focus on implementing the principles of Just-in-Time (Lean Production), Total Productive Maintenance, Total Quality Management, and Total Employee Involvement. Each approach offers an array of the Productivity tools that are well-known for their significant shopfloor results: Quick Changeover, Mistake-Proofing, Kanban, One-Piece Flow, Problem Solving with CEDAC, Design of Experiments, Autonomous Maintenance, Visual Controls, Quality Function Deployment, Ergonomics, Standardization, and more.

Contact the PCG to learn how we can customize our services to fit your needs.

Telephone: 1-800-966-5423 (U.S. only) or 1-203-846-3777
Fax: 1-203-846-6883